# RAISING SILENT VOICES

## Educating the Linguistic Minorities for the 21st Century

**Henry T. Trueba**

*Graduate School of Education*
*University of California*
*Santa Barbara, California*

**Heinle & Heinle Publishers**
A Division of Wadsworth, Inc.
Boston, Massachusetts 02116 U.S.A.

Director: Laurie E. Likoff
Production Coordinator: Cynthia Funkhouser
Cover Design: 20/20 Services, Inc.
Compositor: Crane Typesetting Service, Inc.
Printer and Binder: Malloy Lithographing, Inc.

Raising Silent Voices: Educating the Linguistic Minorities for the 21st Century

Library of Congress Cataloging in Publication Data

Trueba, Henry T.
    Raising silent voices : educating the linguistic minorities for
the 21st century / Henry T. Trueba.
        p.  cm.
    Bibliography: p. 187
    Includes index.

    1. Education, Bilingual—United States.   2. Linguistic minorities—
Education—United States.   3. Education, Bilingual—Law and
legislation—United States.   4. English language—Study and
teaching—United States—Bilingual method.  I. Title.
LC3731.T697   1989
371.97'0973—dc19                                              88-28982
                                                                  CIP

ISBN 0-8384-2709-X

Printed in the U.S.A.
63-26128                                              98 9 8 7

To the memory of don Joaquin Torres Trueba,
my father, and doña Refugio Eguiarte de
Torres Trueba, my mother.

To other immigrants whose troubles I shared, and to
all the people of the United States whose help
and support persuaded me to love this
country and make it my own.

# Preface

In the face of the twenty-first century we have today the unique challenge of educating linguistic minorities who in many cities are becoming the majority. The children who will be in the next century's schools have already been born and, without their knowing so, their educational career may already be "at risk." Many of these children are recent immigrants and do not have a voice, at least not in English. They are still unaware of the price they will have to pay in school and society because of their linguistic and sociocultural differences. Their silence today about our tardiness to respond to their social, economic, emotional, and, especially, their educational needs, and our misgivings regarding their place in public schools and their potential contributions to our society will speak eloquently tomorrow. In the twenty-first century, these children's voices will be heard as they ask for explanations and solutions, effective educational policies, and a fair share in the social and economic benefits given to other members of American society. But this book is not an indictment of public education, nor is it a quick-fix recipe for solving educational problems. Rather, it is an invitation to think critically about schools from the perspective of linguistic minority children and their teachers. The book attempts to offer not only food for thought but also practical suggestions and exercises to help us face the challenges of tomorrow with more confidence.

If we reach the decision to recognize the problems of linguistic minority students and acknowledge their demographic, economic, and cultural contributions to our aging society, we must proceed with caution. We must not act out of compulsion, reacting defensively to an educational system that has neglected large numbers of minority students or that has remained anachronistically segregated and insensitive to the cultural differences and value orientations of contemporary students. There are no easy ways to achieve the systematic reform needed to improve public education.

This book makes a realistic assessment of who linguistic minorities are and describes some of the problems they experience in school. It asks questions about the nature of the instructional process and alternatives available to improve it. The book speaks to educators—teachers, administrators, and other school personnel—but particularly to the teachers and administrators of schools with heavy concentrations of linguistic minority students. These pages are intended to invite reflection on the intimate relationship between language, culture, and cognitive development. Teachers' voices are also heard in this book: their concerns (at times bordering on

frustration and despair) regarding the impossibility of the task, their need for professional and spiritual support and appreciation of their capabilities, and their wish
for additional flexibility in the organization of instruction. Most importantly, teachers' call for a more humane teaching environment in which they feel safe, and
wanted, as well as rewarded in their efforts to teach by the commitment of students
to learn.

The first four chapters of this text offer a historical and theoretical framework
for analyzing school work and its outcomes for linguistic minority students and
their teachers. They suggest potential explanations for differing minority achievement, types of educational programs designed to meet the presumed needs of
linguistic minorities, and legislative and political support for these programs in the
context of the American democratic system. Chapter Five examines the nature of
the instructional process. Chapter Six integrates the concerns of teachers into the
idea of professional empowerment, its meaning, and possible instruments to be
used to accomplish it. Chapter Seven, the final chapter, examines the actual execution of the curriculum design, including the planning, implementation, and evaluation of programs for linguistic minorities.

The issues discussed here point to the need for educators to arrive at a consensus
regarding fundamental principles guiding educational practice for linguistic minorities (and other students as well). To invite discussion and move toward consensus,
the volume proposes some general ideas about the nature of these principles. Linguistic minority students must be assisted to attain critical thinking skills (as demonstrated in academic tasks), communicative competence in English and in the
home language, and high levels of literacy, especially in domains required for
academic achievement. Furthermore, these students will achieve if they are given
opportunities to internalize cultural values required for the acquisition of a second
language and a second culture: English communicative competence and English
literacy skills.

Many teachers are to be given credit for the herculean efforts they have made
to meet the demands of teaching linguistic minorities in our schools. They often
feel isolated and unfairly treated when they advocate for alternative (but in their
view, more effective) means of instructing linguistic minority students. If public
education is in crisis, it is not because of the teachers but in spite of their efforts
in environments that are often unsuitable for teaching. This book makes a plea to
create local centers for teacher assistance and support.

Educational research in the last decade has begun to recognize the need to
engage in cooperative efforts with teachers in the school setting, and to be less
prescriptive and simplistic. Some of the literature from the social sciences warns
us about the foolishness of arrogant scholars who pretend to know the answers or
who reduce everything to psychometric scores. This book presents case studies,
teachers' and students' testimonies, personal accounts of school events, and other
less orthodox strategies to invite reflection. It also offers summaries, exercises, and
relevant readings at the end of each chapter. It is this author's hope that the reader

will pause to think, regardless of whether he or she agrees or disagrees with the ideas presented. Best of all, if as a result of such thoughtful consideration the reader makes a commitment to share generously of his or her knowledge, cultural values, and skills with linguistic minority persons, the book's purpose will have been accomplished.

# Foreword

In *Raising Silent Voices*, Henry Trueba makes good use of his training and experiences as an anthropologist, but his purposes are those of an educator who wants to improve education and thereby improve society. His conceptual and methodological armamentarium is from sociocultural anthropology, with a leavening mix of ideas and information from psychology, philosophy, and sociology, as well as from sociolinguistics. This centered eclecticism gives the book a certain character: solid but variegated and stimulating.

His major thesis is that linguistic minority children are not disadvantaged so much by language handicaps as by the manifold contexts of their experience in our confused but hopeful society. His is no value-free stance, but he supports his value orientations and judgments with disciplined inquiry and objectively ordered data. He does not blame teachers, or schools, or, least of all, children or their families for failures in schools or for school failures. He searches for root causes and conditions in the transactions of daily life and of biographies in and out of schools. Having identified some of these causes and conditions, he then recommends action and suggests to readers how they may inform themselves further about the issues he has raised and their contexts. This balance of inquiry, analysis, and ameliorating recommendation leads one to a hopeful rather than a desperate attitude, which is remarkable in view of the immensity and complexity of the problems his presentation uncovers. He makes a statement on behalf of teachers who face the challenges of communicating through a language and culture foreign to many of the children in their classrooms. He explores the roles of teachers, their value systems, and their need to reflect upon and analyze how cultural assumptions affect teachers' perception of students' capacities and performance.

Having worked as Visiting Professors with Henry Trueba in his own context at the Office for Research on Educational Equity at the University of California, Santa Barbara, we know firsthand of his whole-hearted dedication to the improvement of the quality of the school experience for linguistic minorities in our society. No one knows better than he that the problem is not one for the schools and for educators alone. And no one knows better than he that the answers to our problems are not in this or any other book. But the questions have become more clear and the outlines of some solutions and answers are beginning to take form.

*Raising Silent Voices* will help anyone to orient himself or herself to the problems of linguistic minorities in our schools, and the problems of schools and teachers involved with linguistic minorities. No other complex of problems is of greater import for the future of education in our society. The twenty-first century will be an era of failure and despair if we do not succeed in creating and sustaining conditions for equity in our schools. Linguistic minorities are growing rapidly, particularly in relation to nonminority populations. They will be the majority, in fact already are, in many school districts. If our schools fail with this dynamic population, our social order will be grievously weakened and our culture impoverished. The American way of life has always been in process—in creation, not created. It energizes itself by furnishing hope for all that life can be better than it is. To some this means assimilation: a loss of identity and difference. To others this means disintegration of the core of American culture. These are narrow views of the American reality, for that reality itself is shaped as the incorporation occurs. Our multifaceted cultural dialogue, with its babel of voices, will continue to expand opportunity for personal and social improvement for all of us if we can better understand the existing barriers to full participation by linguistic minorities, and if we can learn to act on the basis of that understanding. This book is a significant contribution both to this understanding and to the possibilities for action.

*George and Louise Spindler*
*Stanford University*

# Acknowledgments

I feel a deep sense of gratitude to George Peter Murdock—he passed away a few years ago after making outstanding contributions to the social sciences—whose energies and personal support facilitated my professional development and my adjustment to life in the United States. I also have a debt of gratitude to Professors George and Louise Spindler for their continued encouragement and inspiration. I feel fortunate to have recently rediscovered George and Louise as friends and colleagues. Much of the content of these pages is the fruit of long conversations with them; at every step of the development of this volume, their theoretical guidance and critical comments stimulated my thinking. George and Louise graciously agreed to write the Foreword, and this is also sincerely appreciated.

While I take full responsibility for my statements with all the shortcomings, biases, and errors that often accompany similar efforts, I also must recognize the intellectual support, comments and information given to me by many colleagues. First and foremost, the logical consistency and clarity in the work of the Spindlers compelled me to look further and with additional cultural sensitivity into the social and cultural context of knowledge acquisition.

The work of many other colleagues has also had an impact on my thinking about linguistic minorities. Just to mention a few, the written work of Fred Erickson, Ray McDermott, Michael Cole, Ron Gallimore, Roland Tharp, Norman Gold, Fred Tempes, Guadalupe San Miguel, and other scholars provided me with essential insights and stimulated my thoughts during the many lonely hours of writing and correcting these pages. I want to thank the Newbury House/Harper & Row reviewers and editors; without their criticism this volume would have never reached a level of clarity, cohesiveness, and balance. It was not easy to handle their detailed comments, and yet they were right on target. Many other colleagues and friends have also given generously of their time offering feedback, suggestions, materials to read, and moral support during the writing and rewriting of this book. For their editorial work and general support I want to thank Dr. Concha Delgado-Gaitan, Carolyn Benson, and Gail Baxter.

To Mary McConkey and Elena Horak, who patiently, scrupulously, and efficiently helped me in putting together, duplicating, organizing, and sending out this manuscript to readers and editors, during its various phases of development, my sincere gratitude. To Beatriz Jamaica, who, without ever complaining, assisted me with last minute chores such as checking references, retyping sections, and taking responsibility for a thousand details, my most sincere thanks.

Finally, I also feel indebted to Ardie, my wife, and to Phillip and Laura, my children, who tolerated my absence for months in good spirits. I could not close without expressing my love and dedication to the schoolchildren and teachers who opened their lives to me and shared with me their happy and less happy moments in school.

# Contents

# List of Tables and Figures

# 1

# Sociocultural Integration of Minorities and Minority School Achievement

This chapter explores two fundamental questions: Who are the linguistic minorities? And why do most of them do poorly in school? The problem of defining linguistic minorities is fraught with difficulties. One problem is the assessment of linguistic proficiency in languages other than English. Another is the verification of ethnic identity and degree of assimilation into mainstream American society. Are Chicanos and Native Americans, who have maintained their own ethnic identity and language (at least for ceremonial purposes and for intragroup communication), "linguistic minorities"? If these persons lose their language completely but retain their culture and ethnic identity, do they cease being "linguistic minorities"? If certain children are monolingual in English, but their parents and relatives speak another language at home, particularly during the children's early socialization period, are they members of linguistic minorities?

The narrow definition used by the federal government identifies individuals who "are not functional in English" as linguistic minorities. This definition results in conservative estimates of the numbers of linguistic minority schoolchildren. The first part of this chapter will provide some factual information about linguistic minority children in the United States, followed by an examination of the nature of education problems of linguistic minorities.

The multiethnic nature of American culture is selectively being changed by new waves of immigrants and ethnic minority groups who have different collective and personal experiences. The narrow conception of some social scientists in their analyses of the academic problems of minority students has led us to believe that many ethnic groups have a language problem, or a problem with communicative competence. There is evidence to suggest that a relationship exists between broad sociological, political, or economic factors and the different success rates of certain minority groups adjusting to our society.

This chapter explores the cultural basis for differential academic achievement of minority students, focusing on the cultural conflict experienced and accommodations made by both the minorities and the school personnel working with them. It points to the need for *all* Americans from both ethnic and mainstream groups to cope with the rapid cyclical changes and selective continuity of values crucial to the social order and power structure of our culture. Because the "problem" of minorities is no longer a minority problem alone, but is now an issue for all members of American culture to deal with, this chapter focuses on the structural (systemic) features that seem to facilitate or hinder the adjustment of minority children to our society, and specifically to our schools. The emphasis is necessarily on the school because the school has consistently played a crucial role in the transmission of cultural values, helping to perpetuate social norms and principles. Indeed, the school is the gateway to mainstream America for ethnolinguistic minorities. If the gate becomes too small, teachers may function as gatekeepers and create a large mass of alienated Americans.

To avoid such a situation, social scientists, through various complementary approaches but often using competing theoretical frameworks, attempt to develop explanations for the success or failure of minority groups in school and society. In order to accomplish this goal, they aim to:

1. Offer a better explanation for how educational institutions function and how they are viewed by linguistic minorities in the context of their entire sociocultural experience.
2. Explore current instructional practices used to teach linguistic minorities, particularly those with special needs.
3. Describe the social and cultural characteristics of the minority family, and the process of a student's transition from the home to the school learning environment.
4. Suggest instructional practices that maximize minority students' learning potential.
5. Explore the nature of learning problems.
6. Study classroom organization and student participation.
7. Assess the level of children's literacy in English.

We need to know specifically what these children can and cannot do. What skill and performance level is displayed in academic tasks? How do first- or second-language proficiencies affect children's performance? How do different language groups react to specific participant structures created by the teacher; for example, does a child behave differently during math and reading classes? What are language minority children's learning styles? How do they experience stress and cope with it? What specific problems do they have in the context of academic activities? What classroom or other arrangements allow them to achieve the most, with maximum satisfaction? In brief, what can teachers and children do differently in order to obtain optimal instructional effectiveness? By answering these questions, researchers can develop explanations for the success and/or failure of minority students in school.

Social scientists want to identify characteristics of the academic problems manifested by minority children. They are asking additional questions such as the following.

1. Do the learning problems of some minority children increase with time? Such problems may result in lack of participation, inability to understand or follow directions, or difficulty in articulating (oral or written) concepts related to academic content. If these problems are exacerbated with time, early diagnosis and remediation are desirable.
2. Do these problems seem to be related to children's general maladjustment to school and society? If so, these problems may be manifested in pervasive, undefined fears or stress, or in confusion related to time fragmentation and shifts in contexts for learning. Again, early intervention is indicated.
3. Is children's use of English clearly insufficient for effective functioning in school? If English remains at the surface of the communicative process and fails when needed for critical analysis of text (and other cognitively demanding tasks), use of the home language may be more effective.
4. Is there an overall deterioration of minority children's cognitive, linguistic, and academic skills, as demonstrated by an inability to cope with stress in school and by increasing psychological and social isolation? At this point, effective remediation may be too late.
5. How does the institution handle children experiencing such problems? School personnel must explain children's underachievement. To understand any explanation, researchers must note the underlying assumptions guiding institutional policies. Some typical assumptions may be that the children are to blame for their lack of achievement and poor adjustment; tests conducted in English are appropriately used to assess children's abilities; and school personnel do not hold the responsibility for children's failures. Researchers must also note whether efforts are made to work with the ethnic community, especially with parents.

## WHO ARE THE LINGUISTIC MINORITIES?

According to the 1980 U.S. Bureau of the Census data (as cited in the 5th Annual Report of the National Advisory Council for Bilingual Education, 1980–1981, and published by the Bureau of the Census 1983, and 1984; see Tables 1.1, 1.2, and 1.3) the language minority population (that is, people whose mother tongue is other than English, regardless of their proficiency in English) in the United States was about 30 million (projected to reach about 40 million by the year 2000) with a school-age population of 3.5 million children. The population of limited English proficient (LEP) students, which was 2.4 million in 1980, is conservatively projected to reach about 3.5 million by the year 2000, not counting the children of undocumented workers.

The Spanish-speaking LEP student population, which is now about 80 percent of the total LEP student population, has unique characteristics, is concentrated in the southwest and northeast part of the country (see Figure 1.1), and deserves special discussion. According to the 1980 U.S. Census (Walker, 1987), there were 13.2 million Spanish-speaking persons in this country, not counting undocumented workers. As the National Center for Education Statistics indicates:

**Table 1.1.    LINGUISTIC MINORITY STUDENT POPULATION WITH LIMITED ENGLISH PROFICIENCY, AGED 5–14 (IN THOUSANDS)**

| | Projections | | | | | |
|---|---|---|---|---|---|---|
| | 1980 | | 1990 | | 2000 | |
| Language | N | % | N | % | N | % |
| Spanish | 1727.6 | 72.2 | 2092.7 | 74.8 | 2630.0 | 77.4 |
| Italian | 94.9 | 4.0 | 100.1 | 3.6 | 109.6 | 3.2 |
| French | 89.0 | 3.7 | 93.9 | 3.4 | 102.9 | 3.0 |
| German | 88.8 | 3.7 | 93.7 | 3.4 | 102.6 | 3.0 |
| Filipino | 33.2 | 1.4 | 35.0 | 1.2 | 38.3 | 1.1 |
| Chinese | 31.3 | 1.3 | 33.0 | 1.2 | 36.2 | 1.0 |
| Greek | 26.5 | 1.1 | 27.9 | 1.0 | 30.6 | 0.9 |
| Vietnamese | 24.9 | 1.0 | 26.2 | 0.9 | 28.7 | 0.8 |
| Navajo | 24.3 | 1.0 | 25.6 | 0.9 | 28.1 | 0.8 |
| Polish | 24.0 | 1.0 | 25.3 | 0.9 | 27.5 | 0.8 |
| Portuguese | 23.8 | 1.0 | 25.1 | 0.9 | 27.5 | 0.8 |
| Yiddish | 22.5 | 0.9 | 23.7 | 0.8 | 26.0 | 0.7 |
| Japanese | 13.3 | 0.6 | 14.0 | 0.5 | 15.3 | 0.4 |
| Korean | 12.2 | 0.5 | 12.8 | 0.4 | 14.1 | 0.4 |
| Not accounted for and other | 158.5 | 6.6 | 167.5 | 6.0 | 192.9 | 5.4 |
| Total | 2394.2 | | 2795.9 | | 3400.0 | |

*Source*: Adapted from National Advisory Council for Bilingual Education, 1980–81.

In 1976 there were 3 million Hispanic children enrolled in elementary and secondary school programs, 6 percent of the total school-age population. Of this group, 63 percent (approximately two-thirds) are Mexican–American, 15 percent are Puerto Rican, 5 percent are Cuban, and 16 percent are of other Hispanic background (Walker, 1987:18).

Population trends indicate a rapid increase in the Hispanic population relative to other minorities and to overall population growth within the country. We know that Hispanics coming from monolingual Spanish-speaking homes form a substantial group of recent immigrants but there are as yet no reliable data on their exact numbers (O'Malley, 1981; Ulibarri, 1982; Duran, 1983; Walker, 1987). What is clear is the overall underachievement of Hispanics in schools, as documented by many recent scholars (Duran, 1983; Walker, 1987). The latter authors indicate that Hispanics in the early 1980s have fewer median years of schooling (10.3) than non-Hispanic whites (12.5) or blacks (11.9), and that the dropout rate for Hispanics aged 14–25, including those who have already left school by their fourteenth birthday, is 40 percent.

The work by Carter and Segura (1979), Brown et al. (1980), Davis et al. (1983), Duran (1983), and Suarez-Orozco (1986, 1987, in press) indicates that Hispanics aged 14–19 are 50 percent less likely than non-Hispanics to complete high school. Duran (1983) points out that Hispanic underachievement patterns in elementary and secondary schools continue through college. Brown et al. (1980) suggest that Hispanic students nationwide who report spending about the same amount of time on their homework as their Anglo counterparts show a significantly lower academic achievement.

Consistent with the above information is the work by other scholars who indicate that Hispanics rarely pursue college majors in engineering (2.4 percent), the biological sciences (2.2 percent), or the physical sciences (0.8 percent); and that only a small fraction (1 percent) ever obtain a Master's degree in biology, physics, or mathematics (Walker, 1987).

Our rapidly evolving, modern, industrial world shows evidence that vast economic and sociocultural changes can lead to widespread poverty, outbursts of violence, and even international conflicts. Many parents are forced to uproot and move their families to other countries in search of safety, better economic opportunities, and peace. Thus stable, affluent countries continue to attract immigrants from developing countries. Two minority groups—immigrants, and economically disadvantaged in-country ethnolinguistic minorities—face similar problems, but react differently to the problems and challenges of integration as they strive to become part of mainstream society. Minority groups must acquire special knowledge in order to function effectively in the political, economic, and educational institutions of the host society. This challenge is uniquely difficult for a social group whose entire cultural system is at odds with that of the modern industrial society. This may be the case with some rural peoples who have been isolated from modern technology.

In most countries that document large numbers of immigrant linguistic minorities within their populations, there are attempts to curb migratory waves by ensuring assimilation or returning them to their country of origin. There are also countries such as the United States, Australia, New Zealand, Canada, and Mexico in which past conquests and colonial occupations account for a significant number of unassimilated indigenous communities.

In some instances these peoples are descendents of the original, indigenous populations of the land, who lost not only their freedom and their socioeconomic organization to the European invaders but also much of their culture and collective will to survive; thus some of these groups remain in social, cultural, and economic isolation. So we find that both immigrant and indigenous minorities must face the problems of adjusting to the demands of modern technological societies and of redefining their cultural self-identity. Entry into the host society and educational or economic achievement are not equally accessible to these minorities. Some minority people are individually and/or collectively more successful than others. In fact, in the United States some are clearly more successful than the average mainstream Anglo (Wagatsuma & DeVos, 1984; G. Spindler, 1982, 1987; Spindler & Spindler 1987a,b; Gibson, 1987a,b; Ogbu & Matute-Bianchi, 1986). The question is, why?

**Table 1.2. ESTIMATED NUMBERS OF LANGUAGE MINORITY PEOPLE IN THE UNITED STATES, BY AGE GROUP, ENGLISH OR NON-ENGLISH LANGUAGE (NEL) SPOKEN AT HOME, AND LANGUAGE: 1980 (NUMBERS IN THOUSANDS)**

| Language | Total | Children <5[b] | People living in language minority families[a] | | | | | | Other home speakers of NELs |
| --- | --- | --- | --- | --- | --- | --- | --- | --- | --- |
| | | | Aged 5–17 | | | Aged 18 and older | | | |
| | | | Total | Speak English | Speak NEL | Total | Speak English | Speak NEL | |
| Total | 34,637 | 2,562 | 7,948 | 3,466 | 4,482 | 20,616 | 5,549 | 15,067 | 3,511 |
| Spanish | 15,548 | 1,537 | 4,164 | 1,284 | 2,879 | 8,472 | 1,610 | 6,862 | 1,375 |
| French | 2,937 | 147 | 685 | 468 | 218 | 1,776 | 772 | 1,004 | 328 |
| German | 2,834 | 120 | 594 | 401 | 193 | 1,773 | 727 | 1,046 | 348 |
| Italian | 2,627 | 86 | 437 | 285 | 152 | 1,871 | 637 | 1,233 | 233 |
| Polish | 1,285 | 31 | 166 | 123 | 43 | 916 | 310 | 606 | 172 |
| Chinese languages | 769 | 58 | 152 | 37 | 115 | 476 | 44 | 432 | 84 |
| Filipino languages | 713 | 70 | 168 | 104 | 63 | 423 | 64 | 359 | 52 |
| Greek | 548 | 33 | 108 | 42 | 66 | 361 | 71 | 290 | 46 |
| Japanese | 542 | 26 | 98 | 65 | 33 | 358 | 114 | 244 | 59 |
| American Indian or Alaska Native languages | 512 | 54 | 155 | 66 | 89 | 262 | 59 | 203 | 41 |
| Portuguese | 480 | 34 | 103 | 36 | 67 | 307 | 57 | 249 | 35 |
| Yiddish | 430 | 16 | 41 | 22 | 20 | 290 | 76 | 214 | 83 |

| Language | | | | | | | | |
|---|---|---|---|---|---|---|---|---|
| Korean | 384 | 40 | 95 | 36 | 60 | 224 | 42 | 182 | 25 |
| Asian Indian languages | 321 | 41 | 67 | 24 | 43 | 188 | 12 | 175 | 25 |
| Arabic | 312 | 32 | 64 | 26 | 38 | 179 | 37 | 142 | 38 |
| Hungarian | 266 | 8 | 37 | 24 | 12 | 186 | 55 | 131 | 36 |
| Dutch | 252 | 13 | 52 | 36 | 16 | 159 | 54 | 105 | 27 |
| Vietnamese | 250 | 27 | 75 | 14 | 61 | 122 | 15 | 107 | 27 |
| Russian | 232 | 10 | 34 | 15 | 20 | 152 | 34 | 117 | 36 |
| Serbo-Croatian | 211 | 10 | 35 | 16 | 19 | 146 | 35 | 110 | 21 |
| Czech | 194 | 5 | 26 | 21 | 5 | 134 | 46 | 87 | 29 |
| Norwegian | 184 | 5 | 26 | 19 | 7 | 120 | 48 | 72 | 34 |
| Ukrainian | 168 | 6 | 22 | 12 | 10 | 121 | 28 | 92 | 19 |
| Swedish | 163 | 5 | 22 | 15 | 7 | 103 | 43 | 60 | 33 |
| Slovak | 141 | 2 | 15 | 12 | 3 | 106 | 40 | 66 | 19 |
| Armenian | 127 | 6 | 20 | 7 | 13 | 89 | 14 | 75 | 12 |
| Persian | 138 | 10 | 24 | 7 | 17 | 76 | 14 | 63 | 28 |
| Thai | 127 | 17 | 31 | 11 | 21 | 66 | 14 | 52 | 13 |
| Finnish | 111 | 3 | 16 | 13 | 3 | 74 | 26 | 48 | 19 |
| Lithuanian | 104 | 2 | 11 | 8 | 3 | 73 | 21 | 52 | 17 |
| Other languages | 1,726 | 108 | 404 | 216 | 188 | 1,015 | 428 | 587 | 198 |

[a] Families in which one or more family members speak a non-English language at home.
[b] Children one or both of whose parents speak a language other than English at home.
Note: Entries may not add up to total because of rounding.
Source: U.S. Bureau of the Census, 1984.

**Table 1.3.   ESTIMATED NUMBERS OF LANGUAGE-MINORITY PEOPLE IN THE UNITED STATES, BY AGE GROUP, ENGLISH OR NON-ENGLISH LANGUAGE (NEL) SPOKEN AT HOME, AND STATE: 1980 (NUMBERS IN THOUSANDS)**

| State | Total | People living in language minority families[a] | | | | | | | Other home speakers of NELs |
| | | Children <5[b] | Aged 5–17 | | | Aged 18 and older | | | |
| | | | Total | Speak English | Speak NEL | Total | Speak English | Speak NEL | |
|---|---|---|---|---|---|---|---|---|---|
| Total | 34,637 | 2,562 | 7,948 | 3,466 | 4,482 | 20,616 | 5,549 | 15,067 | 3,511 |
| California | 6,915 | 624 | 1,640 | 591 | 1,049 | 3,943 | 734 | 3,208 | 708 |
| New York | 4,514 | 304 | 926 | 323 | 603 | 2,753 | 589 | 2,163 | 531 |
| Texas | 3,802 | 391 | 1,052 | 258 | 794 | 2,086 | 310 | 1,775 | 274 |
| Illinois | 1,805 | 137 | 392 | 161 | 231 | 1,090 | 285 | 804 | 186 |
| Florida | 1,634 | 87 | 310 | 110 | 200 | 1,053 | 227 | 826 | 183 |
| New Jersey | 1,594 | 100 | 336 | 134 | 203 | 1,022 | 264 | 758 | 136 |
| Pennsylvania | 1,293 | 60 | 253 | 143 | 110 | 841 | 328 | 513 | 140 |
| Massachusetts | 1,074 | 56 | 215 | 110 | 105 | 679 | 203 | 475 | 124 |
| Michigan | 954 | 53 | 204 | 125 | 79 | 596 | 215 | 381 | 101 |
| Ohio | 914 | 50 | 203 | 118 | 85 | 572 | 228 | 345 | 89 |
| Arizona | 727 | 74 | 200 | 72 | 127 | 397 | 77 | 320 | 57 |
| Louisiana | 699 | 44 | 174 | 125 | 49 | 425 | 146 | 279 | 56 |
| Connecticut | 637 | 35 | 133 | 63 | 69 | 406 | 120 | 286 | 64 |
| New Mexico | 618 | 62 | 170 | 60 | 109 | 341 | 47 | 294 | 45 |
| Colorado | 475 | 37 | 120 | 74 | 46 | 268 | 81 | 188 | 49 |
| Washington | 452 | 33 | 103 | 58 | 46 | 260 | 95 | 165 | 55 |
| Wisconsin | 438 | 22 | 90 | 57 | 33 | 266 | 108 | 158 | 61 |

| | | | | | | | | | |
|---|---|---|---|---|---|---|---|---|---|
| Maryland | 415 | 24 | 96 | 51 | 45 | 257 | 96 | 161 | 38 |
| Virginia | 392 | 27 | 95 | 53 | 42 | 229 | 91 | 138 | 41 |
| Indiana | 381 | 26 | 95 | 53 | 42 | 225 | 93 | 132 | 35 |
| Minnesota | 374 | 18 | 76 | 52 | 24 | 223 | 94 | 129 | 57 |
| Hawaii | 360 | 23 | 72 | 44 | 29 | 233 | 64 | 169 | 32 |
| Georgia | 277 | 18 | 71 | 44 | 27 | 163 | 81 | 82 | 25 |
| Missouri | 270 | 16 | 64 | 40 | 24 | 162 | 75 | 87 | 29 |
| North Carolina | 273 | 17 | 68 | 43 | 26 | 162 | 85 | 78 | 26 |
| Oregon | 227 | 17 | 52 | 30 | 22 | 128 | 49 | 78 | 30 |
| Rhode Island | 224 | 11 | 43 | 24 | 18 | 147 | 42 | 105 | 24 |
| Oklahoma | 212 | 17 | 53 | 33 | 20 | 120 | 49 | 70 | 22 |
| Maine | 187 | 10 | 42 | 30 | 13 | 114 | 35 | 79 | 21 |
| Kansas | 185 | 14 | 43 | 26 | 17 | 107 | 42 | 65 | 21 |
| Utah | 184 | 21 | 49 | 32 | 17 | 98 | 38 | 60 | 17 |
| Tennessee | 179 | 11 | 46 | 29 | 17 | 107 | 58 | 50 | 16 |
| Iowa | 174 | 10 | 40 | 25 | 15 | 102 | 47 | 55 | 22 |
| South Carolina | 157 | 10 | 42 | 27 | 15 | 91 | 49 | 42 | 14 |
| New Hampshire | 153 | 7 | 33 | 24 | 9 | 95 | 32 | 63 | 17 |
| Alabama | 152 | 9 | 39 | 25 | 14 | 92 | 51 | 41 | 12 |
| Kentucky | 132 | 9 | 34 | 21 | 12 | 78 | 42 | 36 | 12 |
| Nebraska | 124 | 8 | 26 | 18 | 9 | 74 | 30 | 44 | 16 |
| Nevada | 121 | 8 | 27 | 16 | 11 | 71 | 25 | 47 | 14 |
| North Dakota | 119 | 5 | 24 | 21 | 4 | 73 | 25 | 48 | 16 |
| Mississippi | 100 | 7 | 28 | 18 | 10 | 58 | 31 | 27 | 7 |
| Idaho | 88 | 9 | 23 | 13 | 9 | 46 | 18 | 29 | 10 |
| Arkansas | 85 | 6 | 22 | 14 | 8 | 51 | 26 | 25 | 7 |

*(Continued)*

**Table 1.3.** (*Continued*)

| State | Total | Children <5[b] | Aged 5–17 | | | Aged 18 and older | | | Other home speakers of NELs |
|---|---|---|---|---|---|---|---|---|---|
| | | | Total | Speak English | Speak NEL | Total | Speak English | Speak NEL | |
| South Dakota | 84 | 6 | 20 | 13 | 7 | 48 | 16 | 32 | 11 |
| West Virginia | 81 | 4 | 19 | 12 | 6 | 51 | 26 | 25 | 7 |
| Alaska | 74 | 7 | 20 | 10 | 10 | 40 | 11 | 28 | 8 |
| Montana | 71 | 5 | 16 | 11 | 5 | 42 | 17 | 24 | 8 |
| District of Columbia | 70 | 3 | 12 | 6 | 6 | 36 | 13 | 23 | 19 |
| Vermont | 58 | 3 | 13 | 10 | 4 | 36 | 15 | 21 | 7 |
| Delaware | 55 | 3 | 13 | 7 | 5 | 33 | 14 | 19 | 5 |
| Wyoming | 51 | 5 | 13 | 9 | 4 | 28 | 11 | 18 | 5 |

People living in language minority families[a]

[a]Families in which one or more family members speak a non-English language at home.
[b]Children one or both of whose parents speak a language other than English at home.
Note: Entries may not add up to total because of rounding.
*Source*: U.S. Bureau of the Census, 1984.

10

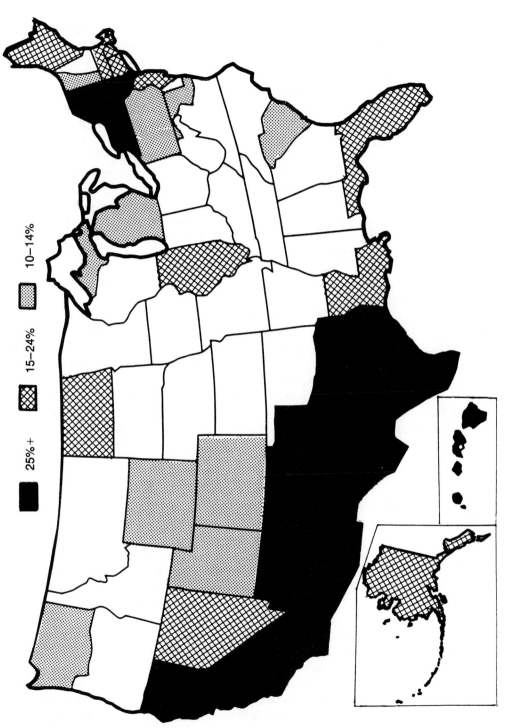

**Figure 1.1.** Concentration of language minorities in the various states: 1980

25%+

15–24%

10–14%

11

At times, immigrants in the United States have faced drastic changes and gone through adjustment crises over a period of several generations. Sometimes second and third generations have lost their language and culture, but still have not been integrated into mainstream American society. Their continued marginal status must be explained. In many respects, alienated second- and third-generation immigrants have more in common with the low-income mainstream disenfranchised poor than with their ethnic counterparts in the host country or mother country. Both the loss of the home language and culture and the social isolation in this country seem to be rooted in similar causes. One of these may be the collective inability of these groups to respond to the social and cultural discontinuities (and rejection) presented by the dominant culture. Both types of groups have in common very low social status, low educational levels, poverty, isolation, and helplessness in the face of rejection. On the other hand, some minority groups seem better suited to adjusting to their new lives in the United States. DeVos (1983) has discussed the success of Japanese Americans. Likewise, Roosens (1987:8) has pointed out in discussing the Japanese that ''. . . the internal logic of large parts of the pre-industrial culture can be harmonized with the modern model much more easily and much more quickly than is the case with others.''

Regardless of their country of origin, linguistic minority families assimilate at different rates into the dominant social and cultural life of modern industrial societies. Their speed of assimilation seems to be connected with their relative familiarity with complex industrial societies and the functions of various institutions such as banks, schools, hospitals, and government. The less acquainted a family is with a pluralist, complex, literate, technologically sophisticated society, the greater the time needed for assimilation. Thus, while families coming from the same country may share overall characteristics of language and culture, they may differ in value orientation as well as in their understanding of how the host society and its institutions operate.

## REASONS FOR ACADEMIC SUCCESS
## OR FAILURE

Academic achievement is only part of the ''success'' or ''failure'' of the overall process of minority integration into industrial societies. The problem of assimilating varied ethnic groups is not unique to the United States and Canada. Indeed, there are waves of migration all over the world. Turkish, Spanish, Moroccan, Italian, and other workers take their families to Germany, Belgium, Switzerland, or France in search of better jobs and educational opportunities. The successful adaptation of immigrant children has been, for the last two decades, the concern of research organizations affiliated with various American, Latin American, and European universities. Since the 1960s the Center for Social and Cultural Anthropology of the Katholieke Universiteit Leuven in Belgium, along with the Indigenist Institute in Mexico, has been conducting migration and assimilation studies. More recently, the Linguistic Minority Research Project at the University of California has created interdisciplinary teams to conduct basic and applied research on linguistic minorities in their homes and at school.

One of the most serious difficulties in such research is defining "success" and "failure," not only from the standpoint of the host society but also in terms of the ethnic groups under study. Another difficulty is creating adequate theoretical approaches that are compatible across disciplines. Social scientists have attempted to explain minority success and failure (academic, social, and economic) using a number of approaches and hypotheses that are not universally recognized as valid. Many of these theoretical approaches are still in their infancy and lack empirical evidence. A brief summary of some of the most important approaches is presented below.

In the last 10 years, sociologists, cultural anthropologists, psychologists, and linguists have been searching for a better understanding of immigrant and minority cultures. Accurate descriptions are seen as a fundamental first step toward understanding the social integration and academic success of minorities. Experts have adopted the use of what is known as an "emic" description, one that presents the perspective of the members of a given linguistic and cultural group (Pike, 1954), in contrast with an "etic" description, which presents an "analytical standpoint . . . [from] outside of a particular culture" (Pike, 1954:10) and is adopted for the purpose of making cross-cultural comparisons.

The same social scientists have also made special efforts to study success or failure from the vantage point of their various disciplines. Their descriptions of how culture has an impact on learning are truly "grounded," meaning they are based on the data collected. In order to understand and explain to others the relationship between culture and learning, they have carefully examined the use of language, assuming along with earlier anthropologists that people "construe their world of experience from the way they talk about it" (Frake, 1964:132).

The emphasis on culture is particularly welcome after years of controversy regarding the relative significance of linguistic factors in determining the academic achievement of minority students. The narrow focus on linguistic differences and the overpoliticization of linguistic models did not lead to a better understanding of the success or failure of linguistic minorities. While excellent research was produced on first- and second-language use in the 1970s and early 1980s, the actual cognitive ability of minority children was not directly addressed until the more recent work of Cummins (1976, 1978, 1981a,b, 1983, 1986), Duran (1983, 1985), Heath (1983), Krashen (1980), Wong-Fillmore (1976, 1982), and other scholars. Language and culture are so intimately related during the process of early socialization that one cannot be studied without the other. Examining language isolated from cultural factors leads to a serious misunderstanding of the minority person's process of resocialization and consequently of integration, knowledge acquisition, and successful participation in the various institutions of the host society.

Leading European social scientists, such as Roosens in Belgium (1971, 1981, 1987) and Zeroulou (1985) and Camilleri (1985) in France, have joined American and Japanese (see Wagatsuma & DeVos, 1984; Ogbu, 1974, 1978, 1981; Suarez-Orozco, 1986, 1987, in press; and many more to be mentioned below) researchers in seeking explanations for the differential scholastic achievement of minorities and immigrants. Their approaches attempt to combine psychological and sociological factors of achievement across cultures. Their overall concern is with the general process of minority integration into modern technological societies, and specifically with cultural adaptation to the host country. In an attempt to explain the success or failure of immigrants, Roosens (1987) presents five different "hypotheses" that capitalize on the ideas of selected American theoreticians. Each of these hypotheses is discussed in some detail below.

## First Hypothesis: Cultural Discontinuities

"The language and cultural differences between the home environment of certain categories of immigrant children and what is taught at school are so great that one may speak of a true educational subordination for the majority of the children, a subordination that they will never be able to overcome in their lives" (Roosens, 1987:4). This hypothesis is congruent with the work of many American scholars currently involved in the applied instructional process (Au & Jordan, 1981; Gilmore & Glatthorn, 1982; Trueba, 1983, 1987a,b; Goldman & Trueba, 1987; Erickson, 1982, 1984; and many more). The main point stressed by Roosens must be kept in mind, namely that "the way the individual reacts to the discontinuity is determinative, not the fact of the discontinuity itself" (Roosens, 1987:10).

We know that social and cultural discontinuities affect individuals and social groups in different ways. Immigrant children from middle and upper classes, regardless of their particular linguistic and cultural backgrounds, seem to adjust faster to modern industrial settings than their lower-income, rural counterparts. It seems that the relationship between social and cultural backgrounds of the immigrants and those of their host society determines the speed of integration and the overall success or failure of the minority group.

What comes with membership in certain social and cultural groups prior to immigration or colonization? What values, knowledge, and skills seem to maximize successful integration into industrial societies, regardless of the cultural discontinuities? How do such values, knowledge, and skills affect the collective response of some minority groups who succeed, in contrast with those who fail? These are as yet unresolved issues.

## Second Hypothesis: Low Status and Income Level

Common to recent immigrants and low-income members of the host society is their lower socioeconomic position in the stratified industrial setting. Undoubtedly, poverty and lower social status have clear implications for participation in educational institutions and for making use of other public services.

Economic means and social status seem to provide a qualitatively different experience to families in such a way that the social order—or disorder—tends to perpetuate itself. Some scholars believe that children of upper-low and middle-class families tend to reach higher educational levels, to network successfully, and to hold power, while children of poor families tend to drop out of school and hold menial jobs. The question is, why? What does income have to do with quality education and subsequent access to positions that enhance opportunity for retaining (or increasing) wealth and political power? Perhaps income determines not only the knowledge and experiences of children but also the way in which these children are treated in public institutions. In schools, for example, the culture of the middle- and upper-middle-class families may determine course selection advice given to children by counselors, the achievement expectations of teachers, availability of key courses through "regular scheduling," and/or the overall access to resources and information required to succeed in school.

While income alone may not seem to explain differential academic achieve- ment, the organization of behavior in the home is characterized by the experiences of, and resources available to, the family. Even acquisition of the mother tongue is contingent upon the access a child has to adults and/or peers who are actively involved with the child in systematic linguistic and social interaction. Neglect and isolation of some children from such interaction is often the cause of "learn- ing disabilities" (Heath, 1983; Cummins, 1986; Mehan et al., 1986; Cheng, 1987; Rueda, 1987; Trueba, 1987a,b, in press; and other authors cited by Roosens, 1987).

## Third Hypothesis: Minorities' Response to Low Status

Independent from economic factors, the collective response to the status as- cribed to some minorities (for example as described by Ogbu and Matute-Bianchi [1986] in the United States in the response of blacks and Mexicans, contrasted with that of Sikhs, Japanese, and Chinese) explains the academic failure of the former groups and the success of the latter in California (Ogbu & Matute-Bianchi, 1986). According to Roosens, "the decisive factor would thus be that one has 'surrendered' and has internalized the failure for reasons of a quasi-caste position that socially and psychologically seals off any way out" (Roosens, 1987:5). The question remains why the response differs.

Both of these groups may be victims of prejudice, but only the former are the victims of "subordination in a system of rigid stratification" (Ogbu & Matute- Bianchi, 1986:87). The former are forced to emigrate, while the latter emigrate voluntarily. The key to understanding the different response of these two types of minorities is the "cultural inversion" of the former, that is, "their own rationali- zation or explanation of the existing social order and their place in it" (Ogbu & Matute-Bianchi, 1986:93).

Several historical and empirical questions need to be addressed in the context of this hypothesis. One is whether the low status ascribed to an ethnic group is equally shared by all members of the group. Are most Mexicans and blacks failing to integrate in the United States? A second question is whether the response of individuals in terms of academic performance and integration into the dominant society varies a great deal from one social group to another within the same ethnic minority. Is it possible that success makes many Mexicans and blacks less visible and that we focus only on those who fail?

A third and related question is whether the seemingly permanent low status of a given ethnic group may in fact hide the rapid integration of individual members while new ones continue to arrive on the social scene. In other words, there may be a relatively rapid assimilation of Mexicans in America, but it may be socially invisible because of the constant flow of new immigrants. Individual mobility and integration may be ignored in the face of continuous arrivals who then hold the low-paying jobs. Ultimately, however, we must still face the question of why some individuals "surrender" while others decide to challenge the status ascribed to them and continue to strive for high achievement, and succeed to some degree.

## Fourth Hypothesis: Parents' Role

Parents' role and disposition are decisive. According to Roosens (and Zeroulou, 1985, cited by Roosens),

> Parents who firmly decide to succeed in the host country and plan and provide for their children a definitive residence and career in that country will act in such a way that their children succeed much better than those of families who see the migration as a temporary phase and that continue to cling to the relations that stayed behind and to their region of origin (Roosens, 1987:5).

This interpretation seems to be in contrast with Ogbu's conception of high-achieving immigrants in the United States—Chinese Americans, for example—who maintain as reference groups for success or failure people of the home country, and who do not allow what are called "degradation incidents" (instances of racism and other humiliating events, as described by DeVos, 1983, 1984) to decrease their self-esteem. For Ogbu (1978), these students succeed because they see themselves as temporary immigrants in the United States, and are high achievers in comparison with their peers in the home country, to which they plan to return.

## Fifth Hypothesis: Genetic or Inborn Characteristics

The last hypothesis, which is unacceptable to Roosens, abundantly refuted by Ogbu (1978), discredited by many, and least likely to explain differential success in minorities, is that "inborn characteristics play such a great role that they explain the spectacular successes or failures of certain minorities. . . ." (Roosens, 1987:5). Inborn characteristics are the inherited physical and mental endowment of individuals that supposedly translate into higher levels of intelligence and achievement for some social groups but not for others. Roosens points out that this hypothesis is clearly without scientific foundation, although from time to time it acquires notoriety and is discussed seriously by political activists. The belief held by some white supremacists that race, as narrowly conceived over the last 2,000 years, diversifies levels of human talent into black and white clearly ignores human history, including well-documented evidence of vast differential achievement within each of those two very broad racial groups.

The above five hypotheses attempt to address in a very general way the attempts made by social scientists, particularly those in Europe, to explain complex phenomena relating to the integration of ethnolinguistic and immigrant groups into mainstream industrial societies. These hypotheses place the burden of success or failure on the shoulders of the ethnolinguistic minorities and immigrant groups themselves. It is possible, however, that one side of the integration coin (and only one) is the differential response of minority groups to mainstream society's rigid stratification patterns. The other side of the coin, and probably just as important, is the active role that mainstream society members can play in opening or closing the door to integration. In other words, it is the differential treatment of minority groups by the host society that very likely plays an important role in the integration of minorities and helps to determine their overall success or failure (G. Spindler, 1987).

## SOCIAL INTERACTION AND LEARNING: A VYGOTSKIAN APPROACH

Roosens' hypotheses deal with the general process of cultural integration and the resulting academic outcomes. They do not address the specifics of academic success or failure in terms of the particular achievement levels, knowledge, motivation, skills, endurance, and other requirements for success. In other words, the specific context of academic success or failure is not discussed. Nevertheless, the perspectives of Roosens and Ogbu have made a significant contribution to anthropology and education by calling our attention to the broad cultural and sociological factors affecting the overall mainstreaming of minorities.

These broad factors differentially affect minority groups as well as individuals within a single minority group. A complementary perspective, logically following that of Roosens and Ogbu, is proposed by scholars in the United States who, recognizing the significance of the broader theoretical perspectives (social, economic, and others) suggest that a "context-specific" approach, which views the psychological reality of knowledge acquisition in its immediate social and cultural context, would bring about a further understanding of the varied achievement among minorities (Diaz et al., 1986). This approach, based on the studies of Vygotsky and other Soviet scholars, can be summarized as follows: "If all children exhibit similar linguistic and cognitive capabilities required for literacy and school achievement in the home environment, why do they exhibit vast differences in ability and academic performance in school?'' (Trueba 1986:256).

As previously mentioned, central to the discussion of minority student achievement is the body of literature developed by Vygotsky, a Jewish Russian sociohistorical psychologist who died in 1934, and those inspired by him. Having experienced prejudice and social injustice, and having closely studied children with learning difficulties, Vygotsky proposed a new way to assess children's potential.

Contrary to the thinking of western psychologists, Vygotsky postulated a notion of cognitive development rooted in social interaction and inseparable from social development. Thus, he opposed the use of standardized tests to measure intellectual ability and presented an alternative assessment of differential learning potentials through the notion of a personal "zone of proximal development" (ZPD). This is the sum of experiences, background knowledge, and conceptual synthesis with which the individual approaches the task of inferring meaning from social interactions. He defined it as ''. . . the distance between the actual developmental level as determined by independent problem-solving and the level of potential development as determined through problem-solving under adult guidance or in collaboration with more capable peers'' (Vygotsky, 1978:86).

In this approach, social scientists view success or failure as related to the communicative process, which is central to the process of socialization and acculturation. Context-specific approaches are based on the ''ethnography of communication'' (Gumperz & Hymes, 1964, 1972), as well as on the concept of ''education as cultural transmission'' (G. Spindler 1955, 1982, 1987; Spindler & Spindler, 1987a,b). These scholars ask: Why do some individuals seem to acquire and accept sociocultural knowledge readily, while others have problems in doing so? More specifically, what are the educational problems and needs of linguistic minorities in this country? What should educators do in order to make the instructional system more responsive to these minorities' needs?

Particularly relevant to the context-specific approach is the theoretical perspective of Vygotsky (1978) and scholars whose work is based on Vygotsky's theories. Their efforts are focused on the development of higher psychological functions (Scribner & Cole, 1981; Griffin et al., 1981; Cole & D'Andrade, 1982; Cole & Griffin, 1983; Wertsch, 1985). One of the common assumptions is that language and communicative competence are critical for the development of higher psychological abilities. Another assumption is that this development is possible only if children participate in culturally meaningful activities. It is also assumed that development consists of an increased ability to manipulate symbols and use them in inter- and intrapsychological operations (Wertsch, 1985). Symbolic systems, especially language, are presumed to mediate between the mind and outside reality. Consequently, the role of teachers in helping children to understand symbolic systems is of crucial importance. Recent studies (Rueda & Mehan, 1986; Trueba et al., 1984; G. Spindler, 1987; Spindler & Spindler, 1987a; Trueba, 1987a,b, in press) combine current anthropological, sociological, psychological, and linguistic methods with Vygotsky's theoretical framework.

Vygotsky's sociohistorical school of psychology departs significantly from traditional western thought in that it requires the child to take an active role in determining his or her level of activity and to engage in a mental or social activity congruent with his or her ZPD. Activity is understood as an intellectual and social task composed of action and operations, which can be interpsychological (carried out in interaction with others) or intrapsychological (carried out inside the mind). For children to play an active role and work effectively within their ZPD, they must move continuously between the interpsychological and the intrapsychological realms. In effect, every developmental step is mediated in social situations by inter- and intrapsychological activities (Griffin et al., 1981).

If we assume, within this theoretical perspective, that all children normally succeed in learning if given the opportunity to interact socially within their ZPD, it follows that failure in learning is "systemic." It is not an individual failure, but a failure of the social system to provide the child with an opportunity for social intercourse. This "systemic failure" is a social phenomenon understandable only in its own historical, economic, and political context. It is not the failure of a single social institution, such as the school, or the result of faulty instruction alone. In fact, the failure may exist in the classroom, home, workplace, community, and/or society at large. Consequently, in order to overcome systemic failure one needs to change the system by means of planned (social) instructional interventions in the various learning contexts (Cole & Griffin, 1983; DeVos, 1980, 1983).

## The Nature of Learning Problems Revisited

Within the theoretical framework of Vygotsky, children's inability to handle oral language, text, and other symbolic systems is rooted in the failure of society to provide them with opportunities to engage in the social and cognitive activities necessary for learning within their ZPD. The socialization process of these children is flawed by prejudice or neglect. To prevent this, one must begin by adequately socializing minority individuals for success in the most important learning environments, the home and the school (G. Spindler, 1987). The formation of academic concepts is based on formal schooling and requires mastery of the use of taxonomic systems (systems that classify objects according to certain properties). Thus, in jobs requiring the grasp of taxonomic systems and an ability to process knowledge, schooled populations outperform cognitively nonschooled populations (Cole & D'Andrade, 1982). Ultimately, however, cognitive development is manifested in higher-order mental functions that are rooted in social interaction. This theoretical position is called by Vygotskians "culturally- or socially-based notion of cognitive development," and it has important implications for the study of linguistic minority children's adjustment to the culture of their schools.

Researchers guided by the context-specific approach and by a neo-Vygotskian perspective are not satisfied with information resulting from making general inquiries. What teams of researchers and practitioners (especially teachers) seek is a sequence of specific interactional contexts in which children demonstrate their handling of school work. Researchers need information leading to more specific analytical inferences and pragmatic instructional suggestions. The following four points based on limited study (Trueba, 1983; Trueba et al., 1984; Mehan et al., 1986; Rueda & Mehan, 1986; Trueba, 1987b; Jacobs, 1987; Kirton, 1985; Rueda, 1987, among others) are representative of the findings obtained through the context-specific approach.

1. Children's abstract categories of objects do not seem to correspond to those used by school personnel.
2. Children cannot articulate linguistically the concepts and their interrelationships apparently grasped during instruction.
3. Children's ability to remember curriculum content appears erratic and unpredictable.
4. Domain-specific skills in math, reading, or writing develop at different rates and correspond to children's English language proficiency.

While individual differences in learning ability and style may be evident, it is also important to identify characteristics shared by all children. These include lack of exposure to experiences relevant to school work, including the language used in classroom activities, and/or the opportunity and willingness to "absorb" American cultural information through school at a pace that permits them to understand such experiences. Empirical evidence supportive of the above generalizations will allow researchers to develop theories that attempt to explain the learning problems of minority students.

For educators to engage successfully in the reorganization of instructional activities, they must first explore different hypotheses concerning the success or failure of minority groups. If, for example, one advances the hypothesis that some minority groups cannot handle psychological stress in the host society and cannot function well in school because of that stress, one could generate further studies suggesting educational practices congruent with the main hypothesis, for example, that stress reduction will enhance learning. One question might be how we can examine the effects of time fragmentation on the development of high stress levels during early attempts by linguistic minority children to enter their ZPD and adjust to a new linguistic and cultural environment.

## THE ZONE OF PROXIMAL DEVELOPMENT IN "DISABLED" MINORITIES

One could try to relate stress and children's inability to learn to a fundamental barrier to entering the ZPD (in Vygotsky's terms): that is, the difficulty in relating previous knowledge and experiences, acquired through the mother language and culture, to the new knowledge and experiences of the school. For example, the researcher could explore the possibility that fragmentation of time during initial experiences in an American school may result in the negative response to social and cultural discontinuities alluded to by Roosens. Within this context-specific approach, one could still pursue specific areas of inquiry that would eventually lead researchers and practitioners toward better instructional design. Such areas of inquiry are reflected in the following questions:

1. Do minority children have the opportunity to understand the nature of different classroom activities, and the transition from one behavioral context to another?
2. Do they experience trauma associated with continual changes of activities without fully understanding the conceptual content or expected behavior?
3. Can English be acquired under high levels of stress resulting from continual fragmentation and trauma?

Teams of researchers and practitioners ultimately need to find more useful theories and possible explanations that permit them to improve instructional design. For example, the team may discover that the child becomes confused because he or she never quite understands either the content of the instructional activity or the expected behavior during such an activity. The function of researchers is to identify the role that culture plays in the acquisition of knowledge and in the overall emotional and intellectual development of students.

In Table 1.4, an attempt is made to combine both of the principal theoretical approaches discussed here. You will notice that the view of the child as a member of an ethnolinguistic group in four main interactional contexts has a parallel chronological (horizontal) continuity in each of those contexts. On the other hand, you will notice that the relationships between synchronous interactional encounters affect each other. It is true that the prearrival experiences of immigrant and linguistic minority children determine their interpretation of the initial encounters, their attempts at mainstreaming, and later on their response to cultural discontinuities (that is, their final success or failure). However, appropriate interventions can change this socialization for failure into programming for success.

If one of the most important conditions for overcoming learning difficulties as a minority child is to build adequate one-to-one relationships with adults and peers who play the role of teachers, in order to break the vicious cycle of stress, trauma, miscommunication, and poor performance, a risk-free and stress-free learning environment must be created. In this environment there is no failure nor penalty for poor performance, and there is ample opportunity to grasp the full social and cultural context of learning activities. A flexible learning environment using available cultural and linguistic resources, including those more familiar to the child, will then permit the child to link past learning experiences (along with cognitive taxonomic system acquired earlier) and new ones.

The actual documentation of minority children's stress in school is relatively

**Table 1.4. LEARNING TO SUCCEED: INTERACTIONAL CONTEXTS AND STAGES OF SOCIALIZATION**

| Interactional contexts | Stages of socialization | |
|---|---|---|
| | Construction of success | Outcomes |
| Community | Community-based counseling, legal and mental health services, basic exposure to public institutions (banks, schools, hospitals, etc.) through literacy classes. Message: "America is multicultural and your ethnic community is part of America." | Selective assimilation patterns through active participation in interethnic public activities. Collective presence in various institutional positions and roles. |
| School | Use of peer group to reinterpret degradation events and to create a climate of acceptance for cultural differences. Message: "Minority students belong here and can achieve with peer support." | Acceptance of potential success of minority students on the part of school personnel and peer groups. Increasing influence of interethnic peer groups in support of academic success. |
| Home | Reach out efforts to help parents become strong school allies. Friendly communication for the purpose of creating a support system for the minority student. Message: "You and your child belong in our school." | Selective adult support for student. Reorganization of home life style to help student engage in academic work and provide emotional support. Knowledge of the function of school and roles of school personnel. |
| Self | On a one-to-one basis, reinterpret past experiences, overcome impact of degradation events, and engage in learning activities through personal relationships with teachers and peers. Discover actual and potential academic skills. Message: "You can succeed if you are willing to seek help." | Redefinition of and acceptance of self. Control over stress and commitment to academic work. Increased cognitive and linguistic skills to articulate abstract thought. Social skills to handle academic problems and engage in learning relationships. |

scant. Earlier studies (for example, Trueba, 1983) seem to suggest that children attempt to cope with stress in three main ways:

1. By withdrawing from painful encounters and isolating themselves from the world around them;
2. By compensating with excessive and anxious efforts to participate, often mimicking behaviors that are not yet fully understood (pretending to read or write, for example);
3. By choosing to participate under protest and demonstrating their anger outwardly.

Other information obtained from recent studies (Trueba, 1983, 1987b; Mehan et al., 1986; Rueda & Mehan, 1986; Jacobs, 1987; Kirton, 1985, 1987; Rueda, 1987) may permit speculation about some of the mechanisms used by children to cope with culture shock perceived as "mental assault," as well as with the actual unfolding of the process of becoming disabled in school as part of the adjustment to the new society. Table 1.4 will help the reader to make some general observations by using a central hypothesis based on a limited number of current studies.

## The Stress Hypothesis

The observation of high levels of stress in minority students classified as "learning handicapped" and/or "language impaired," who have no apparent use of effective coping mechanisms, leads me to believe that there is a psychological reinforcement of stress associated with communicative exchanges, particularly in the classroom. While there may be a history of stress accompanying the early exposure to the new culture, which can result from prearrival traumas ("degradation incidents") or other psychologically devastating experiences, something must occur during school encounters to create an undue increase in stress, manifested in uncontrolled body and eye movements and an inability to perform relatively simple tasks.

The following observations have been made, based on recent studies (Trueba, 1983, 1987b; Mehan et al., 1986; Rueda & Mehan, 1986; Jacobs, 1987; Kirton, 1985, 1987; Rueda, 1987), regarding the devastating impact of excessive and uncontrolled stress in minority children during school, as they attempt to enter their ZPD and engage actively in learning activities.

1. Many of the "learning-disabled" children under study have learning disabilities that have increased through time, and are manifested in behavior such as lack of participation, inability to understand learning tasks, and inability to articulate meaning in oral or written form.
2. Disabilities seem to be related to children's general adjustment patterns to school culture. Many children suffer pervasive fears as they move from

one task to another. The level of stress seems to increase with the continual shift in interactional contexts.

3. School participation through the medium of English remains superficial and clearly insufficient for effective participation in academic activities.
4. There is progressive deterioration of many minority children's cognitive, linguistic, and academic skills. They find it difficult to engage in social intercourse as well as to cope with stress. They become effectively isolated academically, socially, and psychologically.
5. The institutional handling of these matters seems to exonerate school personnel and put the blame on children themselves for their lack of achievement and adjustment problems, while perpetuating a blind faith in standardized testing.

These observations are clearly linked to the central issues of the nature of learning disabilities and the lack of optimal conditions to prevent or remedy them. If cultural adjustment to an entirely new set of values is indeed being made through school encounters, a sense of personal competence and self-efficacy is essential to optimize the social participation of linguistic minority students in learning activities.

The disabilities observed in linguistic minority students, based on the limited number of studies mentioned above, have these characteristics:

1. Children's efforts to understand abstract concepts related to instructional taxonomies are not met with help from school personnel, mainly because teachers do not understand children's cultural knowledge and experiences. Consequently, teachers cannot find equivalent taxonomies and semantic categories to help children comprehend new concepts and values.
2. Beyond the expected phonetic difficulties, after several years of exposure to the English language, minority children cannot perform linguistically at the expected level because they have not fully grasped the meanings and relationships of concepts that are alien to them. These concepts were never explained to them by teachers in culturally comprehensible terms.
3. Children's ability to remember (short- and long-term memory) appears erratic and unpredictable to teachers because it is still erratic and undefined in their minds. The reason for this lack of definition is that no one has given them the cultural equivalent of those concepts in a meaningful situational context.

Excessive and persistent stress in school has serious consequences for children trying to adjust to a new cultural environment. First, it makes academic activities traumatic and the transition from one activity to another difficult to understand. Next, stress makes efforts at communication ineffective. It also makes the establishment of lasting learning relationships most difficult. Finally, stress results in the acquisition of English being painfully overextended. The child never quite understands either the classroom content (which is already foreign in many aspects) or the expected behavior. This confusion causes stress that peaks when the child is forced to perform while still unfamiliar with the cultural context. This stress will also reappear and increase with every attempt at participation in school activities. Critical to an understanding of the isolation of these children is that any attempts to express themselves, to inquire and to negotiate meaning socially, can replicate the trauma of previous experiences. It becomes a vicious circle of stress leading to poor participation, to embarrassment and confusion, and resulting in the inability to deal critically with text. Reading and writing require an understanding of the relationships of language to logic in specific instructional content areas. Wrong inferences, confused semantic ranges, inappropriate use of oral or written forms, and the relentless pace of instruction can create unbearable levels of stress.

In general, classroom instruction is perceived by many minority "learning-disabled" students as rigidly managed, fast-paced, and meaningless. Students may also see the lesson content as carefully packaged to conform to a previously approved curriculum. Minority students cannot be socialized rapidly enough for the main-stream organization to work as well for them as for mainstream students. Classroom participation by minority students is often marginal, involving acts of "passing for" a competent student (to use the term coined by Rueda & Mehan, 1986). For example, minority students pretend to understand, comply, write, read, or compute, when in fact they are painfully aware of their inability to function in the classroom.

A careful analysis of minority "learning-disabled" students' compositions, and of their repeated attempts to read, reveals a progressive deterioration in their literacy skills. It is not simply a matter of text becoming more difficult from year to year, because in some instances children remain in the same grade and deal with the very same exercises. One explanation for this phenomenon is that children's motivation to engage in literacy activities is conditioned by the expected rewards. If the rewards do not compensate for the pain, there is no good reason for a child to try to learn. Many minority children have stopped attempting to "pass for" competent students because they do not want to continue to fail. In fact, there should be nothing surprising about the desperation of some students who talk about killing themselves.

The problem is clear: some culturally different children cannot adjust rapidly to a new cultural system and are penalized by becoming officially incompetent and disabled. What is the solution? How do we maximize these children's talents and engage them in rewarding learning experiences? We must understand that children who are culturally and linguistically different, and therefore prime candidates for the label "learning disabled," need learning environments that encourage the use of native language and culture as a means to continue the learning process started at home. Use of the native language also encourages a smooth transition from the home to the school culture. The school problems of "handicapped" minority children seem to stem from their "conspicuous inability" to handle what seem to us to be "simple" academic tasks. In reality, these tasks are far from simple when they have a cultural wrapping that is misleading and difficult to grasp. The "rules of the academic game," that is, the norms of appropriate behavior, are neither clearly understood nor accepted, because these very behaviors attempt to replace many previously acquired values of appropriate adult–child and child–child behavior. Furthermore, the content and substance of much of the academic endeavors in elementary education assume cultural knowledge and life experiences that many minority children do not have. Reflecting on the ideas and hypotheses presented above, what can we do to maximize minority children's learning potential? What are our best strategies for classroom instruction? What should teachers do to become more effective in the classroom?

## CONCLUDING THOUGHTS

Academic achievement appears to be linked to successful integration into the host society, which is, in turn, a complex and difficult process taking place at different levels: at the larger macrosocial level, as part of a group of immigrants that has low social and economic status and is viewed with certain prejudices; and at the school level, where there are rigid norms of behavior and instructional principles tailored to fit middle-class, mainstream populations. Competitive performance is extremely important in school, and testing is the most common mechanism used to assess children's performance, classify them accordingly, and declare them academic successes or failures.

In the efforts by social scientists to understand academic success or failure, two main complementary approaches have emerged as the most useful. The first is the broad psychosociological approach outlining social, economic, and educational factors that are part of the infrastructure of American society and determine the social status of minorities along with their relative access to resources. The second approach, which recognizes the importance of the broad psychosociological factors, focuses on the context-specific learning setting, that is, on the mechanisms that allow an individual to obtain the necessary social and cultural knowledge as well as the cognitive skills to learn. One of the most crucial steps in the initial acquisition of skills required for learning is gaining the ability to establish dyadic and peer learning relationships.

If we take the perspective of the linguistic minority child, we realize that, without having any say in the matter, he or she is uprooted from a familiar environment, placed in a strange and often radically different learning environment, and asked to learn a new language, acquire new values, and perform in competition with natives who already have significant advantages (particularly in the form of linguistic, social, and cultural knowledge). As the linguistic minority child attempts to adjust, he or she finds it extremely stressful to communicate as well as to meet the expectations of adults and peers.

Linguistic minority children need to cope with stress and they face serious social and psychological challenges (including a redefinition of self during the transition from home culture to school culture) in establishing these learning relationships. Communicative ability (requiring linguistic, social, cultural, and cognitive skills) is critical in the process of self-redefinition and adjustment. Curriculum content and level of performance are secondary during the initial phases of adjustment; consequently, priority should be given to increasing students' participation in communicative activities.

## RECOMMENDED EXERCISES

In order to synthesize the content of this chapter, the readings suggested below, and the relationship of this chapter to the following chapters, students (preferably in small groups) should complete one or more of the following exercises.

1. Conduct a series of observations in a school, focusing on a specific class-room or set of activities. One concentration could be on a typical day in the life of a minority child. Describe what the child does, with whom he or she interacts, how he or she participates in various activities, and how peers and teachers behave towards him or her.
2. Interview a teacher of linguistic minority students. Prepare in advance a series of questions with a particular focus. For example, you may want to ask the teacher why he or she wanted to work with minorities; how well she or he knows the students, their families, cultures and backgrounds; and what problems she or he finds in dealing with them, along with what solutions she or he has found.
3. Write *your* summary of the possible explanations for the underachievement of minority students. Obtain an interview with a school principal. Ask him or her to react to these explanations, to give you his or her own explanations, and to share some documentation demonstrating his or her point of view.
4. Conduct a brief ethnic and linguistic survey of an area known for its ethnolinguistic diversity. Map it out, organize door-to-door inquiries, tab-ulate results, and write a report. As you conduct your informal survey, observe differences in life styles, income, use of space, and different or-ganization of household groups (number of families per household or lan-guages used in the home, for example).
5. Conduct library research, using data from the Census, State Department reports, and other sources to assess the ethnic and linguistic distribution of a region, its occupational profile, demographic trends, and other social and cultural characteristics. Compare the demographic trends in your region to trends in other regions or in the country at large.
6. Organize a panel discussion of students in your institution to discuss the issues of linguistic minority achievement locally and the social, political, and economic factors affecting their achievement. Document the diversity of opinions among participants and contrast their views with those of the researchers about whose work you have read.

## RECOMMENDED READINGS

Carter & Segura, 1979
Cheng, 1987

Cole & D'Andrade, 1982
Cole & Griffin, 1983
Cummins, 1986
Delgado-Gaitan & Trueba, 1985
DeVos, 1984
Deyhle, 1987
Erickson, 1984
Freire, 1973
Gilmore & Glatthorn, 1982
Goldman & McDermott, 1987
Goldman & Trueba, 1987
Ogbu, 1974, 1978, 1982
Ogbu & Matute-Bianchi, 1986
Rueda, 1987
Rueda & Mehan, 1986
Scribner & Cole, 1981
Spindler G., 1982, 1987
Spindler & Spindler, 1982, 1983, 1987a,b,c,
Suarez-Orozco, 1987
Trueba, 1983, 1986, 1987a,b
Vygotsky, 1978
Walker, 1987
Wertsch, 1985

# CHAPTER
# 2

# Language, Culture, and Schooling

There is an intimate relationship between language and culture. Without language, culture cannot be acquired effectively nor can it be expressed and transmitted. Without culture, language cannot exist. The linkage between language and culture in the process of knowledge acquisition, as well as in the context of the whole development of young humans, cannot be stressed enough. While there is no contention about this linkage, its nature and consequences need to be addressed.

## LANGUAGE AND COMMUNICATION IN SCHOOL

Language—defined as a communications system consisting of arbitrary symbols used by humans to organize, structure, and store experience, knowledge, and concepts—is not only an integral part of human culture and a distinctive characteristic of humans (in contrast with other primates and mammals) but also an instrument of communication that has changed and is continuously changing life styles and conditions for the entire human species. Language is the primary instrument with which we express and transmit culture, maintain it, teach it, and adapt it. Characteristics of human speech are that it is patterned, structured, and predictable, and as such suitable for the articulation of concise, coded formulas, complex experiences, taxonomies, and classes of phenomena and objects. Language helps us to link past and present experiences and place them in the mind in neatly structured categories, ready to be used. Human speech is an integral part of human social intercourse, and as such it cannot exist in isolation, independently from social interaction. Consequently it is regulated, changed, and interpreted through social intercourse.

Indeed the history of mankind is reflected in such linguistic phenomena as bilingualism, language contact, minority languages, dialects, immigrant languages, literacy languages, code-switching, language interference, motivational stereotypes, bilingual proficiency, and others (Haugen, 1978; Kachru, 1978; Fishman, 1978; Trudgill, 1984; Cummins, 1984, 1986; Heath, 1983; Goldman & Trueba, 1987; Trueba & Delgado-Gaitan, 1988). In historic terms, the acquisition of a second language among educated people has been a common phenomenon. The Romans, during the early centuries of our western civilization, adopted their Greek slaves' language and culture, especially their religious beliefs, arts, sports, and science. Roman children were exposed to the Greek language and culture through their slaves who became servants and teachers, and Greek–Latin bilingualism and bi-literacy developed in the early 3rd century A.D. (McLaughlin, 1985).

During the nineteenth and twentieth centuries language teaching changed drastically to an emphasis on learning syntax and morphology, line-by-line translation, phonetics, and repetition of patterns. In recent years, language teaching and learning have focused on verbal exchanges with native speakers in face-to-face interaction and in culturally relevant (real life) contexts. Not until some 20 years ago did more sophisticated techniques for teaching and learning English as a second language (ESL) begin to develop. Phonological accuracy was given much importance, and gave rise to the "audiolingual" method as well as to the foreign language in the elementary school (FLES) programs of the 1950s and 1960s (McLaughlin, 1985).

In the study of education for linguistic minorities in the United States, a common assumption on the part of the public and educators is that the "language problem" of minorities consists simply of a lack of phonological skills and/or linguistic forms (knowledge of syntactic structures and vocabulary), and a lack of "practice" in the use of English. If the diagnosis is "lack of English," then the prescribed remedy is a good dose of ESL conceptualized as "lots of practice in English patterns." The problems for linguistic minority students, however, are far more complicated. A number of social, economic, and political contextual factors, either limit their access to the second language or isolate them culturally and/or motivationally from mainstream groups. Cummins states:

> Recent policy initiatives in relation to the education of minority students in North America and Europe have generally assumed implicitly that such students can be treated as a homogeneous group; in other words, that the same educational policy initiatives are equally appropriate for Chinese, Mexican-American, Portuguese and other groups (Cummins, 1984:96).

In the early 1970s bilingual education was "hailed as new panacea for the academic ills of our economically disadvantaged" without any pondering of the "societal implications and requirements of bilingual education alternatives" (Fishman, 1979:11; see also O'Malley, 1981, 1982; Hernandez-Chavez, 1984).

Two important factors invite reflection:

1. Many minority children who were exposed to ESL instruction consistently over a period of years did not learn enough English to function effectively in English-speaking classrooms.
2. Many other minority children who did learn English continued to have serious adjustments and academic problems in school.

Fishman has eloquently explained why looking at bilingual education as a panacea is only a trap that will surprise us with disillusionment:

The constriction of bilingual education to overcoming "diseases of the poor," distasteful though it may be, has its well-established precedents in other climes and other centuries, but most particularly in Europe since the Reformation, by the fact that the official language of education was not always the mother tongue of students new to the educational system. In such circumstances, whether in early-modern France or Germany, in turns of the century or in the recent-day Yucatan, Manila or Moncton, the same claim has been advanced: start the learner off in the language he knows best. The more rapid progress made as a result, insofar as developing learning confidence and satisfaction is concerned, will then pay off in terms of much more rapid progress when majority language is turned to (and, as some would have it, when more serious educational work is begun). This approach when transferred to the American context, typically claims that "learning English" and "getting educated" are not one and the same and that it is worth pursuing the latter via the mother tongue until the former can be tackled and, indeed, that the one will facilitate the other (Fishman, 1979:16).

Social scientists have pointed out that even within one general community, going from home to school requires in children the acquisition of social and cognitive skills and the internalization of norms of behavior equivalent to a "new" language and culture (Au, 1980; Spindler, 1982; Boggs, 1985; Delgado-Gaitan, 1987b; Delgado-Gaitan & Trueba, 1985; Gilmore & Glatthorn, 1982; Trueba & Delgado-Gaitan, 1988; Tharp & Gallimore, in press). What happens to children who go through more drastic changes, who are removed from their familiar environment and placed in a new social, linguistic, and cultural environment, away from the extended family and friends? How do they acquire the culture of the school through language they do not understand, in circumstances of high stress and alienation? Successful schooling does not necessarily mean accepting the status quo, the power structure, and values traditionally passed from generation to generation. The critical mass of immigrants can demand some changes. In a study of a bilingual programs in central western California, Warren observed the following:

> The principal and the bilingual teachers display the bilingual competence— using two languages to manage their work and social environment. . . . Parents are not content with the traditional assimilative-oriented admonition that their children have to learn English to "make it" in the Anglo-dominated society. They believe the bilingual job market offers far more opportunity for employment and upward mobility—and they observe critically and carefully the qualifications of those among them who move into positions as bilingual aides (Warren, 1982:404).

Despite a more liberal and assertive parental response to "Anglo" educational philosophy and practice, that is, of advocating the use of two languages in instruction and school management, the researcher states his conviction that the school curriculum is fundamentally assimilationist:

> Curriculum systems have been presented as prototypical instructional processes and have been found to be culturally "Anglo" in their socializing effects—oriented towards individualistic achievement values—and (whether presented in English or in Spanish) eliciting from pupils common patterns of adaptive behavior (Warren, 1982:405).

While some children have no problem acquiring a new language and culture, many others seem to find it nearly impossible. The identification of cultural conflict and its relationship to language use is the focus of recent research. Conflicting cultural values as reflected in language use are illustrated by the following examples:

> One cultural difference in language use which has already been mentioned is the difference in voice level normally used by some Native American groups and whites, with Native Americans interpreting the whites' level as anger and hostility and the whites interpreting the Native Americans' level as shyness or unfriendliness. A child who looks directly at the teacher when talking or listening is considered honest, direct, straightforward by most Anglos and as disrespectful by most Mexican-Americans, Blacks, and Native Americans. The child who averts his eyes would be considered respectful by the latter and shifty or dishonest by many Anglos (Saville-Troike, 1979:146).

At the heart of these conflicts is the nature of language as a system of communication and cultural values transmitted through language in the same interactional setting and even in the same communicative act. It is important to discuss the linkage between language and culture in order to understand the problems language minority children often face in adjusting to American schools and society.

Many scholars have explored the relationship of second language development, culture change, and the acquisition of cognitive skills. Cummins (1976, 1978, 1981a,b, 1983, 1984, 1986) has strongly defended the relationship between bilingualism and cognitive growth, and has postulated the "linguistic interdependence hypothesis." This hypothesis states that the acquisition of a second language is contingent upon the full development of the mother tongue. Proficiency in a second language is best acquired through the transfer of linguistic and cognitive competencies gained in the first language. Cummins also distinguishes between "basic interpersonal communicative skills" and "cognitive academic language proficiency." This distinction—which is very difficult to assess—has been disputed by linguists and psychologists on the basis of differential linguistic development in specific interactional contexts (language compartmentalization per domain). No one, however, can deny the existence of different degrees of second-language proficiency and academic performance.

The position that the most effective way to assimilate a language minority group is to create a mandatory language policy enforcing second language acquisition is neither unique to this country (in recent years), nor foreign to Europe, Central America, the Soviet Union and many other regions. The continent of Africa has over 1,000 languages; usually French or English is the language of the school. Mexico has over 100 languages, and Spanish is the language of the school, with the exception of some bilingual programs (in Chiapas, Oaxaca, and northern Puebla, for example). On the continent of South America over 500 languages are spoken; Spanish and Portuguese are the school languages. The Soviet Union has over 50 major school languages, Switzerland has 4 (French, German, Italian, and Romansch), and other countries have regions with two languages, such as Spain (with Basque, Catalonian, or Gallician combined with Spanish) (McLaughlin, 1985).

Language policies change from country to country, but they all have in common assumptions about the power of the language to join or separate people, to open up avenues for assimilation, to increase isolation, or to provide higher or lower social status. The differences between European linguistic minorities and American linguistic minorities, according to Van der Plank, are determined ''by their historical background, ecological character, national aspirations, and above all by their social composition and status'' (1978:423). In the United States, contrary to the situation in Europe, there are no previously established geographic boundaries corresponding to ethnic–linguistic boundaries; indeed some minority groups (the Hmong, as an example) go on to secondary and tertiary migration patterns searching for more suitable social and ecological environments in which to establish their society.

> In America, language is just one of the differentials, among which social class, social values (culture), religion, and possible racial differences are much more decisive for the total processes of assimilation. In Europe, linguistic minorities often differ only in their speech from dominant linguistic groups. Even religious boundaries very seldom fall together with linguistic or with other ethnic (in Europe folkloristic) peculiarities . . . in spite of the incongruence between language and other ethnic markers in Europe, language has proved to be an astonishingly dominant symbol of group identity for more than one-and-a-half centuries (Van der Plank, 1978:424).

The ethnic boundaries in Europe seem to operate at the folk–societal level and are not as clearly defined or as important for social interaction as they are in this country.

Thus, for example, some European countries such as Sweden, Germany, and France provide several hours per week of native language instruction, and their schools are often organized so that the children of guestworkers who speak other languages are grouped together. The policy of encouraging guestworkers to return home after their contracts are over has consequences for school language programs. McLaughlin states: ''In the Swedish context, some instruction in the home language is required for all immigrant children, unless the parents are opposed, or the language is spoken by only a few students in a school district'' (1985:35).

In West Germany, children of guestworkers are educated in separate classrooms with different curricula, teachers, and textbooks, unless the children speak German fluently. If such children are integrated into the regular school system, they will have no opportunity for mother language instruction (Rist, 1979; John, 1980).

In the Soviet Union in 1979 there were over 105 million people belonging to 19 nationalities who spoke languages other than Russian. Of this group, 70 million belong to five main national groups that speak Ukranian, Uzbek, Byelorussian, Kazakh, and Tatar, in contrast with some 137 million Russian speakers. The remaining 35 million people speak 14 other major languages, from as many nationalities, each including at least 1 million people each (McLaughlin, 1985).

The United States has gone through giant swings of the public opinion pendulum, from advocating no explicit language policy, and opposing any attempts to establish one, to the extreme of sponsoring ballots to eradicate the use of languages other than English. In spite of this sentiment against the use of other languages for school instruction, since the early 1960s there has been strong federal support for bilingual education. The question of eligibility of students has been placed in the hands of politicians. Definitions and numbers of eligible children change according to political creed. Wagonner (1984) explains the conflicting figures for school-aged children who speak languages other than English in the home and who are limited English proficient (LEP). In 1978, for example, one branch of the federal government calculated the total of LEPs at 653,000, while researchers, also paid federal monies, presented a more realistic figure of between 3.4 and 6.6 million. Wagonner's rationale for such diverse estimates depicts the variation among LEP categories:

1. Children who speak languages other than English at home rated as speaking English not well or not at all by household respondents (653,000).
2. Children who speak languages other than English at home who are LEP (2,904,000).
3. Children who speak languages other than English at home who are LEP and LEP children who only speak English (3,439,000).
4. Children who speak languages other than English at home and who are LEP, and LEP children whose usual language is English, including LEP children who only speak English (6,634,000) (Waggoner, 1984:12).

The issue, as one studies these diverse criteria, is the degree of English language proficiency, even if English is the only language known by the child. Lack of school English proficiency does not preclude a child from being proficient in the kind of English used by peers or other persons in the outside community. If indeed English becomes the only language of a child because of rapid loss of mother tongue, we have to contend with other serious problems associated with that phenomenon. In general, however, given certain conditions of isolation *and* pressure to assimilate, children tend to lose their mother tongue more rapidly than they manage to acquire the second language.

A figure (reached by compromise) for the number of children between kindergarten and ninth grade who were eligible for bilingual education programs in the United States in 1980 was 1.7 million. This figure is based on the Children's English and Services Study by O'Malley (1982). This study reports that in 1980 there were 600 federally funded programs in 79 different languages for 315,000 children (18.5 percent of the presumed 1.7 million eligible), and that 80 percent of these children were Hispanic. O'Malley reports that in addition to the 18.5 percent receiving some kind of bilingual instruction, 11 percent received instruction in ESL. Finally, O'Malley believes that 58 percent of all eligible children were receiving instruction in mainstream English classrooms, with some remedial English instruction provided in some schools.

If we look at the instructional picture of the 315,000 students in bilingual programs, O'Malley tells us that 77 percent received 5 or more hours weekly of English instruction, and 46 percent of them received more than 10 hours. In 80 percent of those programs classified as bilingual, English was used more frequently than the native language. Halcon (1983) reports that in the Spanish–English Title VII programs surveyed, Spanish language skills were not sufficiently developed or maintained. An overall picture of the type of bilingual instruction provided to language minority children at that time indicates that the native language was used as a means of clarifying or bringing about some understanding when English was not comprehensible.

The figures cited used to estimate the needs of children who do not speak English may appear conservative when we remember the many children of undocumented workers, whose numbers increased during the conservative waves of public opinion against the use of languages other than English, and who consequently are not considered a legitimate part of the school issue of classification.

After years of official support for bilingual education involving a substantial amount of money spent on basic programs, teachers, materials, teacher training programs, the federal government and the public are becoming concerned about their original understanding of the problem of linguistic minorities in school, and about the solution adopted. All the money spent by the government from 1968 to date has reached only a fraction of the eligible student population. It is estimated that federally sponsored bilingual basic programs (for elementary or secondary schools) served only a quarter of a million school-age children. To compound the problem, many of these programs have had to face other difficulties, such as lack of funds, trained personnel, and political support within the school itself. Even those programs that have successfully assisted children to acquire English as a second language have not been able to help these children achieve at the level of the mainstream student population.

No one denies the importance of language, and yet to focus on language alone without examining the social, political, and cultural context is not very useful. Vygotsky gave language an enormous importance in the cognitive development of children:

> The most significant moment in the course of intellectual development, which gives birth to the purely human forms of practical and abstract intelligence,

occurs when speech and practical activity, two previously completely independent lines of development, converge (Vygotsky, 1978:24).

For language minority children to have a fair opportunity to develop their talents, they must also be given an opportunity to integrate "speech and practical activity" in the school setting. Under what conditions can this occur? What are the barriers that impede it? The answer is not in the acquisition of the second language alone, but in the acquisition of the culture of the school. This assumes that children are allowed to become bona fide active participants in the school's culture.

## ACQUIRING A SECOND CULTURE IN SCHOOL

Becoming an active member of a new cultural group requires specific sociolinguistic and cultural knowledge, along with the ability to use that knowledge appropriately in specific contexts. These steps are part of the early socialization process among humans. An integral element of this process is the internalization of values that enhance the survival and well-being of the individual and his or her social unit, such as the nuclear family. American culture is internalized by newcomers in many different ways because culture means different things to different people: a set of values, a common ethos, a democratic philosophy of life, an open political and economic system. Meanwhile, minorities participate in American culture unequally. Minorities also retain different degrees of affiliation with their home culture and of isolation from the mainstream culture. If we see culture not only as a set of cognitive modes but also as a set of values that shape our lives and compel us to behave in certain ways, how can minority groups be expected to participate in American culture? What outlooks, values, and philosophy do they share with the rest of the members of American society? If there is a multicultural America, in what ways is it cohesive? What is the role of the school in the creation and maintenance of a single nation?

From the standpoint of the "learning-disabled" minority child, the complex world of symbols (including language) represents America in concrete interactional settings. The contrast between the symbols acquired at home and those acquired in school may create sharp behavioral conflicts that require selective change and adjustment. In the classroom, the structure of academic tasks, the use of power by authority figures, the role of teachers and principals, and the behavior of mainstream peers all send minority students indirect messages about their own incompetence and the lack of value of their home culture and language. School socialization involves "meta-messages" as part of the "hidden curriculum" (Warren, 1982) that makes school a pivotal social institution for expediting the acculturation of minority children. The new values are inculcated in the organization of school activities and reward system. A case in point is the intensive competition around which the entire American school system is built.

## The Culture of Competition

Teachers are true heroes who must take the brunt of demands, attacks, and failures. Nothing presented in these pages should be interpreted as an attempt to blame teachers or to point at flaws in their characters, commitment, or skills. What teachers do and are taught to do is actually congruent with expectations of American culture; indeed, it is a reflection of the mission society has imposed on schools and the role society has ascribed to the teacher as the main architect of a child's education.

Competition is at the heart of democratic societies with open social and economic systems that maximize individual freedom and free enterprise. In fact, some scholars argue that schools and classrooms are organized so as to meet the demands of the economic world. This is precisely what makes the work of teachers so much harder. Goldman and McDermott state:

> In a school system that has all children pitted against each other in the name of celebrating the best, we have become preoccupied with documenting and sorting out the half of our children who do not do as well as their fellow citizens. The sorting function of schools is never far away from any classroom. This makes teaching a most difficult task (1987:282).

Their argument goes on to recognize that while competition can be helpful in some settings, it can also be destructive, and is quite possibly becoming more so in the schools, which have been burdened with the responsibility of sorting out children for their place in life. This responsibility forces teachers to rely on head-to-head competition and put up with the embarrassments of differential pupil success. As Goldman and McDermott remind us:

> We do not want to forget, however, that within the largest frame of reference, competition and evaluation make the school well-tuned with the more forceful institutions of American life, most particularly the dog-eat-dog world of business (1987:283).

The stress involved in competition is considerable for all children, but even more so for the linguistic minority child who feels disadvantaged from the start because of linguistic and cultural differences. Indeed, many of these children face serious cultural dilemmas because they are caught between two conflicting value and behavioral demands.

In academic competition, there are sometimes more losers than winners. The direct result of omnipresent and excessive competition of the type described by Goldman and McDermott (1987) is to create a stratified group within the school, replicating the social strata of larger society. According to these authors, teachers considered that competition would increase student motivation to participate in learning activities. Many minority children come from home cultures in which socialization efforts are oriented toward working cooperatively and performing inconspicuously. These children find it very difficult to enter a culture of competition. Looking at the home and family settings of the students, we may find genuine insights into so-called "school problems" (Trueba, 1983, 1987a,b). The information discovered in the home is crucial in helping teachers and children to cooperate in the communicative process of teaching and learning during the complex years of linguistic and cultural transition.

A preoccupation with American culture has attracted brilliant minds throughout this century. Anthropologists and psychologists have attempted to present a configuration of American culture from many different perspectives (Boas, 1928; Dollard, 1937; Warner, 1941; Mead, 1943; Kluckhohn, 1949; and many others cited by Spindler & Spindler, 1983). Earlier anthropologists wrote on consensus and continuity and the characteristics of the "ethos of American culture," emphasizing the virtues of honesty, motivation to achieve, equality, optimism, and conformity (Mead, 1943; C. Kluckhohn, 1949; F. Kluckhohn, 1950; Gillin, 1955). More recent anthropologists discuss American culture in specific communities and make comparisons cross-culturally in a number of current studies (Spindler & Spindler, 1983). *Americans Together*, by Varenne (1977), a study of a midwestern community that focuses on social interaction, communication, values, rituals, and ideology, stands out in clear contrast to previous studies because it shows how midwestern American communities have changed ". . . in the direction of loosening boundaries between social classes, statuses and roles, sexes, families and identities" (Spindler & Spindler, 1983:51).

The Spindlers suggest that Varenne's (1977) model of community is timebound, but biased towards a description of the flow of interaction in its immediate context, perhaps overlooking "stability, boundedness, and structure" (Spindler & Spindler, 1983:55). In contrast to Varenne's work stands *America Now*, a holistic study by Harris (1981), which attempts to explain some of the characteristics of American culture:

> Technological breakdown from errant toasters to space capsules, as well as uncivil help, the shrinking dollar, women's liberation, gay liberation, rising crime rates, and religious movements in the phrasing of material determinism (Spindler & Spindler 1983:52).

My interpretation of the work by George and Louise Spindler leads me to emphasize the diametric opposition in American culture between an egalitarian philosophy, based on our democratic political and economic system, and the concentration of power in large, internationally based American corporations, which can bypass our complex system of checks and balances. Another diametrically opposed relationship exists between the individual and the ethnic community. Hatch's (1979) description of a rural town is characterized by an attempt to understand "the deterioration of small-town life in America" (Spindler & Spindler, 1983:53).

The "dialogue" (to use the Spindlers' phrase) or the diametric opposition alluded to above, between individualism and conformity, consensus and debate, continuity and change, is at the heart of American culture. The conflict between individualism and conformity appears in the context of the civil rights struggle and the intolerance of cultural and linguistic differences. The American national character is described as guided by rugged individualism, militancy, and rejection of authority, which surface in conjunction with the rejection of traditional values (Hsu, 1953, 1972). The Spindlers (1983) argue that this characterization cannot be generalized, and that it entails some historical misinterpretation of the overall national picture. They recognize, however, the differential accommodations of the various groups in conflict with the "power structure." In accordance with the conflicting currents of tolerance and intolerance for linguistic and cultural differences are current efforts to emphasize national unity through enforced mandatory use of English for most public services (especially those related to health and legal issues), civil activities, and school instruction.

The variety of case studies in the Spindlers' review and analysis (1983) indicates the controversy over opposing themes throughout our history, when the intensity of the debate varies periodically and moves from one issue to another: from English language policy to employment, to education, to low-income minorities, to control of our borders, to the gay movement and women's liberation, to governmental policies on AIDS research and testing, and many others.

Anthropologists have gradually focused on specific institutional settings in which cultural transmission is one of the primary purposes. The examination of general transmission and changes in American cultural values (G. Spindler, 1955, 1977, 1987; Spindler & Spindler, 1987a,b) evolved into a study of specific transmission mechanisms within educational institutions (Peshkin, 1978; G. Spindler, 1982, 1987; Gilmore & Glatthorn, 1982). The transmission and change of American culture may also result in the perpetuation of a particular socioeconomic stratification, the loss of ethnic ties and ethnic identity, and an increased isolation on the part of some ethnic minority groups.

## Transmission of Culture in the School

Linguistic minority students may notice upon arrival at the new school that teachers control all the details of classroom activities. Students ask permission to talk, they observe different norms of behavior in specific school contexts, and they imitate behaviors. Newcomers may also notice that teachers control the posture and physical movements of students in class, as well as their access to others, the manner in which requests are made, and the overall participation of students in academic activities. Asian, Native American, Hawaiian, and other minority children may notice that adult control is reinforced by training children to follow "directives," and that children do not take offense or grow embarrassed if they are singled out for discipline or performance purposes.

Lack of conformity with mainstream cultural and linguistic norms on the part of the linguistic minority child sends a signal of alarm to the teacher. It may mean "potential trouble," "lack of discipline," or "failure to achieve in English at the level of mainstream children," all of which are immediately interpreted as personal and institutional failures. Concern on the part of school personnel results in the setting up of the entire machinery of testing and assessing children's "intelligence" through traditional standard English tests.

The usual process is this. First, teachers, psychologists, the principal, and other school personnel communicate informally, and later formally—through memos carefully worded for legal protection—the message that a given child is not performing at the expected level, and that she or he therefore "may" be "learning disabled." The next step consists of developing a consensus about the assessment and classification of the child's presumed handicaps. This step leads to a formal referral, a formal declaration by the school psychologist, and a joint ratification by school "experts." The child's problem is cited as the rationale for recommended treatment (special education classes, speech pathology help, tutoring in English or math, family conference, or additional referrals). These steps have serious consequences for day-to-day interactions between teachers and children and often send messages to children that they are "incompetent" or "potential trouble."

## ADJUSTMENT TO A NEW CULTURE THROUGH REFLECTIVE CULTURAL ANALYSIS

Stating the problem and some possible explanations for its existence is always easier than offering a solution. Social science research is entering a phase of development in which its potential applicability is viewed as a strength, in that it permits a real-life examination of whether or not a theory works. Anthropology is no exception; its recent major accomplishments bring about a better understanding of culture and its role in determining behavior, knowledge acquisition, and successful adjustment to new environments.

This section reflects some of the theoretical advances best represented by the work of George and Louise Spindler and their associates. My interpretation of their concept of culture, the role of culture in the development of learning handicaps or achievement problems, and the need for reflective cultural analysis is only tentative. It integrates various theoretical contributions of the Spindlers on the one hand, and neo-Vygotskians on the other hand.

Culture consists to some extent of "the organization of activities that one engages in that result in one's acquiring possessions, recognition, power, status and satisfaction" (Spindler & Spindler, 1987b:2). There is, therefore, a clear relationship between the choice of specific activities and the individual's cultural values to be enhanced by the expected outcomes of these activities. Furthermore, the acquisition of cultural knowledge and values includes learning how to select those activities with the greatest potential for enhancing cultural values (power, recognition, status, satisfaction, possessions, or any other desirable ends).

The Spindlers note that because modern societies are subject to rapid changes, cultural knowledge and values become rapidly outdated. This forces an individual to lose his or her culture before he or she has mastered the original set of values or internalized the linkages between activities and expected outcomes. Such internalization takes place during early socialization (Spindler & Spindler 1965, 1987a, b; G. Spindler 1974a, b; L. Spindler 1978, 1984).

As observed by George and Louise Spindler in their Remstal study in Schonhausen, Germany, in the face of sociocultural change, people manage to retain their deeply rooted enduring self. The enduring self is "equated with ideal-romantic instrumental choices and rationalizations" associated with images of the land and village life, in contrast with their situated self, which is "equated with the pragmatic modality" associated with images of urbanized lifestyles in an industrial society. This and similar findings led the Spindlers to develop the concept of "instrumental competence" (1987b:4), which is discussed below.

## Instrumental Competence and Learning Disabilities

If we assume that all children develop a sense of self-esteem and competence as a result of their success in mastering certain tasks, it follows that failure to perform at the expected level has a negative effect on self-esteem. This process is described by the Spindlers as follows:

> Minority children with various socio-cultural backgrounds attend schools predicated on mainstream, largely middle class, and largely white Anglo Saxon North European Protestant cultural assumptions. Such children acquire deficits in self-esteem damaged not only by actual failure but also by negative perceptions and low expectations of them by teachers and other students (Spindler & Spindler, 1987b:5).

There is, however, a complex mechanism of high self-esteem maintenance that permits children to search for alternative sources for competency and for success, in contexts other than school. Therefore, as part of the situated self described earlier, the minority child seeks to develop self-efficacy (a component of self-esteem) in areas of experienced success. George and Louise Spindler define this concept as follows: "We define self-efficacy as a prediction that one will be able to meet the demands of the situation effectively. . . . Self-efficacy in our terms is an expectation that one can exhibit instrumental competence in the appropriate contexts" (1987b:6). Therefore, the situated self can gradually accommodate demands for additional instrumental competencies by selectively taking activities in which he or she can predictably demonstrate self-efficacy. Success is clearly a necessary condition for the retention of high self-esteem.

Cultural change can place self-esteem in serious jeopardy. Adjustment to new settings may require a thorough reorganization of cultural priorities and acquisition of new instrumental competencies. Children in new settings need to experience academic success; otherwise, there is no reason for them to engage in such activities. Continued failure preempts the individual's motivation to become involved in an activity.

If the main reason for the poor academic performance of "learning-disabled" minority children is their lack of opportunity to develop needed instrumental competencies and self-efficacy, it follows that one of the main tasks in reflective cultural analysis (RCA) is to help teachers develop effective instructional strategies based on an understanding of the cultural roots of academic failure. There is a reason why minority children have been deprived of the opportunity to master the instrumental competencies required in school: these competencies are functionally relevant in a culture that is unknown to the minority child. We discussed earlier the minority child's excessive stress from lack of instrumental skills that go with such knowledge or values. The proposed solution is "cultural therapy" for their teachers, and for the children too.

## The Nature of Reflective Cultural Analysis

The concept of RCA presented by George and Louise Spindler (Spindler & Spindler, 1982; G. Spindler, 1974a,b; L. Spindler, 1984) is best understood in the context of their study of *Roger Harker and Schonhausen: From Familiar to Strange and Back Again* (1982). Roger Harker (a pseudonym) regarded himself as a competent and caring elementary school teacher who volunteered for the study to improve his "professional competence." George Spindler worked intensively with him for 6 months collecting autobiographical and psychological data, ratings of him and interview data obtained from administrative superiors, self-evaluation comments, observations of his interaction with children, notes from interviews with each child, including student ratings, and sociometric data describing children's interactional networks (Spindler & Spindler, 1982).

Roger Harker was considered one of the "most promising" and best organized teachers, "sensitive to children's needs," "fair and just to all of the children," and knowledgeable. His group, crossing social strata and ethnic boundaries, was composed of Mexican Americans, Anglo Europeans, and Japanese Americans:

> He ranked highest on all dimensions, including personal and academic factors, those children who were most like himself—Anglo, middle to upper-middle social class, and, like him, ambitious (achievement-oriented). He also estimated that these children were the most popular with their peers, and were the leaders of the classroom group. His knowledge about the individual children, elicited without recourse to files or notes, was distributed in the same way. He knew significantly more about the children culturally like himself (on items concerned with home background as well as academic performance), and least about those culturally most different (Spindler & Spindler, 1982).

According to the children he was not always fair and just. He had "special pets," his view of children's networks was in conflict with that of the children themselves, and "his negative ratings proved to be equally inaccurate":

> Children he rated as isolated or badly adjusted socially, most of whom were non-Anglo and non-middle-class, more often than not turned out to be "stars of attraction" from the point of view of the children. . . . He most frequently called on, touched, helped, and looked directly at the children culturally like himself. He was never mean or cruel to the other children. It was almost as though they weren't there (Spindler & Spindler, 1982:26).

The Spindlers conclude that this young man "was confirming the negative hypotheses and predictions" made earlier, and that he "was informing Anglo middle-class children that they were capable, had bright futures, were socially acceptable, and were worth a lot of trouble," and indeed, Roger Harker "did not know that he was discriminating" (Spindler & Spindler, 1982:26). The major insight in the discussion of Roger Harker is that "he was locked into a self-reinforcing, self-maintaining sociocultural system of action, perception, and reward," and the ethnographer working as consultant and researcher with him "had to make the familiar strange to him in order to have any effect" (Spindler & Spindler, 1982:29).

It is precisely in this context that RCA must take place. This is fundamentally based on what Freire has called "conscientization" (1973), which is a process of bringing to the surface of our awareness our own cultural identity in its historical, sociocultural, and political context. The RCA approach can be applied to teachers and students. The example given by the Spindlers shows that discrimination does not have be a vicious and direct effort at hurting someone else; it can be the most spontaneous reaction in response to culturally determined perceptions of other peoples. On the other hand, on the part of the minority student, the lack of self-esteem, which is at the basis of the conflict experienced in the transition from home to school, is internalized as a mirror image of what the teacher thinks. Freire and the Spindlers share a broad sociohistorical and cultural perspective, as well as the assumption that academic failure is not necessarily the fault of the individual, but also the result of many extrinsic social forces. These approaches demonstrate deep concern for social equity and justice, and for universal human rights to one's own space, language, culture, and freedom. What is unique to RCA as described by the Spindlers is its theoretical framework and ethnographic documentation taken from cultural anthropology.

Cultural knowledge is selectively acquired in such a way that it becomes "self-reinforcing" and normally it presupposes the individual's commitment to engage in certain activities. These activities are perceived as leading to the mastery of those instrumental competencies that enhance the pursuit of cultural goals. The mastery of specific instrumental competencies must be perceived by the individual as having a direct effect on the pursuit of specific cultural goals. Such goals are congruent with culturally preestablished order of priorities in values. Roger Harker's cultural values determined his ranking order of students' competencies and self-worth. The reinforcement and attention he gave to culturally similar pupils mirror his value structure. By the same token, minority children's response—their very motivation to acquire certain instrumental competencies—is based on the assumption that such competencies match minority home culture values, and the expectation that with these competencies children will attain goals relevant to their individual and collective cultural survival.

It seems reasonable to expect that in order to establish a process of RCA for schoolchildren, the trainer of teachers, counselor, psychologist, or principal needs to reflect on:

1. What American culture is and how it is transmitted, and what instrumental competencies are required to adjust successfully to American schools;
2. What type of school activities require cognitive and social competencies, and on what cultural values motivation to engage in these activities is based;
3. What the culturally established value priorities are in American culture, and what conflict there is with priorities established by minority families;
4. What specific goals (for example, literacy in English) are pursued through the choice of certain school activities that have no corresponding value in the minority home culture;
5. What potential areas of conflict in values and philosophy exist between mainstream children and minority children, as evidenced from exhibited teacher–child and child–child interaction.

If we see America as multicultural, pluralistic, and ethnically diverse, does it make sense to speak of a single American culture? The debate about what American culture is can be summarized by these eloquent remarks by George and Louise Spindler:

> Despite these objections, we say there is an American culture. We claim that there is an American culture, because ever since pre-Revolutionary times we have been dialoguing about freedom and constraint, equality and difference, cooperation and competition, independence and conformity, sociability and individuality, Puritanism and free love, materialism and altruism, hard work and getting by, and achievement and failure. It is not because we are all the same (we are not) or that we agree in most important matters (we do not) that there is an American culture. It is somehow that we agree to worry, argue, fight, emulate, and agree or disagree about the same pivotal concerns (Spindler & Spindler, 1987c:5).

For the Spindlers, the essence of American culture is in dialectic exchanges that determine the prevalent values, behaviors, beliefs, and symbolic systems in American society. Because education is viewed as "cultural transmission" and "learning and transmission are never separated," schooling provides calculated interventions in the learning process (Spindler & Spindler, 1987c:6) that are central to RCA. Conscious and reflective analysis of cultural conflict presupposes a profound understanding of one's own culture—in our case, an understanding of American culture in its broader sociohistorical context—and its role in establishing the perceptions of others who do not share our culture. The purpose of RCA is not necessarily to change teachers or students, but to help them understand the cultural differences and the judgements made on the basis of cultural values. If the teacher misunderstands the child's home environment, the teacher cannot assist this child in the acquisition of missing instrumental competencies. The nature of cultural conflict and of the means necessary to resolve it requires RCA. The solution may indeed require some change in both the minority child and school personnel.

Ultimately, the purpose of cultural reflection and analysis is to internalize the nature of American culture and the place of minority cultures within it. In order to obtain an insight into both mainstream American culture and the place of ethnic cultures, it may be necessary to use ethnographic techniques to gather and analyze cultural knowledge and values, including the sources of cultural conflict in specific school contexts.

## Mechanisms for Reflective Cultural Analysis

To explain the dialectic nature of American culture and its historical, technological, industrial, and pluralistic context the Spindlers have discussed American culture as it exists in our society. They have emphasized values that give the individual the freedom to choose between opposite or alternative philosophical and pragmatic positions, as long as these positions are compatible with our Constitution. There is, therefore, an inherent and continuing debate just in being American. This "dialogue" is centered around the degrees of freedom that an individual can be given without infringing upon the rights of others, and the awareness that freedom, dialogue, and debate have social and personal consequences, such as reciprocal rights and obligations, and respect for the rights of others to disagree and exhibit diverse behavior. Diversity (within the limits of the Constitution) is further restricted by social, economic, and political sanctions. Therefore, there is enormous pressure on minority children and their families to conform, assimilate, and embrace middle-class values.

Given the diametrically opposed elements of American culture, cultural therapy requires adaptation of the instruments to be used by the teachers of culturally different students, according to the school and students' home learning environments. Of primary concern, at this point, is to describe some instruments relevant to teachers without discussing the details of their adaptation and use. I will list several instruments used successfully by the Spindlers (1987c) and other scholars. Some general strategies in using these instruments in the concrete situations of learning-disabled minority students and their teachers will also be included. The multiple use of these instruments in traditional anthropological research will be recognized by many; they are now being used by various groups of teachers during pre-service and in-service training.

**The Reflective, Cross-cultural Interview Procedure**    The reflective inter-view procedure can be used in working with teachers. Its appropriate use requires some interviewing skills and cultural sensitivity. In addition, audiovisual materials relevant to cross-cultural comparisons are needed. Teachers from one cultural setting are invited to view videos, films, and pictures of their counterparts in other cultural settings. For example, the Spindlers asked German teachers to react to films of American classrooms, and American teachers to react to films of German class-rooms. This technique facilitated teachers' responses, eliciting rich cultural material without causing self-consciousness. This type of contrast between the two cultures invites teachers to provide a rationale for inculcating specific cultural values.

A variation of this technique (Trueba et al., 1984) consisted of presenting teachers with videos, films, and pictures of the home cultural environment of their students and asking them about students' values in contrast with those of the teachers. Issues of home discipline, respect for adults, interactional styles with peers, home responsibilities, play behavior, and the home reward system became extremely useful to teachers in organizing their instruction. Such a technique requires a stress-free, spontaneous interactional environment that permits teachers to share their reactions without penalty or embarrassment. Ultimately the purpose of this instrument is to help teachers identify the value priorities in their students' culture in contrast with their own. To achieve this purpose, teachers can use their training in observing and reflecting on the activities they become involved in every day. To make legitimate inferences about the cultural knowledge presupposed in aca-demic tasks, and to make appropriate use of this knowledge in the organization of instruction, teachers need to understand students' home culture.

The recent work of Fujita and Sano, comparing and contrasting American and Japanese day care centers, is a good example of the use of this instrument for inviting reflection on the ethnocentricity of cultural values in determining our views on culturally different individuals:

> To discern different educational assumptions operating under the two systems
> [the American and the Japanese], we describe a research procedure, "reflective
> cross-cultural interviewing," which George and Louise Spindler coined. Ac-
> tivities at both centers are recorded on videotapes. Both American and Japanese
> videotapes are shown to the teachers in these two centers. Watching these
> videotapes with the teachers, we first interviewed the teachers concerning their
> explanation of their own activities. Then we asked them to compare the Amer-
> ican and Japanese day-care centers shown on the tapes. Therefore, we have
> used these tapes as evocative stimuli to let the teachers talk about their cultural
> assumptions (Fujita & Sano, 1988:74).

Naturally, in order for this technique to work well the teachers are invited to redefine their role and explore their cultural assumptions to help them internalize this role, rather than acting casually or automatically. The tolerance for cultural differences and the acceptance of alternative instructional models readily follows reflection.

**Instrumental Activities Inventory**    The instrumental activities inventory has been used by the Spindlers in a number of research projects, most recently in their study of German and American schools. The inventory is created with the assistance of teachers for the use of children. Its appropriate use requires a cross-cultural perspective and knowledge of the cultures being compared. Through the use of pictures and sentences, students are asked to select desired scenarios for a number of activities in the home, work environment, school, and church. Children are asked to explain why they chose one scenario over another.

This inventory is part of the instrumental model alluded to earlier in which the choice of activities implies the pursuit of specific cultural values. The focus of the instrument is the contrast between cultural values, and the possible incongruities in moving from one culture to another. One of its most productive uses is in the study of the self, including self-esteem, situated and enduring self, and self-efficacy. With the instrumental activities inventory the teacher can identify areas of cultural conflict as well as other areas needing attention during the face-to-face interaction with students. Also using this instrument, the teacher can redesign her or his instructional activities to meet the needs of particular students.

**Personal Journal**    Teachers who keep a personal journal of their teaching activities can be trained to follow trends, understand relationships between behavioral phenomena, identify cycles of academic progress in children, and better manage their time and personal talents. Writing an ethnographic journal must be clearly geared toward exploring specific issues with specific students. One of these issues is to monitor the relative academic progress students make, their commitment to engaging in academic activities, their responses to the organization of instruction, to peer feedback, and to other school circumstances.

The most important benefits of this journal for the teacher are to document in detail the adjustment process of each student, assess the impact of specific teaching strategies, and identify relationships between the teacher's method and student's response. The insights teachers get from writing about their daily teaching activities are most valuable. Indeed, teachers learn to think critically about their teaching only when they begin to write reflectively, on a regular basis, about their teaching. Writing a personal ethnographic journal also has a healing effect. Teachers working with culturally different children are subject to many pressures and frustrations. Learning to bring these feelings to the surface and articulate them is, for some teachers, not only a learning experience but a matter of psychological survival. Giving feedback on these journals and the judicious use of their content requires a great deal of tact on the part of the therapist as well as trust on the part of the teacher.

**Peer Support and Assessment Procedures**   One of the greatest needs of teachers is to have a support system. This system may be in the form of a peer group to turn to in case of emergency, a group of friends with whom to share successes and failures, a coaching group on which to try out new lessons and teaching methods, and/or a friendly evaluator who can give constructive criticism. For teachers to function as a support group, it is necessary that they have in common similar working environments, educational philosophies, and teaching goals. It helps if they work with similar age groups and subject matter. A support group often needs direction, training, and supervision from more experienced peers or administrators. The purpose of this group of people is that they observe each other in the process of teaching, analyze the instructional process, and assess the teaching effectiveness, including any need for change. Group activities in curriculum design are recommended. The focus of group observations is the multifaceted teaching/learning interaction. It includes:

1. Teaching and learning styles.
2. Students' differential participation.
3. Students' performance.
4. Teachers' performance.
5. Possible improvements in the selection and organization of content in recognition of students' cultural background.

The teacher support group should gradually become self-sufficient and meet regularly under an informal but effective governance agreement. From time to time a small group of teachers should invite other similar groups to exchange information and explore new alternatives. The use of audio- and videotaping can be very helpful in observing and analyzing the instructional process in order to design appropriate curricula.

Ultimately, the insights resulting from RCA depend on the use of instruments and procedures that enhance teachers' new learning and conscious awareness of their cultural assumptions, in contrast with assumptions made by persons from other cultures. Understanding the cultural conditions necessary for minority children to adjust and achieve in school also requires an understanding of teachers' cultural conditions for becoming effective instructors and designers of curricula for specific groups of students. Naturally, the use of the above instruments and procedures must be adapted locally after some experimentation.


## CONCLUDING THOUGHTS

Neither language nor culture can be neglected, nor can one be separated from the other. Appropriate use of language implies communication that is grammatically correct and culturally meaningful. This type of communication requires sophisticated social and cultural knowledge. Changes in language mirror sociocultural and political changes. The effective use of the home language and of the mainstream language for instruction requires a certain degree of biculturalism. Specific usages in language mirror cultural and social values.

If one takes the position that the acquisition of a second culture and second language are interdependent and have in common similar requirements, one can assume that in order to develop a second language (the language of mainstream society) it is necessary to become somewhat acculturated into the second culture. Furthermore, if one accepts the theory that for certain social groups the development of a second language requires a threshold of proficiency in the home language (Cummins, 1981a,b; Gold & Tempes, 1987), it is essential for linguistic minority children to continue to develop their learning skill through the home language and culture, and later to transfer instrumental competencies to the second language and culture.

American culture, as internalized in public schools, involves intensive competition and dialogue on opposite extreme positions tolerable within the Constitution. This "dialogue" between diametrically opposed alternatives, between conformity and individualism, consensus and debate, freedom of the individual and respect for the rights of others, between tolerance of cultural or linguistic differences and intolerance, is at the heart of American democracy and of the culture of the schools.

In order to increase tolerance of linguistic and cultural differences, and to maximize the learning potential of minority children, qualitative research approaches, such as the reflective cultural analysis (RCA) are particularly helpful because they increase reflective awareness of how our cultural system determines our perceptions of other peoples' competencies. Some of the interview and videotape techniques and some of the survey instruments associated with the RCA have produced excellent results in comparative cross-cultural studies by identifying the implicit cultural assumptions and value judgements determined within one's own culture (Fujita & Sano, 1988).

## RECOMMENDED EXERCISES

In order to comprehend the content of this chapter, several of the following exercises can be helpful.

1. Follow up one of the RCA exercises from the previous chapter and present your findings to a group of friends whose cultural assumptions differ due to differences in social class, ethnic background, and/or religion. Analyze their interpretations and reactions.
2. Visit a classroom and interview the teacher. Your job is (1) to summarize the organization of classroom activities and norms of behavior in the classroom, explaining why those rules are so important and how they relate to the teacher's culture; and (2) to identify instances of cultural transmission in which the teacher explicitly socializes children into particular values.

3. Observe a classroom and describe the pecking order, as well as the differential behavior of a teacher according to this order. Does the teacher give up the floor or provide rewards and penalties according to this order? Are there any blind spots or "invisible students" whom the teacher does not appear to notice?

4. From any public political speech, church sermon, newspaper editorial, or other similar material (movie, TV program, etc.), identify the most typical American cultural values that are exalted and presented as characteristics of our society, in contrast with those of the other peoples with whom we compare ourselves.

5. Observe several interactional events in school in which language minority students use English. Describe their language proficiency and/or problems in communication with English-speaking persons. Describe a particular incident of miscommunication and explain it.

6. Obtain and analyze an English composition written by an LEP child. What is different in the organization of sentences and the use of linguistic forms? In spite of the errors, do you understand what the child meant? Do you think the child understands what is being discussed? If not, what are the areas of confusion or ambiguity? What is the relation between the inappropriate use of language and the child's lack of cultural knowledge?

## RECOMMENDED READINGS

Au & Jordan, 1981
Brown et al., 1982
Cheng, 1987
Cummins 1976, 1978, 1981a,b, 1983, 1986
Delgado-Gaitan & Trueba, 1985
Diaz, Moll & Mehan, 1986
Erickson, 1984
Gibson, 1987a,b
Goldman & Trueba, 1987
Halcon, 1983
Krashen, S. 1981a,b
McLaughlin, 1985
Mehan, Hertwick & Meihls, 1986
O'Malley, 1982
Ogbu, 1974, 1978, 1981
Ogbu & Matute-Bianchi, 1986
Rueda and Mehan, 1986.
Spindler, G., 1974a,b, 1982, 1987
Spindler, L., 1978, 1984
Spindler & Spindler, 1982, 1983, 1987a,b,c
Suarez-Orozco, 1987
Trueba, 1983, 1986, 1987a,b
Vygotsky, 1978
Walker, 1987

# CHAPTER 3

# Instruction for Linguistic Minority Students: Theoretical Principles, Curriculum Design, and Teacher Preparation

Language minority students are characterized by having a language and culture different from those of the school and mainstream society. The crucial assumption is that to learn one must understand what is being taught through the language of instruction, that is, the instruction must be linguistically and culturally meaningful. Curriculum design is a general term that includes broad pedagogical principles (the theoretical foundations of formal instruction), and some types or classes of structural arrangements that determine the teaching–learning activities, as well as the use of particular teaching methodologies.

## BASIC THEORETICAL PRINCIPLES

The conceptual framework for the curriculum design presented here is based on the California State Department of Education publications (1981, 1983, 1986). This framework is formed by the work of Cummins, Krashen, Diaz, Moll, Mehan, Ogbu, Gold, Tempes and other theoreticians. Cummins (1979, 1981a,b, 1983, 1984, 1986) has dealt with the criticisms against bilingual education and the false assumption that in order to solve the achievement problem all we need to do is "to provide language-minority students with maximum exposure to English" (1986:20).

According to Cummins, the instructional solution depends on the extent to which school reflects the following four characteristics:

1. Minority students' language and culture are incorporated into the school program.
2. Minority community participation is encouraged as an integral component of children's education.

3. The pedagogy promotes intrinsic motivation on the part of students to use language actively to generate their own knowledge.
4. Professionals involved in assessment become advocates for minority students rather than legitimizing the location of the "problem" within the students (Cummins, 1986:21).

These statements illustrate the position advocated by Cummins (1981a,b, 1983, 1986), Krashen (1981a,b), Fishman (1976, 1979), Moll (1986), Hakuta (1986), Dolson (1985), Diaz et al. (1986), Hornberger (1988), and many other scholars who strongly support the theoretical assumption of instructional meaningfulness stated earlier. In fact, we can safely state with Cummins that "for dominated minorities, the extent to which students' language and culture are incorporated into the school program constitutes a significant predictor of academic success" and that students' school success "appears to reflect both the more solid cognitive/academic foundations developed through intensive first language instruction and the reinforcement of their cultural identity" (1986:25).

The conceptual framework for the development of instructional models and instructional methodologies can be summarized in the five pedagogical principles that Gold and Tempes (1987) cited as the theoretical foundations for their recent Case Studies in Bilingual Education:

1. The bilingual threshold: For language minority students, the development of proficiencies beyond a minimum threshold in both the native language and in English has a positive effect on academic achievement.
2. Dimensions of language: Language proficiency is the ability to use language for both academic purposes and basic communicative tasks.
3. Common underlying proficiency: For limited-English-proficient students, reaching the threshold of native-language skills necessary to complete academic tasks forms the basis for similar proficiency in English.
4. Second language acquisition: The basic communicative competency in a second language is a function of comprehensible second-language instruction and a supportive environment.
5. Beyond language: The perceived status of students affects the interaction between teachers and students among students themselves. In turn, student performance is affected (Gold & Tempes, 1987:5–6).

These five principles emphasize the importance of the home language and require "substantial amounts of instruction in and through the home language, and the teaching of initial reading and cognitively demanding subjects through the home language" (Gold & Tempes, 1987:5–6). The use of the home language presupposes the incorporation of the home culture, along the lines of the Kamehameha Early Education Program of Hawaii (Au & Jordan, 1981; Boggs, 1985; Tharp & Gallimore, in press). This incorporation requires that the teaching methodologies take into consideration culturally conditioned learning styles, in an attempt to develop "additive" rather than "subtractive" bilingualism (Lambert, 1981):

Educators' role definitions in relation to the incorporation of minority students' language and culture can be characterized along an "additive–subtractive" dimension. Educators who see their role as adding a second language and cultural affiliation to their students' repertoire are likely to empower students more than those who see their role as replacing or subtracting students' primary language and culture (Cummins, 1986:25).

The "bilingual threshold" has been at the core of the work by Cummins and other scholars (Cummins, 1981a,b, 1983, 1986; Krashen, 1981a,b; Fishman, 1976, 1979; Moll 1986) that has been discussed earlier. It shifts the emphasis from English language development to general language development, and postulates the transference of cognitive skills and subject matter knowledge from the home language to English. This principle is also congruent with the "meaningful academic interaction" principle mentioned at the beginning of this chapter.

The principle of "language dimensions" reflects previous distinctions between interpersonal communicative skills (presumably for tasks demanding low levels of cognitive skills) and for academic purposes (requiring sophisticated cognitive skills to handle difficult taxonomic and problem-solving tasks). These dimensions reflect a continuum in the developmental process, rather than two categories of linguistic skills. This distinction is particularly important in the discussion of tasks requiring high levels of literacy.

The third principle, "common underlying proficiency," directly addresses the issue of language interdependence and the transference of cognitive skills acquired in the home language to be used in the second language, provided the individual goes beyond a minimum threshold of language development. Mastery of the home language's structures is a necessary condition for the acquisition of the second language, as well as for the transmission of knowledge (through instruction in the second language) and the corresponding acquisition of knowledge by the student. Thus, until there is sufficient knowledge and control of a common language between teacher and student, there cannot be a meaningful reciprocal academic interaction.

The fourth principle, "second language acquisition," depending on both "comprehensible" second language instruction (from the perspective of the student) and a supportive environment, points to the complex interrelationship between contextual factors on which motivation to learn a second language is based, and the meaningfulness of interactional exchanges in the second language. This principle is consistent with all others and has important implications for instruction. A problem exists when instruction is "meaningful" or "comprehensible" for one group of students, but not for another. Another problem is that in order to assess comprehension levels one needs to test students and testing itself has other serious problems at the early stages of exposure to a second language.

Finally, the "beyond language" principle goes beyond the status of students and speaks to the entire "cultural ecological approach," or the societal forces that determine differential achievement levels of minority students (Ogbu, 1974, 1978, 1987a,b). While, in general, students' ability to achieve in a second language and achieve academically is partially explained by the societal forces (historical, economic, and social factors) determining the status of minority groups, the actual performance of minority groups can be changed through interventions. It is subject to local circumstances and context-specific interaction (including the effectiveness of instruction).

Recent guidelines developed by the Office of Educational Equity of the Massachusetts Department of Education have adopted the spirit of the these five principles. A document entitled *Educating Linguistic Minority Students* (Glenn, 1988) articulates a policy whose purpose is to guide classroom teachers and bilingual program directors:

> The primary issue for many linguistic minority students is that their verbal proficiency in any language is insufficiently developed. Their education is threatened, not because the home language interferes with English, but because neither language has been adequately stimulated in their early experiences. With appropriate instruction and a well-organized curriculum children of every kind of background and social class can develop competence in using two languages. Development of the home language may contribute to higher-order competencies in English as well (Glenn, 1988:3).

The statements about language in this document must be understood as presupposing an intimate relationship between language and culture, as well as between language and cognition. Indeed, the policy statement alludes to students' need for a period of intense intellectual stimulation and verbal communication in the home language as a condition for the acquisition of English as a second language. It advocates "programs which provide rich language experiences in the home language as well as in English" (Glenn, 1988:4).

The central principle of meaningful academic interaction is pursued in the "reciprocal interaction model" (Cummins, 1986:28), which corresponds in general terms to the "context-specific approach" described by Diaz et al. (1986). This approach is an application of the socially based theory of cognitive development advanced by Vygotsky and current neo-Vygotskians (see Chapters 1, 2, and 5). The practical implications of this approach are discussed by Cummins:

> The use of this model in teaching requires a genuine dialogue between student and teacher in both oral and written modalities, guidance and facilitation rather than control of student learning by the teacher, and the encouragement of student/ student talk in a collaborative learning context (1986:28).

Another practical implication of such a model is the role that assessment plays in the educational process. While in the past psychological "assessment has played the role of legitimizing the disabling of minority students" (see, for example Mehan et al., 1986; and Rueda, 1987), psychologists could take an advocacy role:

In this case, their task must be to delegitimize the traditional function of psychological assessment in the educational disabling of minority students by becoming advocates for the child in scrutinizing critically the societal and educational context within which the child has developed (Cazden, 1985).

This involves locating the pathology within the societal power relations between dominant and dominated groups (Cummins, 1986:30).

The principles enunciated and discussed above strongly promote the acquisition of English skills through ESL instruction and subject-matter classes starting from the earliest stages of exposure to school, and carried out in a variety of school contexts: formal instruction (grammar-based and subject oriented), music, art, physical education, and informal face-to-face interaction.

Although not directly stated in the five principles, the implied spirit of the emphasis on the home language requires some partnership with the family and community. The linkage of instructional programs with the family is viewed as essential by the proponents of this basic theoretical framework. The relationship and adjustment from family to school and from school to family is two-way; consequently one must ensure that the ''culture of the school'' is not perceived as threatening the culture of the family:

Linguistic minority parents often welcome an opportunity to learn how to support the development and academic success of their children, and to make a contribution to the school. Outreach to the home (not simply translating notices!) and a willingness to advise and assist with a variety of adjustment problems are important (Glenn, 1988:6).

Also implicit in the philosophical conception represented by the five principles and the notion of minority empowerment as described by Cummins (1986) is the prevention of minority segregation, which tends to be perpetuated over stages of the life cycle and across institutional settings (Ogbu, 1974, 1978, 1987a,b; Glenn, 1988). Thus the effort to integrate linguistic minority students with other students is seen as compatible with the above emphasis on language development (both the home language, L1, and the second language, L2):

It is not enough to put students together; if integration is not carefully planned and managed it may increase negative stereotypes and decrease the willingness of linguistic minority students to use English. There is a considerable body of research on pedagogical techniques that lead to mutual respect and shared learning (Glenn, 1988:9).

## CURRICULUM DESIGN

The curriculum design presented here is an adaptation of the design presented by Gold and Tempes (1987) and is based on the five basic principles discussed above. Table 3.1 reflects a strong emphasis on the development of the home language skills without neglecting the use of comprehensible input in English as a second language.

This curriculum design, which is general on purpose, proposes three types of instructional delivery each with different language use: instruction in the home language, in sheltered English, and in mainstream English. Gold and Tempes distinguished four phases of English language proficiency: (1) non-English proficient (NEP); (2) limited English proficient intermediate (LEPI); (3) limited English proficient advanced (LEPA); and (4) fluent English proficient (FEP). The use of the home language decreases with the proficiency in English. Sheltered English is proposed for the first three phases of the English language proficiency ladder, and is discontinued for FEP students. Mainstream English goes from use in teaching art, music, and physical education in phase I, to use for all subjects in phase IV, except for an enrichment language arts course in the home language. In contrast, the home language is proposed for all key subjects during phase I, and continues for language arts and social studies for FEPI students who make the transition to math and science taught in sheltered English. Gold and Tempes make an important clarification:

**Table 3.1.  CURRICULUM DESIGN**

| Phase of English proficiency | Principal language of instruction | | |
| | Spanish | Sheltered English | Mainstream English |
| --- | --- | --- | --- |
| I. Non-English proficient [beginning] | Language arts Mathematics Science/health Social studies | ESL | Art Music Physical education |
| II. Limited English proficient [intermediate] | Language arts Social studies | ESL Mathematics Science/health | Art Music Physical education |
| III. Limited English proficient [advanced] | Language arts | Transitional language arts Social studies | Art Music Physical education Mathematics Science/health |
| IV. Fluent English proficient | Language arts [enrichment] | | Art Music Physical education Mathematics Science/health Social studies Language arts |

> The time required to move from Phase I to Phase IV might be as short as two
> or three years for some students, but the majority of students are likely to require
> five to seven years to reach Phase IV (1987:9).

It can be assumed that the assessment of a student's proficiency in English
determines the mode of delivery and the balance between home language, sheltered
English, and mainstream English. As the student progresses he or she will also
participate more fully in the mainstream English instructional mode. The curriculum
design proposed here was implemented by the following five demonstration projects
sponsored by the California State Department of Education: The Mission Education
Center in the Mission district of San Francisco, the Huron elementary school in
Coalinga, the Eastman Avenue elementary school in Los Angeles, the Furgeson
elementary school also in Los Angeles, and the Rockwood elementary school of
Calexico. Planning for these projects began in 1981–1982, English assessments
were collected in the spring of 1982, and the first federal grant (and Elementary
and Secondary Education Act [ESEA] Title VII funds of $200,000) was received
at the beginning of fiscal year 1983–1984. In these schools target students were
primarily Spanish-speaking LEPs. State Department officers had ambitious goals
for these projects:

> We purposely stated student performance goals in an unusual manner to dis-
> tinguish the planned analysis from that done for most experimental designs,
> and to enable us to convey the goals simply and clearly to teachers, students,
> parents and others. Goals were initially set for oral English, and for reading
> and mathematics achievement in English. The target for student achievement
> was the performance of English speaking students [the national norm on achieve-
> ment tests] (Gold & Tempes, 1987:17).

The goals of the officers were ambitious and their level of confidence in the
theoretical framework and in the competence of the persons involved was high.
They reasoned that given sufficient time, careful monitoring of program implementation would lead to success. Time, however, was not as essential as were
experimental designs:

> We were not specifically interested in the *rate* of gain per year; rather we
> posited—consistent with the theoretical framework (California State Depart-
> ment of Education, 1981)—that the desired student outcomes in an ideal pro-
> gram of bilingual education would be obtained only after several years of
> appropriate instruction. We recognized the time required for adequate instal-
> lation of any educational innovation, and anticipated that it would take limited-
> English-proficient students *three* years of appropriate instruction to reach oral
> English fluency, but *seven* years to reach academic achievement in English
> comparable to that of the national norms (Gold & Tempes, 1987:18).

The projects are still in progress. The sites were selected in 1981–1982 and
results indicate very positive trends where the implementation steps were followed
appropriately (see below).

The concrete objectives related to English language acquisition and academic achievement have been defined by Gold and Tempes as follows:

> One hundred percent of the limited-English-proficient students will acquire basic communicative skills in English within three years. The instrument used to measure this objective will be the Student Oral Language Observation Matrix and the standard for attainment will be scores of four or five in all categories, with the exception of pronunciation which may be rated three (Gold & Tempes, 1987:19).

The five categories of the student oral language observation matrix (SOLOM) (Zehler, 1986) each have a maximum score of five, thus 100 percent of the LEP students are expected to obtain a minimum score of 19 by the third year of the program.

The goal for academic achievement has been stated as follows:

> After seven years in the program, at least 50 percent of all students initially identified as limited-English-proficient will score at or above the 50th percentile in the areas of reading and mathematics on the Comprehensive Tests of Basic Skills (CTBS), a nationally normed, standardized test administered in English (Gold & Tempes, 1987:20).

The study presented by Gold and Tempes shows that students performed beyond the original expectations of the researchers. The curriculum design was "substantially implemented in three of the five sites, partially implemented in one site, and implemented fully only for Phase I at one site" (Gold & Tempes, 1987:14). The five school sites were among the top 4 percent of schools in the state with the highest enrollment of LEP children. In fiscal year 1983–1984 the Mission Education Center had 282 students, Huron elementary school 780, Eastman Avenue school 1,720, Ferguson 588, and Rockwood elementary school 650; a total of 4,010 LEP children.

Two years after the new curriculum was implemented, the reading scores for the students originally identified as LEP's in kindergarten were as follows:

> 44 percent of second grade students who were initially identified as limited-English-proficient were scoring at or above the 50th percentile in reading. Thirty-nine percent of the third graders were above percentage of third graders scoring at or above the 50th percentile. And the trend was one of improvement. The percentage of third graders scoring at or above the 50th percentile increased from 16 percent in 1982 to 27 percent in 1983, 36 percent in 1984, and 39 percent in 1985 (Gold & Tempes, 1987:20).

The mathematics scores (in English) mirrored students' performance in reading:

> By the Spring of 1985, the project clearly met its goal of fifty percent of students originally identified as limited-English-proficient scoring at or above the fiftieth

percentile in mathematics. In fact, three-fifths or more of the students who enrolled as limited-English-proficient students in Kindergarten consistently met the criterion in mathematics at all grades from second through sixth by the Spring of 1984 (Gold & Tempes, 1987:20).

These results are an eloquent tribute to the caring, hard-working, and competent teachers of these schools, as much as to the conceptual design of the curriculum and its efficient organizational implementation. What did the teachers have to learn in order to implement the curriculum design? How did they acquire the necessary knowledge and skills? Specifically, how did they handle the home language instruction and the sheltered English strategies? Teacher preparation is by no means confined to traditional university training and a liberal educational philosophy. It goes beyond.

## TEACHER PREPARATION

The areas requiring special training for teachers include[1] intensive language training in the home language of the students,[2] systematic presentations on topics related to the five principles of the theoretical framework,[3] instruction on the teaching of literacy in the home language and in English,[4] the teaching of children's literature in the home language,[5] the teaching of instructional methodologies including sheltered English instruction, and[6] a series of organizational meetings to coordinate efforts and operationalize the instructional goals.

Teachers' attitude toward the home language is characterized by acceptance and support, especially if the home language is a nonstandard variety. However, teachers make the commitment not to mix English with the home language during instruction and to promote strongly the development of English through ESL classes and other subjects. English instruction begins with art, music, and physical education classes that provide rich contextual cues to help students understand language.

Teachers must also have high expectations of linguistic minority children and full confidence in their ability to learn. Both language attitude and confidence in the students are built on a deep understanding of the strong theoretical framework exemplified by the five basic principles. In the projects directed by Gold and Tempes, the work constituting the core of theory and research in bilingual education was the object of extended pre-service and in-service training activities sponsored by the California State Department of Education. In addition, the required home language skills were obtained through special training in Mexico. With the assistance of the Secretaría de Educación Pública, during the summers of 1984, 1985, and 1986 teachers received intensive exposure to the professional use of Spanish in specific instructional contexts, especially for the teaching of reading, mathematics, science, and children's literature.

To further obtain full support from parents and school personnel, the State Department of Education organized several meetings during the year and informal visits to exchange information and materials and to resolve any problems surfacing during the implementation. Finally, a quarterly bilingual newsletter was created to keep school personnel and parents informed and actively involved in program implementation.

An example of a program that fosters parental involvement is the Carpinteria preschool program, discussed by Cummins (1986). It has two strong components. One was the development of the Spanish language, which "was used constantly for conversing, learning new ideas, concepts and vocabulary, thinking creatively, and problem-solving," and "parental participation in their children's education" (1986:31–32). Cummins states that this example shows that educational programs can make a difference, and concludes:

> In this article I have proposed a theoretical framework for examining minority students' academic failure and for predicting the effects of educational inter-ventions. Within this framework the educational failure of minority students is analyzed as a function of the extent to which schools reflect or counteract the power relations that exist within the broader society. Specifically, language-minority students' educational progress is strongly influenced by the extent to which individual educators become advocates for the promotion of students' linguistic talents, actively encourage community participation in developing students' academic and cultural resources, and implement pedagogical ap-proaches that succeed in liberating students from instructional dependence (Cummins, 1986:32).

There is no ambivalence in Cummins' position regarding the nature of pre-dominant "educator/student interactions" that characteristically disable some mi-nority students. "Objective" evidence, that is, evidence obtained from standardized tests (normed in other than minority populations) is gathered to show that the linguistic minority group is inferior and as such justifies the group's exclusion from academic activities designed for mainstream children. All of the above is compatible with the "lip service paid to initial L1 instruction, community involvement, and nondiscriminatory assessment . . ." (Cummins, 1986:32–33).

## Instructional Practices

Instructional practices, or the adoption of specific teaching strategies, are determined by the goals of the program and the theoretical assumptions linking instructional means to expected outcomes. The practices discussed here are con-gruent with the three modes of delivery mentioned earlier, and reflect a particular theoretical framework. The intensive use of the home language, for example, during the early stages of transition from the home to the school learning environment (the position presented by Gold and Tempes and adopted here) is viewed as the first and most crucial step in the acquisition of English literacy. The basic assumption is that first language development is highly instrumental in second language ac-quisition. In order for the child to make sense of instruction, he or she must receive "comprehensible input" (Krashen, 1981a,b). Verbal communication must be purposive, meaningful, stress-free, and creative. Performance should follow competence; that is, first the child internalizes concepts and procedures, and later the child uses those concepts and procedures in social interaction.

Instruction through the home language (the first of the three modes of delivery, see Table 3.1 above) is always focused on the subject matter, kept separately from English, and devoted to the acquisition of knowledge, critical thinking skills, and the pursuit of children's inquisitive search for answers related to the subject. There is no special attention to correcting errors in the use of the language, or in developing a standard form of the home language (even when this option is open). Errors are tolerated in order to focus on the content of instruction and the meaningful and interactive participation of children in the acquisition of knowledge.

If sheltered English is the mode of delivery (see Table 3.1), the emphasis is on providing children with enough contextual clues that permit them to discover patterns and meanings to disclose for them the content of the lesson. There is no emphasis on correcting their errors in English, although input is always given in correct English through rich contextual information.

Rather than modeling "grammar" in the reading lesson, teachers are expected to communicate the content of the lesson through the language experience and other approaches. The same instructional strategy is appropriate when the third mode of delivery is used: mainstream English.

The issues of the separation of languages in bilingual programs and of focusing on the content of the communication, rather than on the form of the language, are strategies consistent with the theoretical framework presented above and supported by work by Cummins (1976, 1978, 1979, 1980, 1981a,b, 1983, 1984, 1986), Krashen (1981a,b), Skutnabb-Kangas (1978, 1984), Wong-Fillmore (1976, 1982), Chamot (1983), and, more recently, Gold and Tempes (1987).

Instructional practices in other types of programs may emphasize a quick and complete transition to the second language on the basis that for some children who have already developed fully their home language and whose home learning environment provides them with intensive literacy experiences in the mother tongue, instruction in the second language is more appropriate.

There are different types of immersion programs (California State Department of Education, 1984; McLaughlin, 1985). McLaughlin describes early total immersion programs, early partial immersion, delayed and later immersion, and immersion in two languages. Immersion began as an experiment created by parents, educators, and researchers hoping to resolve "the French-Canadian problem" by integrating Canada's French- and English-speaking populations socially and culturally. Immersion programs are based on the premise that the acquisition of L2 is essentially identical to the acquisition of L1; that is, it is acquired in natural settings where communication takes places within appropriate social contexts.

Immersion programs are characterized by the primary use of a second language (often the mainstream language) from the first day on by instructors and students. Unlike the so-called "submersion" programs (see contrast between these two types in Cohen, 1975; Skutnabb-Kangas, 1978; and particularly McLaughlin, 1985), immersion students normally have no prior proficiency in the language of instruction. In Canada, English-speaking pupils enter with a similar level of proficiency in French as a second language. In some cases native French speakers are permitted to serve as teachers' aides and role models (Lambert, 1984). Children are taught all subjects in French. There are other more subtle differences, however. Anglophone students are conscious of the higher status of their home language, and continue to engage in home language literacy activities at home.

The theoretical premise of immersion schooling is articulated by Lambert as follows:

> The concept of immersion schooling was based on a very important and fundamental premise—that people learn a second (or third) language in the same way as they learn their first; that is, in contexts where they are exposed to it in its natural form and where they are socially motivated to communicate. From the first encounter immersion teachers use only the target language. They clearly, patiently and repetitively focus on the development of a basic vocabulary in the new language, relying, with the youngest age groups, on plastic art materials, songs, and animated stories. But from the start, the learning of language per se is made quite incidental to learning how to make and do new and interesting things (Lambert, 1984:11–12).

Concentrating on the mastery of the subject matter and making the learning of another language incidental are characteristics of immersion programs that distinguish them from traditional foreign language teaching programs. Lambert feels that:

> The immersion experience also fosters particular sociopolitical insights that monolingual mainstreamers would likely never develop. For example, the immersion children come to the realization by the end of elementary school that peaceful democratic coexistence among members of distinctive ethnolinguistic groups calls for something more than simply learning another's languages (Lambert, 1984:15).

By the third or fourth grade, once they have secured enough oral and written proficiency in the language of instruction, children receive intensive exposure to formal home language development and its use in content areas. Results have been consistent over the past 15 years. Pupils are taken to a high level of functional bilingualism and biliteracy without falling behind in the content areas of the curriculum. There is also no evidence of any cognitive deficits, mental confusion, or loss of ethnic identity associated with these programs. Anglophone students learn to appreciate the language and culture of French-Canadians without sacrificing their own culture. What makes this program unique is the requirement of infrastructural and cultural elements peculiar to the binational character of Canadian society. This is precisely what makes successful replication in the United States highly unlikely.

Lambert believes that "a number of interesting variants or adaptations of immersion programs are emerging in the United States, and these, along with the full immersion programs, will in time be evaluated and judged . . ." (1984:17), if we keep in mind the contrast between additive versus subtractive forms of bilingualism:

> We have referred to the process of developing the bilingual and bicultural skills of English-speaking North American children as an additive form of bilingualism, implying that these children, with no fear of ethnic or linguistic erosion, can add one or more foreign languages to their accumulating skills and profit immensely from the experience—cognitively, socially and educationally, and even economically. . . . The development of strong skills in a second socially relevant language expands the repertory of skills of these children. These skills do not detract from the children's English home-language base, but rather enable them to maintain at least normal progress. For these children and their parents, it becomes clear that the learning of the second language in no way portends the slow replacement of the first or home language, as would be the case for most linguistic minority groups in North America that are pressured to develop high-level skills in English at the expense of their home languages (Lambert, 1984:19).

Hernandez-Chavez (1984) believes that if immersion programs were adopted for mainstreaming linguistic minorities in the United States, the results would be subtractive bilingualism:

> Immersion education appears to contain all the proper ingredients for meeting the expressed goals of effective English acquisition, for avoiding academic retardation, and for providing an environment of "sensitivity" toward the native language and culture of the students. Nevertheless, important and crucial differences exist between immersion programs for majority and minority language children. . . . In the case of the majority language children, the central purpose is to achieve *enrichment or additive bilingualism*. The second language is an addition to the child's native language skills . . . In contrast, the overriding goal of immersion for language minorities, as is beginning to be advocated by certain policymakers in the United States, is *displacement bilingualism*, or, as it has been called subtractive bilingualism . . . (Hernandez-Chavez, 1984: 151–152).

Along the lines of the reasoning presented by Ogbu in his discussion of "caste-like minorities" (1974, 1978, 1981, 1982, 1983, 1987a,b), Hernandez-Chavez (1984) argues that the historical evidence of "repressed ethnolinguistic groups" (giving as examples those mentioned by Ogbu: Native Americans, Puerto Ricans, Chicanos, Hawaiians, and Filipinos), have been forced to lose their language and culture. Consequently, the type of immersion programs that would be implemented in this country would foster the loss of the home language, academic achievement only through English, and the acquisition of mainstream culture and language (Hernandez-Chavez, 1984).

What types of social and philosophical changes and what conditions would make it possible to implement immersion programs whose goal is additive bilingualism? Can we adapt some of the pedagogical principles and instructional practices from immersion programs and apply them to bilingual programs in the United States? The work by Gold and Tempes reflects an effort in that direction by emphasizing the home language and its maintenance, even after English proficiency has been obtained. Clearly, however, the social and political context of multilingual America is such that an "immersion philosophy" of the type advocated by Lambert may be unrealistic as a viable curriculum alternative for most linguistic minority children.

The danger of creating "submersion" rather immersion programs, that is, programs in which the child's language and culture are displaced, must be emphasized. There are fundamental differences between these two types of programs. While immersion education is optional, protects the high status of the home language, assumes no significant differences in second language proficiency among students, and is based on high motivation, teacher expectations and parental support, submersion education is obligatory, stresses the low status of the home language and its eventual loss, has no parental support, low teacher expectations and low student motivation (Cohen, 1975; Skutnabb-Kangas, 1984; McLaughlin, 1985).

Controversy and research have produced a healthy dialogue and improvement in instructional practice. The impact of immersion education in this country was translated into comparative studies of first- and second-language acquisition and new approaches such as the total physical response, the natural approach, and the functional approach.

**Total Physical Response**   This requires the association of language with action-reinforcing meanings. For example, when someone points to something and makes a request, physical action adds to his or her meaning. The assumption is that communication is not only linguistic but also kinetic. Demonstration through physical action and pictures has proven effective in teaching second and third languages to adults.

**The Natural Approach**   This also originated from the comparison between first- and second-language acquisition. Findings indicated that to maximize second-language acquisition, the teacher should provide students with contextual and extralinguistic cues that will permit them to make inferences beyond their actual knowledge of the language. Consequently, this approach does not emphasize acquisition of grammatical structure, but effectiveness in face-to-face communication, which had been emphasized by Genesee (1981), Genesee et al. (1975), Lambert and Tucker (1972), and Lambert (1984).

**The Functional Approach**   The functional approach (Chamot, 1983) focuses on the linguistic knowledge children need in order to function effectively in the instructional setting so as to learn academic content and participate actively in learning activities. The assumption is that to acquire critical thinking skills children must receive "comprehensible messages." This linguistic knowledge may include categories of time and space, taxonomies of objects, relationships between groups of individuals, and semantic and syntactic classifications, all of which permit children to function effectively in the classroom, especially in literacy contexts. Chamot's view is based on the work of Krashen (1981a,b) and is consistent with the distinction between conversational and academic language skills presented by Cummins (1976, 1978, 1981a,b, 1983, 1986). The use of a second language for the cognitively demanding tasks characteristically required in current instructional tasks presupposes a threshold of home language development (as discussed in the five principles defended by Gold and Tempes, 1987).

According to Chamot (1983), application of the functional approach requires a careful analysis of children's linguistic proficiency as demonstrated by satisfactory performance in academic tasks, meeting instructional objectives, and dealing competently with text and other instructional materials. These skills and competencies should exist in minority students at levels comparable to those of mainstream children before minority children are transferred to all-English classrooms. Individual instruction is compatible with the functional approach, and can be adopted as one of its integral components in classrooms with children from different sociocultural backgrounds. The criteria for a child leaving a language minority program should be the demonstration not only of English skills but also of competent academic work in English.

## Teachers' Base Knowledge

Teaching is a science and an art that includes a very substantial amount of knowledge and skills in areas previously neglected during teacher preparation. Shulman contends that if teachers do not think critically and are content with focusing on performance, learning will suffer. What characterizes Shulman's position is a crucial insight into pedagogical processes:

> The conception of pedagogical reasoning places emphasis upon the intellectual basis for teaching performance rather than on behavior alone. If this conception is to be taken seriously, both the organization and content of teacher education programs and the definition of scholarly foundations of education will require revision (Shulman, 1987a:20).

When teaching is successful and children achieve in school, we tend to forget the critical role and the efforts of teachers as professionals. Good teachers have a knowledge and skill base that permits them to communicate subject matter effectively. Shulman (1987a) describes the identified major categories of this knowledge as follows:

Content knowledge

General pedagogical knowledge, with special reference to those broad principles and strategies of classroom management and organization that appear to transcend subject matter

Curriculum knowledge, with particular grasp of the materials and programs that serve as "tools of the trade" for teachers

Pedagogical content knowledge, that special amalgam of content and pedagogy that is uniquely the province of teachers, their own special form of professional understanding

Knowledge of learners and their characteristics

Knowledge of educational contexts, ranging from the workings of the group or classroom, the governance and financing of school districts, to the character of communities and cultures

Knowledge of educational ends, purposes, and values, and their philosophical and historical grounds (Shulman, 1987:8).

When children fail in school, we tend to be quick to examine teachers' performance to see what went wrong. The basic facts point to a fundamental truth: children come to school with skills and backgrounds to which school personnel respond in different ways and that result in different levels of achievement. In the organization of programs for linguistic minority students, many things can go wrong that are beyond the control of the teachers. There are, however, some important lessons to learn from cases in which failure occurs. The purpose of examining the following case study is to reflect on the nature of the teaching process and the role of teachers and to learn some lessons regarding the role of language and culture in school achievement.

Sockett argues that Shulman's position ignores the complex and diverse social, cultural, and educational context of "the human beings who are learning, individually and in groups:

Shulman is aware of this "outrageous" complexity in teaching as an *activity* but not as an *occupation*. Thus, Shulman's team attempts to keep the collections of descriptions and analyses of excellent teaching "highly contextualized, especially with respect to the content-specificity of the pedagogical strategies employed." Unfortunately, they neglect the parochialism of the occupation's context (Sockett, 1987:209).

Sockett is attempting to bring the discussion of teacher preparation to the gut level of the reality in which teachers often have to work. Teaching is far more than a technical activity. As part of our cultural values related to schooling, teaching is governed by the moral principles and the moral language alluded to by Shulman. According to Sockett's critique (1987:212), "Moral language describes both educational *ends* (ideals, goals, and so on) and *means* (the techniques, strategies, and repertoires)." Thus:

> If we are to develop a comprehensive understanding of teaching, we need to cut loose from our poverty-stricken, paratechnical language, not the least if we are to educate student teachers to understand their situations within an appropriate moral framework. . . . Shulman's concern with a developmental model of teachers as professionals moving toward codified wisdom-in-practice, and his rejection of tacit knowledge as lacking explanatory power for the public, suggest that his perspective on teaching, as an occupation incorporating an activity, is too much driven by the demands of public explicability and *assessment*. . . . Professionalization, Shulman is saying, demands an account of the knowledge base of teaching. That knowledge base frames both teacher education and teaching practice. Standards for accreditation, certification, and hiring rest on an explication of the knowledge base (Sockett, 1987:213–215).

This discussion is particularly important for our purposes since the teachers of linguistic minority children have been the focus of intense scrutiny. Efforts to improve the education of these children have targeted the teachers. New examinations, assessment instruments, accreditation requirements, and dialogue over the future of teacher education for the country at large show that Sockett's concerns have serious implications for linguistic minorities. The mechanisms adopted in Texas and California, among other states, to control the quality of teacher preparation and classroom instruction have resulted in selective exclusion of ethnic minority teachers whose main asset is to understand the social and cultural context of minority children. The relative importance placed on codifying teachers' knowledge seems to be the instrument for controlling the profession in ways that may take away the role models minority children are finally getting in schools. Positing that researchers determine how practitioners should be trained, evaluated, and retained or dismissed, seems to stress further the existing dichotomy between research and practice (Sockett, 1987).

Shulman responded to Sockett by emphasizing the "centrality of knowledge, reason, and judgement," the "predictable regularities" in the life of American schools and their curriculum, and the "tendency to endorse the virtues of chaos and flux" in those who emphasize the diversity in educational contexts (Shulman, 1987b:474–475). Shulman agrees with Sockett's view that researchers and practitioners must work in teams and that the knowledge acquired by teachers during training should be applied in specific ways to specific audiences. Indeed, by the very nature of the studies he conducted, his intent was to find effective ways of teaching diverse student populations:

> The studies ranged from one to two years in length and were conducted with students from three different universities. The studies included interviews and

observations, intellectual and personal biographies as well as observational field notes, structured tasks, and informal discussions. The purpose of the research was to understand the manner in which students, who were already competent in a subject area, became capable of teaching that subject to a variety of pupils. Our goal was to learn how knowledge of teaching developed in new teachers so that we could become more capable of preparing teachers intelligently (Shulman, 1987b:479).

Sockett's concern with teachers as a professional community and with their professionalism is a genuine and generalized one. The collective rights and obligations of teachers as professionals to minority students demand that professional development ''be conceived and approached as a matter for all within the community, whether they are researchers, novices, administrators, or general practitioners'' (Sockett, 1987:218).

Most teacher educators, and certainly Shulman, would concur with Sockett's final recommendation:

We need support systems to overcome the cellular character of teaching in schools as much as we need them to overcome the insularity of many university researchers and their myopic pursuit of excellence through publication for others in their cell. . . . The focus on teacher education and the knowledge base is worthwhile, but it needs to be set within a comprehensive moral vision of professionalism, and within the moral endeavor that most in the professional community, whether researchers or practitioners, recognize the occupation of teaching to be (Sockett, 1987:218).

In the particular case of teachers in schools with heavy concentrations of linguistic minorities, it seems essential that teachers become active participants in future reform movements and changes in teacher education. Their knowledge and potential contributions will make it possible for future teachers to succeed. All of the following should be at the center of the discussions on the philosophical foundations of future education: Advocacy on the part of educators suggested by Cummins (1986); Gold and Tempes' (1987) recommended partnership between state Departments of Education and school personnel should be extended to the teams of researchers and practitioners such as those led by Shulman (1987a,b); and the collective rights of teachers as professionals emphasized by Sockett (1987).

## Sociocultural Dimensions of Instruction

Anthropological literature has had an impact on the fields of sociology and psychology in important ways. The role of culture in the acquisition of knowledge and the role of culturally defined collective experiences in differentiating one social group from others have become central aspects of modern neo-Vygotskian theory of cognitive development. This theory is called the ''socially based theory of learning.'' Goldman and McDermott's (1987) finding that competitiveness was the central structural element of high school instructional strategies was reinforced by a strong social value placed on ''success'' and ''failure,'' and with the measurement of the degrees of success or failure through tests.

To the documentation of resistance to literacy (Erickson, 1984, 1986, 1987), recent studies have added a discussion of the appropriate conditions necessary to maximize the acquisition of English literacy. This requires injection into the instructional system of linguistically and culturally congruent strategies that smooth the transition from the home to the school learning environments. For example, the work of Au and Jordan (1981), and of Tharp and Gallimore (in press) in Hawaii and southern California fall in this category. Also the work of Delgado-Gaitan with Mexican families in Carpinteria, California (as well as her previous work; see for example, Delgado-Gaitan, 1987a,b), and the study conducted by Trueba et al. (1988) among the Hmong people of Santa Barbara would fall in this category. Finally, the work by Richards (1987) among the Mayan children of Guatemala, by Hornberger (1988) among the Quechua children of Peru, by Macias (1987) among the Papago, and by Deyhle (1987) among the Navajo should be included. All these studies have recently been published or are now in press. Significant about these studies is that they depict the intimate relationship between language and culture in children's processes of cultural adjustment to the schools, as well as the students' need to internalize school cultural values in order to achieve academically.

Fujita and Sano (1988) compared and contrasted American and Japanese day care centers, using the Spindlers' reflective ''cross-cultural interviews.'' They elicited videotapes to be analyzed by Japanese and American teachers of each other's centers. This study permitted us to reflect on the socialization for ''independence'' or for ''nurturing tolerance and cooperation'' characterizing American and Japanese teachers, respectively. Following also the work of Spindler, Borish (1988) used Spindler's model of ''compression and decompression'' cycles to focus on the socialization of high school youngsters on a Kibbutz who endure intense adult-like working experiences ''in their winter of their discontent,'' while getting ready to enter the armed forces. The function of schooling and their relationships with their teachers as friends leave no room for ''dropouts.''

A number of additional theoretical developments in anthropologically inspired field-based studies deal with effective interventions by social scientists in schools, or after school hours, with minority children. These interventions were guided theoretically by the work of Vygotsky (1962, 1978) and neo-Vygotskians (Cole & D'Andrade, 1982; Cole & Scribner, 1974; Cole & Griffin, 1983; Diaz et al., 1986; Moll, 1986; Wertsch, 1981, 1985; Boggs, 1985; Tharp & Gallimore, in press). The interventions were implemented and analyzed according to the models developed by Cole, Wertsch, Griffin, Newman, Moll, Mehan, and others from the Laboratory of Comparative Human Cognition (LCHC), and those of the Kamehameha Early Education Program (KEEP).

We need a better understanding of the educational needs of linguistic minority children, so as to build an adequate learning environment for them at home and in schools. These children need assistance and support during their difficult social and cultural transition. Instruction should be tailored to children's cultural knowledge and experiences, and it should be conducted within a flexible organizational structure in which teachers have a great deal more control of the instructional strategies and activities, and of the use of instructional resources (tutors, translators, parental groups, audiovisual, computer, and other technological facilities, etc.).

Within a socially based theory of school achievement, academic failure and/ or success is not a personal attribute of the student, but the direct result of structural and psychological contextual factors that permit a child to grow intellectually. Indeed, learning successfully always occurs if a child is given the opportunity to engage in socially meaningful interactions within the zone of proximal development, that is, in contextually meaningful activity settings, through "assisted performance" (with the help of others: those in the same social unit). Vygotsky describes assisted performance as the crossroads between learning and cognitive development, whereby "the child performs, through assistance and cooperative activity, at developmental levels quite beyond the individual level of achievement" (Tharp & Gallimore, in press). Students' commitment to engage in learning occurs during the transition from assisted to independent performance, which can be anticipated by the teacher.

How can teachers obtain more effective communication with minority children? How can they develop a close working relationship with them, and, which is most important, how can teachers help children internalize the short-term and long-term academic goals and the cultural values in which these goals are anchored? These are the concerns that surface with a close ethnographic analysis of children's "learning disabilities." These disabilities are an attribute of schools. Children's seeming "unpreparedness" for mainstream schooling is only a measure of the rigidity and ignorance of our school system, which creates a handicap out of social and cultural differences.

According to Vygotsky, success in social interactional contexts has powerful implications for success in academic contexts, including those that are strictly cognitive. Even partial social successes can help children to acquire personality integration and positive self-concept during the difficult transitional period from the home to the school culture.

McDermott offers interesting insight that requires us to reflect on the current status of social science research on the failure of minority students:

> Now I am trying to move beyond the problem of school failure that has grown into a small industry involving millions of people measuring, documenting, remediating, and explaining the habits, values, and skills of minority groups that contribute so heavily to their ranks of school failures. There is a preoccupation among us: Because we claim to offer good education to all and because many minority people seem to reject, we are plagued with the questions of "What is with them anyway?" or "What is their situation that school seems to go so badly?" Their situation! . . . The breakthrough comes when we realize that their situation is not theirs alone; it is ours as well. We help to make failure

possible by our successes. . . . Failure is a culturally necessary part of the American scene. We do not need to explain. We need to confront it . . . ; explaining it will only keep it at a distance, making us its slaves (McDermott, 1987b:361–363).

Within the culturally based theory of academic achievement, which recognizes the intimate relationship between language, culture, and cognition (Vygotsky, 1962, 1978; Wertsch, 1985; Scribner & Cole, 1981; Diaz et al., 1986), a number of important issues relate to the present study:

1. How is the relationship between language and cognition mediated by the culture, and what is the role of culture in the adjustment of minority children? What is a culturally congruent learning environment? How much is the child (and his or her family) to change, and how much is the school to change?
2. If we are to take McDermott's remarks and confront the structural necessity of academic success and failure, can we retain some hope and plan intervention strategies? Or if we accept Ogbu's taxonomy of castelike minorities, is there room for school reform to accommodate the special needs of culturally different children?
3. What kind of organization of instructional activities in school would minimize failure and maximize success in culturally different children?

In all of the above issues we must face the significant role that language plays in instruction and in socialization for academic success. Language and effective teacher–student communication are essential to foster cognitive growth in children. The literacy problems faced by LEP children are related to school personnel's inability to capitalize on children's different experiences, cultural knowledge, and values. It is obvious that without knowing these children's language, teachers cannot bridge the instructional gap and adapt instructional designs for culturally different children.

## CASE STUDY: FOUR LINGUISTIC MINORITY CHILDREN

This study was part of a larger project (see Trueba, in press) focused on 40 language minority children diagnosed as "learning disabled" by school authorities in the La Playa elementary school (a pseudonym) in central west California. The team of researchers included two doctoral students, three teachers, the principal of the school, and this author. We worked regularly on this project at the school and community, spending an of average 12 hours per week per person between September, 1984, and June, 1986. We conducted observations, taped interviews, collected data on each student and his or her family, checked all existing documentation on each case, and reported periodically to the school teachers.

We started by focusing on four children, a subsample of the larger study, to examine in closer detail the profile and interactional strategies of teachers and children: Richard, an 11-year-old Sudanese child who spoke fluent English (with a British accent), and Dinka and Arab languages, placed in a fifth/sixth grade combination class; two Laotian children, Douang, an 11-year-old girl, and Vilaph, a 12-year-old boy literate in French (though this fact was ignored by teachers), both placed in fifth grade; and Carlos, a 9-year-old Mexican boy repeating third grade. The research questions were at the beginning general and relatively simple:

1. What is the nature of the children's learning disabilities? How did the school personnel determine that they were disabled? What is it that these children cannot actually do?
2. What are the patterns of participation exhibited by these children? To what extent are they receiving "comprehensible" input in the classroom, and how do they respond?
3. What is their level of English proficiency both in academic and other activities? Is this proficiency increasing?
4. What types of instructional practices seem to maximize children's participation and learning outcomes?

From the beginning we were concerned that perhaps prearrival traumas and current high stress levels might prevent these children from participating meaningfully in daily academic and social activities. Furthermore, we suspected that their cognitive development may have been slowed during the early adjustment period in this country, and that their increasing social and psychological isolation would hinder their overall long-term cultural adjustment and second language acquisition.

In 1986 La Playa served 591 students, half of whom spoke as a first language one of the following 25 languages: Spanish (101), Hmong (77), Lao (31), Vietnamese (28), Chinese dialects (12), Portuguese (7), Japanese (6), Hebrew (6), Arabic (5), Korean (5), Danish (3), Hindi (3), Croatian (2), Hungarian (2), Indonesian (2), and eight other language groups represented by a single student each: Bengali, Dinka, French, Ilocano, Tagalog, Malaysian, Polish, and Punjabi.

Within walking distance from a major California university, the La Playa elementary school forms part of a beach community composed largely of Indochinese and Hispanic immigrants, transients, students, and low-income persons. Consequently it attracts nonmainstream children. Our main concern was with the first four groups of language minority students, not only because they were the most numerous—237 of the 298 LEP students: 82 percent, but also because they presented the most acute adjustment and achievement problems.

Some 40 children had been identified by the school psychologist, principal, and teachers as having serious adjustment and achievement problems in the English-language classroom. With the help of teachers and other school personnel we identified the four children in this study as needing special attention because of possible signs of maladjustment and deterioration of cognitive skills. After becoming familiar with the details of the student files, we concentrated on a systematic assessment by observing student participation in school activities, both in the main classroom and in small groups for reading, ESL, or special education classes. We followed up with interviews with each student, his or her teacher, the psychologist, the principal, and members of the student's family. Members of the team met periodically to discuss progress and problems in data collection and analysis, strategies for interpretation, and recent literature relevant to our work.

We began to gain a better understanding of why and how these children had become more incompetent and isolated during their transition from the home culture to that of the school.

In general we found

1. Limited (often meaningless) participation in classroom activities, particularly large group activities.
2. Very limited academic productivity when compared with mainstream children, and even when compared with minority children who had rapidly acquired fluency in English.
3. Signs of anxiety, fear, and confusion (often associated with public performances) often alternating with signs of depression and isolation.

The following examples will help to flesh out our observations.

## Richard

Richard, an 11-year-old black Sudanese who speaks perfect British English, was the son of a middle-aged African doctoral student who is the head of a polygamous family and a high-ranking member of the diplomatic service in Sudan. Richard's mother, the first wife of the diplomat, was left in Sudan, while his stepmother (a younger black woman) was chosen by her husband to come to America. Richard was referred to the psychologist because he expressed anger in public, engaged in fist fights, and refused to participate in classroom activities. Otherwise, he seemed to be alert and intellectually aggressive. One day the reading lesson involved American rivers. It was Richard's turn. The teacher asked: "Richard, where is the Mississippi? Point to it on the map." Richard remained silent, and just before the teacher gave the floor to another student, Richard began: "It is indeed the largest American river, but I know the Nile, and it is bigger. . . ." Then Richard surprised the whole class with a detailed description of what the Nile is like, and how people depend on it for their subsistence. The teacher pressed on with the subject of American rivers, and Richard ignored him.

Another day, the teacher made a casual comment about American politics, and Richard began to recite by heart the names of U.S. presidents and made comments on other politicians, such as Tip O'Neill and Senator Edward Kennedy.

Despite this knowledge, Richard's academic performance, tests, homework, and actual participation in the math and reading lesson continued to be marginal or lacking. He would refuse to follow instructions and do some operations when he was in disagreement with the teacher: "Is not that way," he would say, "you do it this way." His aggression and classroom attitude (perceived as arrogance by his peers) resulted in further isolation and lower academic performance. His father, annoyed by teachers' reports and complaints, came over to school to confront the teachers: "If you cannot discipline, I will; if you don't want to hit him, tell him and I will."

## Douang

Douang, an 11-year-old Laotian girl, was placed in fifth grade, despite the fact she hardly read at the second-grade level. Douang was deeply traumatized and would never speak in English, or even in Lao, in front of the teacher. She would whisper in Lao in her friend's ear once on a while. One day, the ESL teacher announced in the coffee lounge, as an important event, that Douang had pronounced a complete sentence, though not very clearly. "Her expressive language is still very weak," the teacher added. No one complained about Douang. Her fifth grade classroom teacher said, "Her attitude and attentiveness are good." She knew Douang was trying. Our observations of the entire class group during the reading lesson indicate that when instruction emphasized taxonomies, or word classes, Douang would get lost and lower her head as if she wanted to avoid eye contact or disengage from the activity. "Children," the teacher would say, "here is the list of words you need to read for your lesson: fuss, snooze, separate, rock garden, marigold, and zinnia. What is snooze?" Douang immediately became restless (moving her feet under the table) and attempted to remain inconspicuous. After a period during which the children read the first paragraph silently, the teacher would ask, "Did you *all* finish?" The teacher quickly read the passage and began to discuss vocabulary. The lesson went on like that while Douang continued to move her feet and shake all over. She seemed to be terrified of being asked another question. At the end of the painful exercise, she returned to her friend's side, seeking some relief.

Douang wrote the following:

When I am 18 I plan to get an car I am going to ride to school I will learn more I think I would go to college or UC I will learn and if I learn college I will graduate. when I am 22 I will found a work to do or learn more english again or I will ask my brother to found me some work to do.

After several days of painful work Douang presented this composition:

At my house we have 13 people in the house and we have three bed room [bedroom] my brother my brothe [brother's] wife sleep in one bed room [bedroom] my brother have a lot of cloth and my bed room [bedroom] is environment [spacious] because we have 7 people in my bedroom and we have lot of cloth to and other bed room have 4 peope [people] sleep in my house is environment.

The compositions from Douang show determination to succeed, regardless of the serious problems she was facing in school.

## Vilaph

Vilaph, a 12-year-old Laotian boy who came to school 2½ years ago, is deeply troubled, but sociable. He has a hot temper and is constantly moving his feet, hands, and eyes. His restlessness increases during forced performance in large groups, for example, in the teaching of reading. His teacher knows that Vilaph refuses and that he kicks the bench in anger. "He is very slow in math, even counting beans and trading for 10 sticks is hard for him," his teacher said, "He learns words by rote, but has no consonants or other phonic skills." Vilaph's friends say that his older siblings yell at him all the time, and hit him often. The main teacher's monthly report read: "Poor Vilaph, he didn't have a clue . . . , but he tried so hard with the less difficult materials I gave him; it was sad . . . Excellent artist and superior motor skills, but something is not attached right." Here is an example of one of his compositions written on Halloween:

> I Buy A pumpkin and I Drow [draw] my punkin [pumkin] face is gross:—One boy came and trick or treat at my hous [house] and the punkin [pumkin] (is took) [?]. The boy ran and throw the candy and the punpkin [pumpkin] laugh.—The boy cry and go homes and tell his mother. Boy come [The boy came] trick or treat, can you give some candy and the pumpking said no and I will give the boy candy to you. They boy wan . . . [?]

The ESL teacher wrote:

> He tries to read, but cannot understand. He is bored. Does not pay attention to directions any more, and he says, "I want to be in Laos. No. I don't want to be anywhere." Then he tells Carlos, (a child in the same class) "fuck you," and they get into an argument. Vilaph's face is red and the veins are clearly protruding. He cannot talk out of anger. Goes out of class and comes back shortly. He apologizes to Carlos, and says to the teacher, "We're friends now."

## Carlos

Carlos was born on the central west coast to a Mexican couple. At the time of this study he was 11 years old, and in the third grade. His father, a divorced and disabled ex-policeman, had a history of emotional problems, and was the only one living at home. Carlos' older brother, now living elsewhere, had been classified as "communicatively handicapped," as was Carlos himself during preschool. This classification was removed at the request of his father in the second grade. He was placed in a bilingual second grade classroom and did very well. Then he was transferred to an all-English third grade and both his attendance and his achievement declined. For several months he missed 50 percent of school days. A new referral for special education classes came with the teacher's statement: "Cannot follow oral directions. Needs a great deal of help. Is easily distracted. He is depressed." My observations showed that Carlos could not concentrate on a task for more than a few seconds. I collected his work for a month and discovered that he was doing exercises from the year before, and that his writing (in content, productivity, and structure) had been superior the year before. He was repeating third grade, and was writing a a composition based on three pictures showing spacecraft looking at the surface of the earth. The first year he wrote:

> The earth was going to is explod the world. And they made a spceship. And they had all ready gone to the other planet. They land already. They planted flowers and trees. And the trees grow with fod and they build ahose [a house]. And they went back to see oh [?] the plant is but it was not thir [there] so they went back home and it was already night so they all went buck [back] to sleep. And it was moring [morning] now und [and] it was breakfast now. And they ate oranges and corn flakes and they drank orang [orange] juice and grape and mil. And they all played a game called steal the bake.

The same assignment a year later was returned blank. He said he did not know what to write. I called him and asked to see his work from the year before; he looked surprised. While serious family and personal problems may explain Carlos' behavior, his overall productivity was clearly down. The interview with his father (which I found extremely difficult, because he pretended not to understand English first, and, later, when I spoke to him in Spanish, pretended not to understand Spanish) revealed that the father justified keeping Carlos at home with "just in case I need some water or something." He seemed to intimidate the child with veiled threats and there were some suggestions of child abuse. However, even in the previous year's composition there was some fragmentation and Carlos' composition was not as good as that of his peers.

## Participation Structures

The above samples show the problems faced by "learning handicapped" children as they attempt to participate meaningfully and the way that school personnel handle these children. Children's participation patterns can be classified into three types (see Trueba, 1983).

**Hypoparticipation**  This is minimum participation, primarily children's inability to make sense of either the context or content of the activity (lack of "comprehensible input" in text, norms of behavior, or expected outcomes). The extreme manifestation is a desperate effort to become inconspicuous.

**Hyperparticipation**  This is characterized by exaggerated attempts at imitating peers' mechanical movements (pretending to read or write), in response to "incomprehensible messages," without their ever being able to grasp the nature of the task or achieve competence in it.

**Selective Participation**  Calculated attempts are made at participating, often under protest, when the student has achieved a certain level of competence, but he or she perceives the activity as difficult and unrewarding. Exercises in reading, writing, or in math are viewed as too difficult, or boring, or risky. The risk of failing is high, and the loss of face is viewed as painful.

Some of these response patterns have been noted by other researchers, for example Rueda and Mehan (1986), who observed speakers of other languages, who were illiterate in English, "passing" for competent readers. All four students described academic activities as too difficult and boring. Richard would sit, yawn, and say quietly, "I don't want to do it." Carlos would just smile, look around, get up, and, if the teacher was looking at him, pretend to write. If the teacher came closer to examine his work, he'd say, "I don't know what to write." Douang would remain quiet, but next morning she would come with several handwritten pages, copied from the dictionary under parental pressure.

During the research period, children's performance deteriorated significantly in two ways:

1. The quantity and quality of written exercises diminished; the problems of fragmentation and meaning became more severe.
2. Actual attempts to participate in classroom activities become less frequent and less assertive, perhaps as the fear of public embarrassment increased.

Douang, however, more recently showed courage to talk to the ESL teacher. She said, "Mrs. X [the math teacher] never speaks to me. I have lots of time with nothing to do." One day she came and said to the ESL teacher, "I don't want to be nothing when I grow up. . . . I loved my horses in Laos. We had a brown and a white one. Love my animals." From that time to the end of the year, Douang just sat, copied simple sentences, and turned in assignments with the same errors. And Vilaph was more emphatic, stating, "I don't want to be anywhere but in Laos." Carlos has continued to miss school frequently, and still smiles, as if he could not find any other way of coping with the world around him.

## Cognitive Taxonomies and Culture

These children's experiences, objects, and thoughts (and their corresponding taxonomies) and the organization of these experiences as manifested in the way they talk about them appear to be far removed from the experiences of mainstream children. Teachers often react as if they are unable to make sense of what children describe and why it is presented as a joke, or in another unexpected context. Teachers feel culturally unfamiliar with the children's world at home in the local community. Communication between teachers and children is defective, superficial, and always under repair. Even oral or written exercises on celebrations that are part of our cultural heritage (at least in the way we celebrate them, for example, compositions on Christmas, Halloween, or Thanksgiving) seem to evoke unexpectedly different fantasies and meanings for linguistic minority children.

There is also quantitative and qualitative evidence of limited productivity on the part of these four children when compared with their peers. Classroom tasks and homework assignments were either incomplete or never presented. Furthermore, both penmanship and structural organization of the English compositions were clearly much inferior: fragmented, with syntactic error (as shown in the above compositions), and in many instances children could not grasp the central meaning or reasoning intended by the teacher.

There are some sad and extreme cases, in which attempts at participating have stopped altogether. The child just keeps his or her head down for the entire period, or sits quietly, daydreaming. The children's ultimate defense seems to be to give up entirely any attempts to understand the world around them, when nothing makes sense. Fortunately there were a number of positive experiences observed. For example, during small group sessions with the ESL and special education teachers, and only when children had been given the opportunity and encouragement to select the content and process of the activity, Vilaph, Carlos, and, to a lesser extent, Douang and Richard, engaged willingly (although for a short time) in academic tasks and presented (albeit full of grammatical errors) wonderful descriptions of their fantasies or experiences relevant to their home countries.

There is some evidence to suggest that these four children and the other children observed were going through cycles from deep depression and mental isolation to a state of panic, and then back again to depression. This was shown in sudden changes from hyperactivity (hyperparticipation) to decreasing efforts to participate, and/or respond to questions (hypoparticipation). Even the children's willingness or ability to focus on simple directions seemed lacking. At the same time, in the presence of certain unexpected stimuli (a loud command from the teacher or the voice of the principal, for example) we observed signs of fear in the form of physical restlessness, unfocused changing gaze, uncontrolled feet and hand movements, frequent need to go to the bathroom, and other expressions of emotional turmoil. This high stress increased during times of performance in front of large groups, and was at times associated with manifest serious embarrassment and attempts to hide, especially if the children were reprimanded. Vilaph and Richard showed their anger, and refused to answer more questions with an "I don't know," which discouraged the teacher from asking again. Carlos and Douang lowered the head and showed a forced smile.

## Language and "Comprehensible Input"

With respect to the control of the English language, these children cannot distinguish semantic ranges in the use of words, identify incorrect syntactic forms (verb tenses, or word order), or articulate accurate descriptions of events orally. Most importantly, they cannot comprehend, separate, or generate concepts that are taxonomically or contextually related. They have not had the opportunity to internalize domains and relationships of related concepts, of different classes of objects (types of flowers, foods, personnel, institutions, etc.), and activities associated with American holidays (Christmas and Halloween). The reason is that these domains and concepts are culturally defined and can only be learned in appropriate social and cultural contexts, not in the classroom. The children's knowledge of the language and academic subjects remained as superficial and approximate as their understanding of cultural domains. In general, these children cannot communicate in English for academic purposes in ways that would demonstrate competency in establishing logical relationships (cause and effect versus simple association in time or space, for example) through specific language structures. It does not mean that these children cannot express those concepts or relationships in other languages. We know they are competent in other languages. Their lower English skills stand in contrast to the fact that all four of them are fluent in other languages.

If the five principles advocated by Gold and Tempes (1987) had been applied in the cases of these children, they would have by now acquired higher levels of English proficiency, and would have been motivated to continue learning. These and other children observed exemplify the results of submersion programs. We have not studied their loss of their home language, but we have evidence that there is a rapidly increasing social distance between them and their parents (who are monolingual in the home language).

The children blame themselves for their failure in school, thus internalizing their "learning disabilities" as a personal attribute, rather than as a result of factors extrinsic to their mental abilities. Often these children would repeat "I'm dumb! I'm dumb!" or they would say, as Vilaph several times did, "I'm going to kill myself."

Insensitivity to the needs of linguistic minority children, and the dysfunctional instructional arrangements chosen in school, lack of political power in minority communities, or the ethnocentrism of American social and educational institutions are probably more logical explanations for the conspicuous failure of these children than any intrinsic characteristics.

## CONCLUDING THOUGHTS

The English-only philosophy reflects the political clouds that have obscured the discussion of important pedagogical principles applicable to all children. These principles have been spelled out by Cummins (1986), who emphatically states that cognitive skills (the ability to structure knowledge and to approach learning tasks effectively) can be best acquired through the native language and then easily transferred to a second language. Use of the native language is best because critical thinking skills and cognitive structuring are conditioned by linguistic and cultural knowledge and experiences that children usually obtain in the home and bring with them to school.

Some general recommendations are in order:

1. Place students in learning environments in which there are opportunities to evaluate and analyze failure and embarrassing (degradation) incidents related to academic performance.
2. Identify the learning skills and levels of students in specific subjects and domains, using their mother tongue, or the language in which they were initially instructed.
3. Construct learning experiences that are meaningful to children and congruent with their cultural and linguistic knowledge, and in which they play an important role in negotiating the content and level of instruction.
4. Sensitize the school personnel to develop culturally based instructional models that are effective for linguistic minorities.

Unfortunately, schools with high concentrations of minority children are unprepared to meet the needs of these students. This fact, however, understandable as it is, deprives many children of using their cultural knowledge and experience. This happens beyond children's control in the social institutions in which they are not socialized; it is not their fault.

## RECOMMENDED EXERCISES

1. Identify several students and faculty familiar with a bilingual program and set up a series of interviews to find out the organization of the program, its modes of delivery, specific use of first and second language, the repertoire of instructional practices, the student population, and the social, cultural, and political context of the program's operation.
2. Select several teachers from one or several bilingual programs and obtain a series of interviews on their theoretical framework, their knowledge of students' background, their teaching practices, and self-assessment of teaching effectiveness. If you can arrange it, plan to visit one of the teachers' classrooms and contrast your interview data with your observations.

3. Involve other peers in the following cooperative venture. You and your team will inquire which is the best state- and/or federally funded local program, contact the program director, and request a copy of the proposal that attracted financial support. After doing a detailed analysis of the proposal, invite the director to meet with your team to explain the concept and operation of the program, and ask his or her permission to visit the program site, if possible.

4. Invite a few classmates or friends to review with you the pros and cons of immersion education as applied in this country. Argue possible ways to assist students in the acquisition of the second language without losing their first language. Describe the conditions for success of such immersion programs, including the theoretical framework, instructional practices, parental support, and materials needed. Argue the advantages such programs can have over other possible program models.

5. Why is comprehensible language input so important in teaching and learning? Is there an important difference between the theoretical position of Cummins and that of Lambert with reference to second-language acquisition by linguistic minorities? If their positions are compatible, what type of program could incorporate both positions, and how?

## RECOMMENDED READINGS

Au & Jordan, 1981
Chamot, 1983
Cummins, 1979, 1981a,b, 1983, 1984, 1986
Delgado-Gaitan, 1987a,b
Deyhle, 1987
Diaz et al., 1986
Erickson 1984, 1986, 1987
Fishman 1976, 1979
Fujita & Sano, 1988
Glenn, 1988
Gold & Tempes, 1987
Hernandez-Chavez, 1984
Hornberger, 1988
Krashen, 1981a,b
Lambert, 1984
Macias, 1987
McDermott, 1987a,b
McLaughlin, 1982, 1985
Moll, 1986
Ogbu, 1974, 1978, 1987a,b
Politzer, 1971
Richards, 1987
Rueda, 1987
Shulman, 1987a,b

Skutnabb-Kangas, 1978, 1984
Sockett, 1987
Suarez-Orozco, 1987, in press
Swain, 1978, 1984
Tharp & Gallimore, in press
Trueba, in press
Trueba & Barnett-Mizrahi, 1979
Wong-Fillmore, 1976, 1982

# CHAPTER 4

# Legislation and Litigation

Legislative movements and judicial trends reflect cycles of liberalism and intolerance, of conflicting philosophies and contrasting language policies regarding the use of English and other languages in public life, especially in educational institutions:

> Fear of "foreign threat" was fed by racism, intense competition for economic survival and mobility, and two world wars. To unify and conform seemed logical answers, and to do so through control by force of law became a strategy of state and local policy makers (Heath & Mandabach, 1983:101).

## HISTORICAL CONTEXT OF MODERN LEGISLATION

During the last 100 years the primary function of the schools has been consistently perceived by citizens as cementing national unity through uniformity in language and culture. The first step for immigrant children in their journey to mainstream America is to learn English. As Heath and Mandabach have put it, English was the "right" language because it was "both a fundamental instrument and a necessary symbol of knowledge and character," to the point that English teachers were viewed as "preachers" of American values and culture (1983:99). The ultimate goal of American youngsters in public schools was to develop an appreciation for the standard English language as a conspicuous demonstration of patriotism. This strong national feeling explains the fact that by 1923 34 states had passed legislation requiring English to become the only language of public instruction, and restricting the use of French, German, and other languages in private schools (Andersson & Boyer, 1971; Drake, 1973; Heath, 1976, 1977; Leibowitz, 1971; Kloss, 1977; Acuña, 1981).

## From 1776 to 1968

The United States has become the home of millions of persons from non-English backgrounds since the seventeenth century. During the nineteenth century, the Germans settled in the Midwest and advocated bilingual schools. In some states, for example, Ohio and Wisconsin, political support and tax monies were used to hire teachers who knew German and to purchase German textbooks in the public schools (Heath, 1978; McLaughlin, 1985). Gradually, as happened in England, English achieved in the United States the undeclared official status it has today, not because citizens were forced by law to use English but because they perceived English as a higher-status language (Heath & Mandabach, 1983). In the 1880s bilingual education was under attack in many cities that began to pass laws prohibiting the use of non-English languages for instruction (McLaughlin, 1985).

The analysis of legislative movements affecting the education of minorities and language policy in the United States is organized by scholars into different chronological periods and trends (Cuban, 1979; Tyack & Hansot, 1982, 1984; Heath, 1976; Heath & Mandabach, 1983; Kloss, 1977; San Miguel, 1983, 1986, 1987). There are three distinct periods: 1776–1849, 1850–1919, and 1920–1968. In the early period, from 1776 to 1849, the founders became acutely aware of the linguistic and ethnic diversity of the first immigrants who became Americans. Their main concern was to create a strong nation that could compete internationally with the industrial European nations of the time. The way to scientific, economic, and military power was unity. Consequently, language diversity was viewed as a threat to unity. There was a tacit agreement that, with the exception of the Native American nations living in the United States, and of the black people who were slaves, all other persons were to share the English language (San Miguel, 1983, 1986, 1987; Heath, 1978; Heath & Mandabach, 1983).

During the second period, from 1850 to 1919, many of the incoming immigrants to cities such as St. Louis, Cleveland, and New York, had come from Ireland and other Catholic European countries. Their strong advocacy for native languages other than English in their private schools alarmed mainstream Americans, who implemented policies limiting the use of languages other than English for classroom instruction. The demand for cultural conformity and exclusive use of English in the classroom found increasing public support by the midnineteenth century. Compulsory education and phonetic standardization go hand in hand with the urbanization and industrialization of the mid-1800s (Heath, 1978; Heath & Mandabach, 1983). English literacy began then to be considered as an instrument of language control and a mechanism for creating political unity. English literacy became a necessary precondition to the right to vote and participate actively in the political process. The annexation of western territories with high concentrations of Native Americans and Spanish-speaking people created a problem; many Mexican people became American citizens overnight without knowing English or being a part of the social and political system. Furthermore, the recruitment of thousands of Asian workers to build the railroads was also perceived as a threat to the political national unity deemed essential to the United States becoming a cohesive industrial and economic power (San Miguel, 1983, 1986, 1987).

Prior to the mid-nineteenth century there was neither restriction nor prescription of the use of English for public instruction and services. The industrial development of the country inspired legislation intended to curtail the social and political participation of speakers of non-English languages, and thus motivate the new immigrants to acquire English. The nineteenth century legislation, however, did not do away with the use of non-English languages by local organizations, private schools, and printing presses, nor even the use of non-English languages in public schools. The use of German, French, and Spanish is well documented (Kloss, 1977; Heath, 1976; Heath & Mandabach, 1983). State laws continued to be published in Spanish, French, and German. In 1890, however, the states of Connecticut, Massachusetts, and Rhode Island made English the mandatory school language. In that same year New York and many midwestern states ordered public schools to use English exclusively for instruction, clearly prohibiting the use of non-English languages for any subject matter. Thirty-nine states passed provisions to undermine the use of non-English languages in private Catholic schools (Heath, 1976, 1978; San Miguel 1983, 1986, 1987). There were formal declarations by California, Texas, Pennsylvania, and Georgia prohibiting the use of non-English language to conduct public affairs.

Economic and political reasons were given to the public to justify such language policies, particularly in the period from 1890 to 1920. In 1919, Nebraska, for example, prohibited the teaching of foreign languages to children below the level of ninth grade, in an effort to ensure that they became fluent in English. These laws were subsequently ruled unconstitutional by the Supreme Court in 1923 (Heath, 1976, 1978; Heath & Mandabach, 1983).

Events during the period from 1920 to 1968 took a more violent turn. In the West, for example in Oregon, laws were enacted in 1922 establishing compulsory school attendance and English instruction for children aged 8–15. Once more, the Supreme Court declared these laws unconstitutional and defended the right to private education in any language. In 1927, legal restrictions imposed on the use of Korean, Chinese, and Japanese in Hawaii were subsequently lifted by the Supreme Court (Heath & Mandabach, 1983).

The struggle for language rights during the last two decades of the nineteenth century and the first two decades of the twentieth century was bitter. Between 1919 and 1925, in states that managed to pass laws against the use of languages other than English in school, at the ballot box, and in the employment office, the state courts sentenced over 1,000 individuals to jail for subversive speech, which was presumed to make individuals suspicious and dangerous. Thousands of cases were litigated between 1920 and 1950 on the grounds that the use of languages other than English was indicative of "clear and present danger." Thus, the power of the state to restrain free speech was justified on the basis of the state's right to prevent potential disorder and crimes, as well as to prevent national anarchy fostered by language diversity (Heath, 1978; Heath & Mandabach, 1983; San Miguel 1983, 1986). As Gonzalez eloquently stated:

> The logic of the monoglots seemed ironclad at the time. If one assumes that
> all beauty, virtue, and merit resides with one language (and the culture[s] it
> reflects), then the operational strategies are likewise clear: ban the use of all

other languages in education and soon all diversity will disappear, harmony will prevail, and the threat of Babelian discord will end. Indeed the linguistic equivalent of book burning worked admirably well. But it worked best with the Northern European immigrants, people who had a degree of cultural affinity and who shared certain priorities and goals in coming to the United States. Equally important, they shared a Caucasian racial history (Gonzalez, 1979:3–4).

The feelings against teaching foreign languages in public schools became strong during the 1930s and persisted until the 1950s. Then the foreign language in the elementary school (FLES) program was initiated, and by the mid-1960s over a million children were receiving foreign-language instruction. Government support through the National Defense Education Act of 1958 supported the training of foreign language teachers and the country was enthusiastic about the teaching of languages other than English (McLaughlin, 1985).

The most recent period, from 1968 to the present, is clearly characterized by ethnic consciousness and freedom of speech. The end of the McCarthy era was marked by a distinction between opinion and action, and the need to exercise greater control of the political power bestowed upon public figures. The momentum gained by the civil rights movement continued to gain support in the courts. Tolerance for the use of languages other than English was also symbolic of the greater tolerance for the cultural differences of Americans who spoke those languages.

However, neither the legal basis for preventing language repression at the federal level nor public opinion was very strong on behalf of the language rights of minorities. Thus, the United States experienced a policy vacuum regarding national language, and a cycle of repression alternating with support for the use of non-English languages. Periods of language repression have tended to coincide with socioeconomic crises, such as peaking unemployment, international financial turmoil, and, at times, unexpected stock market depressions, threat of war, and internal political struggles. In general, scholars (Kloss, 1977; Heath & Mandabach, 1983; San Miguel, 1983, 1986) view the federal courts as holding a more liberal position than public opinion, and of preventing language legislation that may threaten the rights of individuals to their own language and culture. More recently, however, the excessive use of the court system to determine educational policy has alarmed some educators, who are concerned with the transfer of power from educational institutions to the legal system. The Supreme Court has consistently maintained that languages other than English be used for instruction and public service when circumstances demand it. In *Meyer* v. *Nebraska*, 1923, for example, the Supreme Court declared unconstitutional state legislation prohibiting the teaching of foreign languages in the ninth grade. The same court in 1925 (*Pierce* v. *Society of Sisters*) upheld the right of private schools to use non-English languages for instruction.

## From 1968 to the Present

During the civil rights movement, ethnolinguistic minority groups formed political coalitions and lobbied intensively for federal support of bilingual education. Spanish-speaking groups played a key role during this period. Many scholars have helped us to understand the significance of this historical period and its implications for education (Jorgensen, 1956; Fishman, 1956, 1976, 1977, 1978; Leibowitz, 1971; Kloss, 1977; Cummins, 1983, 1986).

A new provision of the previously approved Elementary and Secondary Education Act of 1965 underwent considerable debate before being passed in Congress and signed into law by Lyndon B. Johnson on January 2, 1968. Public Law 90–247 appropriated $7.5 million for bilingual education. The education of linguistic minority children was the focus of the new act. This act was expected to:

1. Accept the formal legitimacy of bilingual education.
2. Recognize the special needs of non-English-speaking children, and the feasibility of providing them with instruction in their own language.
3. Focus on the notion of equal educational opportunity as distinct from equal educational process.
4. Recognize the existence of a substantial number of "national-origin minorities" as political entities requiring special services, different from those offered on the basis of desegregation legislation.

The fundamental purpose of the Bilingual Education Act was stated by the Department of Health, Education and Welfare as follows:

> . . . to enable children whose dominant language is other than English to develop competitive proficiency in English so that they can function successfully in the educational and occupational institutions of the larger society . . . This view of the federal goal regards the use of the home language and reinforcement of its culture and heritage as necessary and appropriate means of reaching the desired end of giving the children from the various language groups proficiency in the dominant language, and not as ends in themselves (Memorandum, DHEW; cited by Gonzalez, 1979:8).

The acute social, economic, and educational problems of linguistic minority families served as a major argument for accepting the legitimacy of bilingual education. In 1960, achievement scores and median years of school attended by Mexican American children were alarmingly low in contrast with national norms. In California, for example, 50 percent of all Mexican Americans 14 years of age and older had not gone beyond the eighth grade, in contrast with 25 percent of the national sample. Several school districts, notably Dade County (Florida) and San Antonio (Texas) developed bilingual programs with monies from private foundations (Ford Foundation, for example), and began to demonstrate high levels of academic success with selected Hispanic student populations. Similar experiments took place in other states, such as California and New Mexico (Salomone, 1986).

Bilingual education in public schools, with the support of the federal government, represents a compromise between opposing educational philosophies that view first languages in different ways. For some advocates of bilingual education, children's first language use is a civil and social right, as well as the best means to high educational attainment. For others, the mother tongue is only a temporary instrument of cultural transition and adjustment into mainstream instruction in English. This debate between "maintenance" and "transitional" bilingual education philosophies continued for years and resulted in policy changes within the Office for Bilingual Education and Language Minority Affairs (OBELMA).

In 1977, as advocates for bilingual education were getting ready to propose their arguments for the second reauthorization of the Bilingual Education Act (which was reauthorized in 1974, 1978, and 1984), the American Institutes for Research (1977a, b) published their evaluation of 38 Spanish/English bilingual projects studied in 1975. About 12,000 children were included in this $1.3 million study commissioned by the U.S. Office of Education. The study severely criticized bilingual programs and, despite methodological flaws and unwarranted conclusions, it raised doubts about the effectiveness of bilingual education (O'Malley, 1977; Trueba, 1979; Salomone, 1986).

The continued attacks from opponents of bilingual education were epitomized by Noel Epstein (1977), previously one of the education editors for *The Washington Post*. The reaction against bilingual education was vigorous and clear (Fishman, 1978). The Title VII Bilingual Education Act was amended and reauthorized in 1978 in a political victory credited to Senators Edward Kennedy (D-MA) and Alan Cranston (D-CA). The act broadened the eligibility criteria to include students who had "limited English proficiency" and low achievement in content areas, regardless of their proficiency in the mother tongue. The amendment also curtailed participation of students who, because of their demonstrated fluency in English, could be transferred to regular classrooms (Salomone, 1986). The advocacy for bilingual education programs in the reauthorizations of the Bilingual Education Act of 1974, 1978, and 1984 was the result of political coalitions recognizing minority political constituencies. The role of English as the unofficial public language has remained unchallenged. Support for transitional programs did not change people's conviction that linguistic and ethnic diversity is opposed to the cultural and political unity in America. This conviction has historically fueled strong sentiments against the public use of non-English languages (Fishman, 1978).

The Bilingual Education Act came as a surprise to many. Still more surprising, 5 years after its passage, was the fact that

> Half of our states and many local education authorities have instituted bilingual education codes or programs of their own (among them California, Illinois, New York, Texas and Massachusetts), and bilingual education has become an

established part of the programs of all major language teachers associations (Fishman, 1979:12).

Mexican Americans viewed the Bilingual Education Act as a national political victory and a means to eliminate some discriminatory practices in the schools. To many linguistic minorities, the use of home languages was promised to increase academic achievement and ensure a more positive self-image, without jeopardizing their acquisition of English. Additional research (Lambert & Tucker, 1972; Genesee et al., 1975; Lambert, 1981, 1984; Lapkin & Cummins, 1984) has strongly supported the theory that learning two languages is cognitively enriching and a more effective approach to achieving academically. More important for the Mexican-American families, "Using their native language in the instructional process also appeared to be promising in helping Mexican American children adjust to the Anglo public schools and to foster pride in their cultural heritage" (San Miguel, 1987:193). Beyond the perceived political benefits, Mexican Americans insisted that effective schooling, given the unique learning needs of their children, required the reorganization of school administration, curricula, and teaching methods:

> In order to fully meet the special needs of these [Mexican American] children the curriculum would have to be reorganized, administrative procedures for identifying and grouping children based on language needs modified, and the retraining of teachers working with Mexican American children initiated. It would also require better relations with Mexican American parents and their participation in schools' activities (San Miguel, 1987:194).

In the end, Mexican Americans and other linguistic minority communities received support and attention. However, public opinion regarding the value attached to the exclusive use of English in regular instruction as a means to protect national unity did not change. The public sentiment regarding the need to change immigrants into bona fide Americans was behind Epstein's attacks against bilingual education. He considered that it was unconstitutional to spend federal funds on "maintenance" bilingual education programs: programs for children who had already acquired enough English language proficiency to function in normal classrooms. Epstein contended that it was not the role of the federal government to reinforce ethnic identity:

> Separating students temporarily in basic skills classes in the native language until they can learn in English, for example, can be justified. . . . But keeping students and teacher segregated to maintain the native language and culture cannot be so justified, and the evidence indicates that most maintenance efforts are highly segregated (Epstein, 1977:4)

Indeed, while one can disagree with the policy advocated by Epstein, the argument that bilingual education can be misused to pursue ethnic segregation is a serious concern, based on documented experiences of bilingual educators in the Southwest.

## LITIGATION AND EDUCATION

The Supreme Court has remained, in general, true to democratic philosophy, and has defended a liberal position regarding minorities. The *Meyer* v. *Nebraska* precedent in 1923 invalidated suppressive legislation prohibiting the teaching of foreign languages. Not only did the Supreme Court take a liberal position, but some of the local courts did also. *Roberto Alvarez* v. *the Board of Trustees of the Lemon Grove School District* (1931) is a case in point. The Bliss Bill had requested the power to establish separate schools for "Indian" children of Japanese, Chinese, and Mexican ancestry on the grounds that all were Indians and existing laws permitted segregated schools for Indians. Judge Chambers wisely ruled against it stating: "I believe this separation denies the Mexican children the presence of the American children, which is so necessary to learn the English language" (Alvarez, 1988).

In 1954, the Supreme Court examined the case of black children who were systematically segregated in the South under the "separate but equal" official policies of the educational system. In the *Brown* v. *Board of Education*, the Supreme Court took the position that refusing students access to any educational institution on the basis of race was a violation of their constitutional rights, even if children in a segregated school system had comparable teachers, buildings, and resources. Racial segregation itself was ruled to be a violation of civil rights and detrimental to students' education in that it denied them access to their peers (Salomone, 1986; Figueroa, 1987).

The impact of *Brown* v. *Board of Education* was felt in the 1967 *Hobson* v. *Hansen* case. Hansen, the Superintendent of the Washington, D.C., schools, at the time, defended segregation on the grounds that ability groups were created as a result of achievement tests. However, the lower tracks were overpopulated by blacks, and the higher tracks by Anglo children. The courts pointed to flaws in testing procedures and interpretation as a measure of children's potential, thus opposing segregation on any grounds.

No other Supreme Court case has had as powerful an impact as that of *Lau* v. *Nichols* (1974). The Supreme Court upheld the right of non-English-speaking students to educational programs designed to meet their particular needs and language skills. The Court's January decision, in the interpretation of Teitelbaum and Hiller, declared it unconstitutional to deprive linguistic minority students of educational opportunities on the basis of language differences:

> The landmark case in bilingual education was *Lau* v. *Nichols*. It squarely presented to the courts the issue of whether non-English-speaking students who constitute national-origin minority groups receive an education free from un-

lawful discrimination when instructed in English, a language they do not understand. The Supreme Court's January 1974 ruling in *Lau* that federally aided school districts must address the needs of their non-English-speaking students continues to reverberate in the halls of educational institutions (Teitelbaum & Hiller, 1979:21).

Unlawful discrimination was understood to take place when speakers of other languages were instructed in English, a language they did not understand. The *Lau* ruling created a presumption in favor of bilingual education (Teitelbaum & Hiller, 1979), without specifying which educational program would best meet the needs of linguistic minority students.

The suit was brought by Mr. Lau on behalf of 1,790 Chinese students who, like thousands of other students, suffered educationally in the San Francisco Unified School District because they did not understand English instruction. Their claims were initially rejected by the Federal District Court, but the plaintiffs appealed the decision. The Ninth Circuit Court of Appeals then ruled that the uniform use of English did not constitute unlawful discrimination and declared that English-language instruction should be upheld (Teitelbaum & Hiller, 1979; Figueroa, 1987).

The plaintiffs, not yet satisfied, presented their case to the Supreme Court. Justice Douglas stated his official position as follows:

> Teaching English to the students of Chinese ancestry who do not speak the language is one choice. Giving instructions to this group in Chinese is another. There may be others. Petitioners ask only that the Board of Education be directed to apply its expertise to the problem and rectify the situation (*Lau* v. *Nichols*, 1974, 414 U.S. 563).

The San Francisco Board of Education responded by providing bilingual–bicultural educational programs for nearly 11,000 Chinese, Filipino, and Spanish-speaking children. According to Teitelbaum and Hiller, it is clear that this Supreme Court ruling viewed the use of English as discriminatory towards minority national-origin children. This interpretation was taken in other court cases challenging English-only instruction for linguistic minorities. For example, the *Serna* v. *Portales* case of 1972 in New Mexico found that students' constitutional rights had been violated and ordered bilingual education programs to be set up. School officials appealed the decision, but the final ruling was in favor of bilingual education.

In 1972 the case of *Aspira of New York, Inc.* v. *Board of Education of the City of New York* (handled by Teibelbaum and Hiller) dealt with the rights of thousands of Puerto Rican and other Hispanic students who were receiving only ESL instruction to bilingual education. *Lau* precedents were highly instrumental in the out-of-court settlement in favor of Aspira. The litigating parties consented to a decree in August of 1974 under which the school board was required to assess Spanish-speaking students' skills in English and Spanish and to provide core instruction in Spanish for those students not fluent in English (Teitelbaum & Hiller, 1979).

In 1977, another court decision was based on *Lau*, the *Rios* v. *Read* case on Long Island. Plaintiffs had requested information on achievement levels, ESL classes, and reading scores, in order to assess whether the school programs effectively promoted English fluency and academic progress of students. The courts referred to *Lau* and ruled that the school district could not interfere with the rights of the plaintiff to check compliance with *Lau* and the educational needs of linguistic minority children.

A detailed analysis of the desegregation cases preceding *Lau* and those that followed is outside the scope of this chapter (see Teitelbaum & Hiller, 1979). It is important to note that all those cases emphasize the fundamental legal principles announced by Justice Douglas. No educational agency ''shall deny equal educational opportunity to an individual on account of his or her . . . national origin by failing to take appropriate action to overcome language barriers'' (Teitelbaum & Hiller, 1979:34–35).

The previously mentioned *Hobsen* v. *Hansen* case was immediately followed in 1970 by *Diana* v. *State Board of Education*, initiated by the parents of nine Mexican American children classified as ''educable mentally retarded'' (EMR) in the Monterey County Schools. These parents argued that the diagnosis was invalid because the children, who were monolingual Spanish-speaking, had been tested in English, and also that the EMR placement had caused them serious psychological damage. Indeed, the children's verbal and nonverbal IQ scores were not only ridiculously low but were incompatible with observations of their interactional competencies (Figueroa, 1987). The abuse of English testing was an issue settled out of court in the *Diana* case. The impact of this settlement is summarized by Figueroa as follows:

> The out-of-court settlement arrived at before Judge Robert Peckham of the U.S. Ninth Circuit Court in San Francisco established a unique set of precedents relative to testing LEP pupils: testing was to be done in the primary language and in English, nonverbal IQ's could be used, all previously diagnosed EMR Chicano children had to be retested paying particular attention to their nonverbal scores, and intelligence tests appropriate for Mexican American children had to be developed, and the representation of EMR Hispanic students in each school district throughout the state had to be monitored to make sure that there were no ethnic disparities of Chicano pupils in EMR classes (Figueroa, 1987:33).

In order to monitor the Hispanic overrepresentation of children in EMR classes, the California State Department of Education proposed to Judge Peckham a formula that resulted in quasi-quotas for Hispanic children in EMR classes.

Repeated requests to review linguistic minority overrepresentation in EMR classes in 1977 and 1978 finally compelled the *Diana* plaintiffs to renegotiate their settlement through the California State Advisory Commission for Special Education.

The renegotiation included a review of competencies in testers, not just properties of the tests, the abandoning of formulas, and the funding by the State Department of Education of new tests for measuring Hispanic children's intelligence.

The 1979 *Larry P.* v. *Wilson Riles* case was originally presented in San Francisco to Judge Robert Peckham's court in 1970 as a class action suit, based on *Brown* v. *the Board of Education* and *Lau* v. *Nichols*, against the San Francisco Unified School District and the California State Department of Education. The plaintiff presented a case very similar to that of *Diana*: a small group of black children had been misclassified as EMR on the basis of invalid IQ tests. Judge Peckham imposed a temporary injunction on the state forbidding the use of IQ tests that did not take into consideration black children's cultural background and experiences. The issue of overrepresentation of blacks and Hispanics in EMR classes and of insensitivity to the culture of these children was underscored by the judge. Against the vote of the State Board of Education, in March of 1984 Wilson Riles appealed the ruling on *Larry P.* The Ninth Circuit Court of Appeals, in 1987, ruled on behalf of *Larry P.*, thus upholding Peckham's decision.

## HISPANICS' STRUGGLE FOR EQUITY

The term "Hispanics" used here refers to the National Bureau of the Census definition, which includes all Spanish-speaking Americans from various ethnic backgrounds: Mexican Americans, Puerto Ricans, Cubans, Central Americans, South Americans, and others. Between 1980 and 1987 Hispanics in the United States increased 4.3 million (30 percent) to a total of 18.8 million (about 12 million are of Mexican origin). They are characterized by low income (with an increase of 24 percent between 1981 and 1986 in the lowest income brackets, three times as many as non-Hispanics), and by lagging behind the income of mainstream populations (U.S. Department of Commerce, Bureau of the Census, 1987). While in general there has been some increase in the percentage of Hispanic persons 25 years old and over with 4 years of high school or postsecondary education (45 percent in 1982, 51 percent in 1987), the overall proportion of Hispanics in that age group who completed 4 or more years of college remained almost the same: 8 percent in 1982 and 9 percent in 1987.

Mexican Americans are the largest linguistic minority in the United States and the fastest growing group. Twenty-five years ago, Mexican Americans became acutely aware of their potential political power and the problems of a social system that did not seem to respond to their needs. Many of them had experienced poverty and oppression (Acuña, 1981; San Miguel, 1982, 1983, 1987). President Kennedy failed to place Mexican Americans in leadership positions. At first, President Johnson seemed to temper the frustration of Mexican Americans over previous unfulfilled promises by implementing federal programs to help minorities, such as the War Against Poverty (San Miguel, 1987). Traditional organizations such as the League of United Latin American Citizens (LULAC) and the American G. I. Forum involved themselves in picketing to demand fair representation of Mexican Americans in federally funded organizations, such as the Equal Employment Opportunity Commission.

The Johnson administration was charged with being insensitive to the needs of Mexican Americans. Johnson ignored Mexican American leaders such as Reis Tijerina from New Mexico, Cesar Chavez from California, and Rodolfo "Corky" Gonzales from Colorado. Mexican Americans' search for political organizations to help them articulate their needs for representation and leadership positions resulted in the creation of La Raza Unida Party. This organization attempted to gather Mexican Americans from different social strata and political philosophies to determine legal interventions in Texas during the early 1970s, with the ultimate purpose of consolidating Mexican and Hispanic organizations facing political attacks and internal division.

## Mexican Americans in Texas

The League of United Latin American Citizens (LULAC), a well-structured statewide organization of American citizens of Mexican descent, was formed in Texas in response to the socioeconomic problems they faced in the first three decades of this century. Citizens of Mexican descent not only suffered economic deprivation but also were judged responsible for the increase in juvenile delinquency, illiteracy, and crime (San Miguel, 1987). Discrimination and use of physical violence against Mexican Texans, and the continual and contemptuous denial of justice in the courts, motivated Spanish-speaking persons to join forces in LULAC. Their goal, as stated by active members, was clearly conciliatory, to allow Mexican Americans to become loyal citizens of the United States (San Miguel, 1987).

Historians have documented the recent efforts of Mexican Americans to flex their legal muscle in an effort to reach educational and political equity. San Miguel (1987) indicated that between 1970 and 1981 93 education suits were filed by the Mexican American Legal Defense and Education Fund (MALDEF) in Texas. Between 1971 and 1975 alone there were 39 desegregation suits. The support of the Ford Foundation beginning in 1968 was instrumental in changing the political and legal picture for Mexican Americans in Texas and the entire Southwest:

> [The Ford Foundation] decided to grant to the Mexican American Legal Defense and Education Fund a sum of $2.2 million to be spent over five years on civil rights legal work for Mexican Americans; $250,000 of the grant should go for scholarships to Chicano law students (San Miguel, 1987:171).

MALDEF's strategy was to file equal educational opportunity lawsuits at all levels, file separate bilingual education cases, file suit in employment discrimination cases, and to challenge discrimination in public education at all levels. These strategies were continued in the early 1970s with court cases such as *Cisneros* v.

*Corpus Christi Independent School District.* The court ruled, on the basis of the *Brown* case, in favor of desegregation of Mexican Americans at work. In 1971 MALDEF sponsored legal cases in Dallas, Austin, Uvalde, Waco, and Corpus Christi, with equally satisfying results.

## Hispanics in California: Proposition 63

Such factors as those discussed above perhaps prompted the 1986 attempts to declare English to be the only official language. This initiative was a reaction against the use of languages other than English in school and in public life. California has the dubious distinction of having always taken the first step either for or against radical (liberal or conservative) positions. The well-known Proposition 63, passed by a large majority in 1987, seemed to many to be an irrational, unnecessary, and racist movement.

The U.S. English group is the largest private organization to move for prescriptive language legislation in the history of this country. The present organization claims 200,000 members who pay dues and operate a political action committee (PAC) to press for adoption of language-related state and federal amendments. Senator Hayakawa (R-CA), Honorary Chairman of the U.S. English Initiative, best articulates the sentiment of this conservative power:

> We have unwisely embarked upon a policy of so-called bilingualism, putting foreign languages in competition with our own. English has long been the main unifying force of the American people. But now prolonged bilingual education in public schools and multi-lingual ballots threaten to divide us along language lines (cited by Galvan et al., 1986:5).

Federal legislation introduced in the 99th Congress to amend the U.S. Constitution, came in the form of a bill sponsored by Steven Symms (R-ID), reading:

> Section 1. The English language shall be the official language of the United States.
>
> Section 2. The Congress and the States shall have the power to enforce this article by appropriate legislation (cited by Galvan et al., 1986:4).

The House Bill, sponsored by Norman Shumway (R-CA), contains section 1 and 2 (this latter as Section 4) cited above and two additional sections, which read as follows:

> Section 2. Neither the U.S. nor any state shall require by law, ordinance, regulation, order, decree, program, or policy, the use in the U.S. of any language other than English.
>
> Section 3. This article shall not prohibit any law, ordinance, regulation, order, degree, program, or policy requiring educational instruction in a language other

than English for the purpose of making students who use language other than English proficient in English (as cited by Galvan et al., 1986:3).

Advocates for the English-only initiative have been accused of not using arguments founded on facts. Of the almost 22 million people 5 years and older living in California in 1980, about 5 million, that is 23 percent, speak a language other than English, yet most of them also speak English; of the 23 percent, only 15 percent were born outside the United States. Like previous English-only movements, the initiative of the 1980s is motivated by fear that the increasing numbers of linguistic minority persons will create a powerful political enclave and take over power. It is also propelled by the belief that these persons constitute an economic burden for tax-paying citizens.

This country is still viewed by modern western industrial societies as the land of opportunity and an exemplary democratic nation. Yet language repression has been stringent and illogical at times. Lack of a clearly formulated language policy has left a national vacuum, allowing public opinion and local institutions to treat citizens who are not fluent in English less equally than those who are. The lack of adequate opportunity to learn English has prevented many individuals from participating fully in American social, economic, and political life. Yet there may be some interesting exceptions in two modern cities, Los Angeles and Miami. The fact that larger clusters of Hispanics reside in those areas than elsewhere in the United States may have permitted individuals to remain monolingual in Spanish and still hold economic and political power. Both cities, however, face strong opposition to the public use of non-English languages, and have considered ordinances restricting the public use of Spanish. The main political purpose of Proposition 63 in California was probably to curtail the use and status of Spanish in public life.

## Liberal Reaction to Proposition 63

After the initial enthusiasm of some and the shock of others following the victory of Proposition 63, a liberal current in defense of non-English languages began to surface from different quarters. Some liberals reacted angrily through the newspapers to charges that the use of non-English languages is socially divisive, unnecessary, or unpatriotic. University professors and other scholars argued that Proposition 63 itself was divisive and dangerous, and they denounced it as an expression of xenophobia and irrational behavior in a country and region that are ethnically and linguistically heterogeneous. More specifically, the proposition produced polarization and tension between adjacent mainstream and Hispanic communities, for example in Ojai, Ventura, and Oxnard in southern California. Furthermore, there was a concern that implementation of Proposition 63 would jeopardize communication associated with public service provided during crisis situations. Public property, health, and even the lives of many citizens could be endangered if immigration, police, and fire department officers, or medical personnel were prevented from using non-English languages during their ordinary operations.

Proposition 63 was perceived as having a punitive intent and being ineffective in the task of assisting speakers of other languages to learn English. As Madrid expressed in his testimony for the Joint Legislative Committee on Proposition 63:

> Many of the fears regarding the public use of languages other than English in the United States derive in large measure from an irrational fear in our society of persons who are different; a lack of understanding of the history of the United States and particularly of the history of language policy; [and] ignorance concerning language use in America today (Madrid, 1986).

Current linguistic distribution in California suggest that 77 percent of the state population speaks only English, 17 percent is bilingual, and about 6 percent speaks languages other than English. There was a very substantial amount of money invested in the media to advocate for Proposition 63, and the votes favored it by a large margin, including the vote of Hispanics.

In 1980 there were 4,965,022 Californians 5 years or older who reported speaking a language other than English. This figure is not much larger than the number of recent immigrants (3.4 million) who came to California in the last five years. Non-English languages spoken in California are Spanish (14.3 percent of the total population), Chinese (1.2 percent), Filipino (1.1 percent), German (0.8 percent), Italian (0.6 percent), French (0.5 percent), Greek (0.2 percent), Polish (0.1 percent), and others (4.0 percent) (Estrada, 1986).

It is paradoxical that while the vote on Proposition 63 was being passed by a sweeping majority, adult education programs in Los Angeles reported that in 1986 alone they had to turn away 40,000 adults seeking ESL instruction because of lack of resources. Many of these adults do feel an enormous pressure to learn English, and they do not know that the de facto language policy in this country is more liberal than newspaper rhetoric would seem to indicate.

## National Status of the Spanish Language

In spite of the attacks against minority languages in Texas and California, Spanish and other languages have enjoyed a quasiofficial status in some areas of public service. This special status, offered because of the large numbers of Hispanic residents and the continuing waves of immigrants from Spanish-speaking countries, is not free of ambiguity or confusion. Keller (1983) offers the following examples as other areas in which the Spanish language has already obtained a de facto quasiofficial status:

1. Spanish-speaking citizens have the right to vote in Spanish. This right is guaranteed by the Voting Rights Act of 1965, as amended in 1975.
2. All LEP children residing in the United States (whether citizens or not)

have the right (not the obligation) to receive instruction in their native language, whenever resources permit. Spanish instruction is often encouraged, at least for a short period of time.

3. In some localities, Spanish is required as a broadcasting medium by Federal Communications Commission policies.

4. The use of interpreters and translators is provided for by civil, criminal, and military codes for speakers of other languages, most frequently for Spanish speakers.

These provisions, which have raised languages other than English to a type of official status in this country, are the response to pragmatic political and economic considerations in favor of effective communication in our public service institutions. More humane consideration for the needs of speakers of other languages has prevailed against the sentiment of traditionally more conservative segments of the population, which adhere to the English-only position as the most patriotic and practical. Tolerance for the use of other languages seems to increase or decrease with national political and economic crises. The following case study illustrates the complexity of the issue of instruction in languages other than English, and the meeting of legal mandates, court decisions, school district resources, and local politics. The case also illustrates the process of political socialization to which parents who speak languages other than English are exposed upon their arrival. Learning the American way means learning how to use legal and political means in order to defend educational equity. Every non-English speaker has the right to obtain an education for his or her children that is as good as the education offered to English-speaking students. The local newspapers have closely followed every episode of the legal struggle described below, between Bahia parents and the school district authorities.

## THE BAHIA PARENTS' CASE STUDY: READING, WRITING, AND RETALIATION

The district had been literally warehousing immigrant children in windowless, crowded rooms with poorly prepared instructors who were monolingual in English. Teachers were struggling to communicate with children who were monolingual in six or seven languages other than English. The Board members knew that some of the schools had at least 75 percent LEP children. Many of these children had been passed from one grade to another without being academically prepared to face the next grade level's tasks. As a result, by junior high school as many as 50 percent were dropping out of school. Language minority parents are often stereotyped as being passive and helpless in the face of conflicts with school districts. The story presented here offers evidence that parents can learn how to apply pressure to the school system to protect their children's rights to meaningful instruction.

The Bahia (fictitious name) School District is one of the largest school districts in northern California, with a substantial linguistic minority student population concentrated in 30 of its nearly 100 schools. Hispanic, Chinese, Filipino, Cambodian, Laotian, Vietnamese, and African immigrant families arrive in the Bahia area without any skills in English.

One of the principals—a Hispanic woman—described the children's predicament as follows:

> You come to school who you are, you don't fit the dominant middle-class culture and you can't speak the language. You never catch up to where you should be, and you're always behind. It's a vicious, vicious cycle.

Based on the *Brown* v. *Board of Education* and *Lau* v. *Nichols* cases, the State of California had passed the Chacon–Moscone Bilingual–Bicultural Education Act in 1976, which mandated the most stringent instructional requirements for linguistic minority children. The Bahia school officials had somehow managed to ignore this act without penalty. At the same time, increasing numbers of Hispanics and Southeast Asian refugees, some of whom belonged to upper classes and had high educational levels in their home countries, began to express to school officials their discontent with the quality of instruction. The officials appeared even more callous in their disregard for national and state bilingual education policies. The U.S. Office of Civil Rights had already cited the Bahia district four times for violations of federal bilingual requirements in 1976, 1980, 1981, and 1984. District authorities always managed to make promises and retain the federal monies intended for bilingual education. These funds were used for other purposes.

In the fall of 1982 a master plan, drafted by a group of local consultants together with parents and assisted by Legal Aid Society lawyers, was submitted to the school district for review at a public hearing. The Associate Superintendent for Curriculum and Instruction stepped in during the public hearing and arbitrarily rejected the draft. In its place, he presented a document produced by the district. This behavior was viewed by many as another ploy by the district to evade its obligations, and people in the community became extremely angry. The Associate Superintendent argued that the district simply did not have the resources to establish bilingual programs for all 37 ethnolinguistic groups demanding such programs. The Bahia district, however, had sufficient resources; it had received over $3 million in federal and state grants between 1982 and 1983 to develop bilingual education.

Once more, parents and Legal Aid lawyers organized and worked assiduously for a year to develop a revised plan, after which they requested that they be allowed to bring it before the school board. They were granted hearings from June to the end of July, 1983. Finally, after intense discussion and lobbying, the school board unanimously approved the first bilingual education master plan submitted by parents, on July 27, 1983. In the meantime, district officials had quietly dismantled the district's Office for Bilingual Education and had reassigned its large staff (43 persons) to other positions. During fiscal year 1982–1983 alone the district had received close to $2 million in state and federal categorical funds intended exclusively for bilingual education. Following the confrontation between school district and parents, the local paper stated:

> Many people—including some Bahia school administrators—are hostile to bilingual education because they see it as squandering scarce resources on immigrant and refugee children that should rightfully be spent on programs for Blacks and other educationally deprived youth. The fact that the money comes from designated sources has been obscured by xenophobia and racism—a time-honored American tradition. (March 1, 1985; the paper's name is omitted to retain anonymity).

Without an Office of Bilingual Education, it was impossible for the district to write grant proposals. Therefore, in 1983, for the first time since 1971, the district received no federal Title VII monies. The district again refused to send the mandatory home language survey questionnaires to students' families, and thus refused to comply with the requirements stipulated by Title VII. Consequently the district was starting the new academic year without knowing the exact linguistic distribution of its student population. The master plan was ignored.

The Bilingual District Advisory Committee (BDAC) filed a complaint with the U. S. Office of Civil Rights, which resulted in a new investigation. In April of 1983 the district was found to be out of compliance with federal requirements once more for failing to send home language surveys to its 50,000 students. These events eventually persuaded parent leaders to seek the support of a small group of families in order to file a class action suit.

The suit, supported by Legal Aid counsels, was directed by two parents (fictitious names will be used throughout this case): Carmelo Gomez, a native of the Philippines and an outreach worker for the Filipino Immigrant Services, and Lupe Gonzalez, a Mexican American parent. Both of them had long been involved in the struggle with the district and had served as elected members of the BDAC. They filed a class action suit against the Bahia Unified School District for denying bilingual instruction to their children and all the 8500 LEP children of the district. The suit, still in litigation, received the last name of a young man who served as a key witness; to protect his identity we will call him Hector Gutierrez here. His leadership was instrumental during the preparation of the case. He was a factory worker, native of Mexico, whose six children were attending the Bahia schools.

In March of 1985, the controversy entered a yet uglier phase. Without the support of the Board of Education, but following the instructions of the Superintendent, the attorney representing the school district filed a countersuit seeking $4 million in punitive damages and $125,000 in general damages from Lupe and Carmelo, and from their head counsel. When asked how the district lawyer expected working-class parents like Carmelo and Lupe to come up with $4 million, he snapped: "How do you know they don't have a fund stashed away somewhere? It does not matter if they can't afford it. It isn't the first time the school district has sued parents, and it won't be the last!'' (local newspaper, March 1, 1985). Indeed, the Bahia School District went on record as being the first district in the country to sue parents for demanding a better education for their children.

Meanwhile, Lupe Gonzalez described his frustration:

> When Carmelo and I first started, we sat quietly and listened to the administrators. But after four or five months we started talking together, and we said, 'Hey, what is this?' Then we started becoming more assertive. That was the problem. We went beyond a certain point that they could allow.

Alarmed and anxious by the countersuit, they asked for community support. The community backed them up, and made their support known to the school board.

According to local newspapers, previous consultants and members of the BDAC had characterized Bahia School District officials as ''hostile to bilingual education because they mistakenly see it as squandering scarce resources'' needed for top priority district efforts, such as programs for black youth (as presented in the local newspaper, March 1, 1985). There was an underlying political struggle between black administrators and advocates of bilingual education. This political problem continued thereafter.

The district's superintendent was viewed by the general public as attempting to intimidate parents to force them to drop the charges. One of the critical mistakes made by the district lawyer was to act without approval of the school board (although subsequently most board members ratified the suit under pressure, a decision they were to regret for months to come). Several board members resigned to protest the arbitrary conduct of the superintendent and the district lawyer. Eventually, the parents managed to put enough pressure on the board to get the superintendent fired. Board members were afraid of being recalled and losing their position under increasing attacks from politicians, public officials, and the press. The board's conduct was characterized as ''atrocious, inexcusable, the worst kind of behavior any public body ever took'' (local newspaper, March 1, 1985).

When Hector Gutierrez saw that his children were not learning in school, he joined Carmelo and Lupe in their negotiations with the Hispanic lawyer from the Legal Aid Society of Bahia County. Hector was described by his lawyers in these terms: ''He is a very hardworking man, and he is determined to build a good life here for his children.''

Subsequent negotiations between the district and Gutierrez' lawyers resulted in an out-of-court settlement, in which the district agreed to drop the suit against Carmelo and Lupe and start implementing the master bilingual plan under the supervision of an ''expert auditor'' who, with the approval of the litigating parties and the court, would supervise the implementation process at each step.

The struggle was still far from over. The district's lawyer was instructed to drop the countersuit and propose concrete suggestions to resolve the bilingual education crisis. The lawyer removed the suit but left standing some minor charges against Carmelo. A Superior Court judge later declared the countersuit and all charges "frivolous and malicious" and ordered the district to pay Carmelo, Lupe, and their head counsel $5,500 in legal sanctions.

The issue faced by the Bahia School District was then whether school officials were permitted to proceed at their own pace, letting yet another year go by, or whether they would have to start hiring the personnel needed. An alleged shortage of bilingual teachers was viewed by parents as a smokescreen. They felt that officials did not want to hire bilingual teachers. The judge who had issued the initial injunction in July of 1984 ordered the district to hire the necessary bilingual staff by February of 1986 and to report to the court on progress made.

The lawyer for the parents urged the judge to start contempt of court proceedings and to appropriate administrators' salaries as fines: "These people are not doing their jobs—they don't deserve their salaries. Something has got to make this district sit up and take notice." As one of the parents commented, "They call this plan the parents' plan, but it is for the children. Racism is alive and well [in Bahia]. We have to prove to the world that a multicultural society can exist with safety, confidence and trust" (testimony from field notes, July, 1986).

In the meantime, the classrooms were undisciplined. A volunteer parent working with Chinese, Hmong, and Laotian children, who was deeply frustrated, shared a number of stories of classroom problems. For example, a Chinese boy, the son of her friend, had gotten into trouble in school. When she entered his classroom it was in chaos:

> All of the children except the accused child were running around the room yelling at the top of their lungs. The boy had been confined to a corner by himself as a punishment. The teacher blew a whistle to get the kids to quiet down. When the parent asked the teacher what the boy had done, she replied that he had refused to give her his ball. The parent replied: "Do you realize that that is the first ball this boy has ever had in his life?" (testimony from field notes, July, 1986).

Obviously the teacher was not fully aware of what that boy had gone through as a refugee on his way to the land of opportunity. Indeed, this teacher, unprepared and inexperienced, was barely surviving in a nightmarish classroom situation.

The Bahia District had continued to use various stalling strategies after firing its superintendent. When the language surveys were finally sent and the counts presented, there were numerous complaints from consultants and local experts about undercounting. Yet the expert auditor and her team were to supervise the district's effort to implement the bilingual education plan. Two years after her selection, and after many frustrating confrontations between parents and the district, the district has managed to slow the process by accusing the auditor of misusing monies allocated to her. The district's new lawyer, new superintendent, and staff have managed to convince the press to make misleading assumptions about the role played by the auditor, blaming her for the district's failure to comply with the plan.

Due to their long and yet unresolved struggle with the district, the parents have become an organized, cohesive, and powerful unit that will not leave the district alone until some changes are made. Indeed, some changes have occurred: several principals have been replaced with more sensitive administrators; many parents have become actively involved in the schools as aides and volunteer helpers; children are treated with more consideration and are taught more effectively; many children have renewed spirit; and many parents have developed their skills in using political power to obtain better education.

## CLOSING CONSIDERATIONS: AMERICAN VALUES AND THE COURTS

American democracy has traditionally attached a very high value to the right to disagree and debate, and to enjoy individual and group cultural and linguistic freedom without jeopardizing the rights of others or our national unity. The struggle for civil rights was supported in the 1960s by an impressive majority of honest, unselfish Americans. They pushed these rights to their ultimate extremes to disagree with the military establishment and the Executive power behind it. The courts moved to more liberal positions in support of language minority education through the use of federal resources. If the prevalence of educational equity values, as part of the civil rights package, required the use of languages other than English (Mercer, 1973; Cummins, 1984, 1986; Rueda, 1987; Rueda et al., 1981), the general population, for the first time in our history, was willing to tolerate the use of those languages for instruction in public schools. That was in the 1960s.

The counterattack was felt soon after. The movement from liberalism to conservatism occurred again in the pendulumlike tradition of American politics. The pragmatic reality of strong support for bilingual education, in its not adequately defined form, caught by surprise many people who continued to demand evidence of ''effectiveness'' of bilingual education in terms of rapid mainstreaming and achievement levels. These people were convinced that use of federal funds was a waste of money and a political compromise left over from the 1960s (Trueba, 1979). Consequently, the English-only initiatives of the 1980s represent extreme political opposition to bilingual education, which is nurtured by a conservative Administration and reorganization of federal institutions in accordance with this new sensibility. The process of dialogue between dissenting parties about social and cultural values is what has characterized American democracy. The exercise of our constitutional right to disagree with Executive and military powers should not and cannot be presumed to be evidence of unpatriotic conduct.

The preceding analysis of the often painful process of a democracy in action, particularly during stressful economic and political times, compounded by rapidly increasing requests from people all over the world to emigrate to the United States, must not obscure the fact that there has been and continues to be a clear link between racial/ethnic discrimination and intolerance for the use of languages other than

English in instruction. The next question is whether such intolerance is any different from the discrimination suffered by women, handicapped persons, and other minority groups. The courts have clearly established a link between civil rights and educational equity, and have explicitly stated that the lack of educational equity (as demonstrated in the use of only English for students who do not understand English) is an infringement of students' civil rights (Cervantes, 1974; Jones, 1976; Figueroa, 1983, 1986; Figueroa et al., 1984).

Perhaps one of the reasons this country has outlived most other democratic systems governing ethnolinguistically diverse populations is that there is freedom to disagree, as well as public support for the use of lawful legal and political means to defend our civil rights. The case study of Bahia illustrates precisely how the media were used by the courts and public opinion to create pressure on a conservatively entrenched school district that showed little sensitivity for the civil rights of the linguistic minority population, as understood by courts (*Brown* v. *Board of Education* and *Lau* v. *Nichols*).

Another important cultural value shared by people in our democratic system of government is the belief that schools are responsible for assimilation of minority students into the mainstream population. In the case of Bahia, a large group of educationally isolated and neglected minority students attracted the attention of liberal lawyers and journalists, as well as the support of public opinion, throughout legal encounters between their parents and school officials. The cases defended by MALDEF in Texas were resolved based on similar support.

This debate is bound to continue for years to come. A recent overall trend of the courts to stay off schools' turf (the courts do not want to tell school districts how to do their job) has created a legal mechanism, illustrated by the Bahia case, in which an auditor is brought in to supervise district compliance. A judge is then made referee for the out-of-court settlement. These mechanisms did not exist during the *Brown* or *Lau* cases. Are the courts intruding on school districts' jurisdictions? Was the civil rights movement responsible for the increased power of the courts to rule on educational matters? These issues will also continue to be debated. The *Larry P*. and *Diana* cases would indicate that the courts have been forced to act on behalf of linguistic minority students, either because of the intransigence and neglect showed by school officials over a long period of time, or because of the intrinsic difficulties surrounding minority education.

It is unfortunate that bilingual education and other educational programs for minority students have become part of a political struggle between opposing groups. Educators and parents have been forced into political camps, and have campaigned for or against these programs, without a thorough understanding of their instructional attributes and characteristics. Perhaps it would be easier to reach a consensus regarding the nature of sound pedagogical principles and practices than to continue to debate such politically loaded issues.

# RECOMMENDED EXERCISES

One or several of the following exercises would help students come into closer contact with the content of this chapter.

1. Attend a court session involving a language minority person and observe the use of translators (if any) and the legal process from the perspective of that person. Describe how, in your opinion, the minority person views the court, and what his or her understanding of the court's proceedings is concerning his or her rights.
2. Examine and analyze a particular aspect of the *Brown* or *Lau* case in detail. Obtain and read part of the deposition and court proceedings, as well as the opinion presented by the judge; dispute the conflicting interpretations of the case by following other court cases, such as those mentioned in the chapter.
3. Collect and analyze the newspaper reports on a particular case involving bilingual education or the use of languages other than English for instruction or public services. What are the arguments people give for and against the use of these languages? What is the expected impact (economic, political, legal, etc.) of the use of other languages?
4. Interview an adult language minority person (through an interpreter if necessary), and determine for yourself his or her need to use the language in such situations as banks, hospitals, school, and church. What would be the impact of his or her not being allowed to use the mother tongue in such situations?
5. Interview an official of a school with a high concentration of linguistic minority students. Ask questions regarding the way in which school personnel communicate with parents and children, and the problems they face if they speak only English but must attempt to meet the needs of language minority persons. What are the options as seen by these school officials?
6. Interview an official of the police or fire department in an area heavily populated by persons who speak languages other than English. Ask the official questions similar to those in item 5 regarding the need to communicate effectively with speakers of languages other than English. Compare and contrast value positions (what they believe should be done) with de facto situations (what they have to do in specific circumstances).

# RECOMMENDED READINGS

Assembly Office of Research, 1986
*Brown* v. *Board of Education of Topeka*, 1954
Cervantes, 1974
Cummins, 1984

*Diana* v. *California State Board of Education*, 1970
Estrada, 1986
Figueroa, 1983, 1986
Figueroa et al., 1984
Galvan et al., 1986
Heath and Mandabach, 1983
*Hobson* v. *Hansen*, 1967
Jones, 1976
Keller, 1983
Madrid, 1986
Mercer, 1973
Rueda, 1987
Rueda et al., 1981
Salomone, 1986
San Miguel, 1987
Teitelbaum and Hiller, 1979
Trueba, 1979
United States Commission on Civil Rights, 1971, 1973, 1974, 1978
U.S. Department of Commerce. Bureau of the Census, 1979

# 5

# The Teaching Process and Classroom Structure

Teachers of linguistic minority students know that their role is plagued by difficulties such as lack of support, materials, training, and general incentives. They also know that these difficulties are compounded by political division and confusion among teachers regarding the educational needs of linguistic minorities.

This chapter will discuss the nature of the teaching process in order to come to grips with issues of teacher preparation and in-service assistance. The chapter deals specifically with four overall themes:

1. Teaching as a process, from the teachers' perspective
2. Social and cultural organization of the classroom.
3. Teaching literacy and critical thinking skills.
4. A comparative case study of literacy in the home environment of three linguistic minority families.

## THE TEACHING PROCESS

What teachers actually do in the classroom is affected by the social context in which they work, the training or socialization for teaching they have experienced, their conception of their role as teachers, the evaluation of their teaching effectiveness, and the assistance given to them throughout their teaching career.

### The Social Context of Teaching

Most teachers in schools with heavy concentrations of non-English speakers understand that linguistic minority students have been uprooted, placed in an unfamiliar environment, and forced to acquire a new language and culture perceived by them as intrusive or as displacing their home language and culture. Many teachers are sympathetic to linguistic minority students' attempts to adjust socially and culturally while striving at the same time to acquire new subject matter. Very few teachers, however, realize that the instructional process itself is viewed by these students as foreign and confusing. The intimate link between language and culture discussed earlier has led practitioners to the current realization that acquisition of a second language and culture for linguistic minority students must be gradual and should not jeopardize their self-esteem or overall adjustment to school and society. There are individual and group differences in the acquisition of the instrumental competencies required in school. Contrary to the expectations of some principals and superintendents, teachers have begun to see, as a top priority for these children, continued learning through the language in which they communicate best, while they also receive assistance in acquiring a second language and culture.

As was also discussed earlier, teachers have been unnecessarily divided over program types and instructional designs because of political pressures created by ill-defined federal and state programs. While programs for linguistic minorities have been plagued by political controversy, consequently placing undue emphasis on language alone (especially on acquisition of the second language through ESL instruction), the main goals of all sound linguistic minority instructional models have been neglected. These goals have been to assist students in the continued development of critical thinking and communicative skills in the mainstream language, and to teach them the effective use of language for acquisition of higher literacy levels. Some say that "nothing" can be done about incoming linguistic minority students, and they give these reasons: the overwhelmingly rapid arrival of many immigrant children from diverse language groups, confusion among school management and teaching personnel concerning programs for linguistic minority students, and/or sheer prejudice on the part of school administrators, combined with lack of resources. In some instances, teachers have been the first to support legal action. Indeed, their legal support of many court cases across the country, particularly since the civil rights movement, has been instrumental in expediting the flow of resources and attention to the academic problems of linguistic minority students.

Teachers are a pivotal force in making a most decisive impact on minority children. Teachers' burdens and suffering, their disappointment and hopes are extremely important to this issue. Just as important are teachers' views about their role, about the social organization of classrooms, about teacher effectiveness, and about the teaching process and intellectual growth of minority children (particularly as related to the acquisition of second-language literacy). Teachers' views are anchored in their day-to-day experience as well as in their continuing search for more effective instructional methods to reach minority children and bring them up to the level of mainstream students. The enormous personal investment of teachers, and the incalculable toll of emotional hardship, is not always proportional to the overall academic performance of linguistic minority students. This is one of the most profoundly disappointing truths about teaching non-English-speaking students in the United States.

## Learning to Be a Teacher

Generations of mainstream teachers in middle-class schools have gone through the exciting years of their training only to face the shock of first-year teaching.

They may confess that they feel afraid, overwhelmed, or unprepared to meet the needs of children and the demands of administrators. The situation in schools with large numbers of linguistic minority students is worse in unique ways. Often large numbers of children from different language groups arrive in a relatively short period of time. Some schools have changed within 5 years from having mainstream student populations to serving diverse linguistic minority groups. Well-trained and experienced teachers become as confused as new teachers when the methods they have used effectively in the past suddenly do not work.

With changes in student population there are, on the part of the students, unexpected behavioral responses to traditional instructional practices. In the first place, teaching has long emphasized performance before a student audience: a one-way communication from the teacher to the students with little opportunity for students to ask questions, contribute alternative answers, or help the teacher by giving feedback. Because there is considerable pressure on the teacher to cover specific segments of the curriculum in certain amounts of time, he or she has to monitor the use of class time and proceed at a predictable pace, regardless of how many students can assimilate the material. Furthermore, the teacher is obligated to follow the curriculum format in such a way that the content is presented outside of specific cultural contexts and without details that might aid understanding. For example, if the lesson is dealing with groupings, graphs, or curves, or with other items to be measured, these items are often culturally unfamiliar or irrelevant to many students. Worse, teachers also have a tendency to use abstract concepts in giving explanations to culturally heterogeneous student populations.

The student's role is, at times, misunderstood as that of a passive receiver of instruction, and the role of the teacher misconceived as being an agent of knowledge transfer to students, rather than as an aid in interpreting meaning and making appropriate inferences. In rethinking the process of teaching, we need to rethink the role of teachers in the classroom and their collective role in society.

## Teacher Effectiveness

The teacher's role, as viewed historically, has been internalized by teachers themselves and put into daily practice (see Shavelson & Stern, 1981; Apple, 1982; Goodlad, 1983; Giroux, 1983; Britzman, 1986). This traditional view places a great deal of emphasis on recitation, presentation of factual information, and quizzing. Teachers rarely feel free to depart from a mandated curriculum or a set of preselected activities that uniformly correspond to an approved lesson plan. Lesson plans permit teachers to plan their engagement in predictable activities ahead of time, even when competition and incessant demands for their attention might leave teachers with a feeling of uncontrollable chaos. The serious disadvantage of having prearranged lessons is that teachers are less likely to listen to children and respond to their questions in a spontaneous fashion. Teachers resort to their repertoire of formulaic responses and rapidly move to their top priority, namely, complete coverage of the curriculum. The contrast between a "good" class and a "bad" one tends to be, from the teacher's perspective, the degree of cooperation children give the teacher, and whether or not they perform the required tasks without interruption so that the entire portion of the curriculum prescribed for that day is covered. If the teacher follows curriculum instruction plans, it is believed that children will learn. This is, of course, an oversimplification, but it brings home an important point: there is a need to engage in reflective interaction and genuine two-way communication with students during instruction. Regardless of common-sense positions that place importance on the active participation of students during instruction, teachers know that teaching evaluations will focus on their performance according to fulfilment of the prescribed curriculum.

Teachers' effectiveness has been operationalized in terms that reinforce their views on the need to adhere to a predetermined curriculum. Shavelson et al. summarize the operational notion of teacher effectiveness as follows:

1. Effectiveness assumes commonality of curriculum goals, objectives, and content coverage across classrooms because one standardized achievement test is used to judge the effectiveness of all classrooms.
2. Effectiveness is strictly summative in this measurement of subject matter knowledge. It is not what students know or don't know that matters, but the accumulated quantity of their knowledge in comparison with students in other classrooms.
3. Performance on the effectiveness measure is equated with knowledge or skill in subject matter. There is no notion of "less than best effort," guessing, partial knowledge, or test-taking skills.
4. Effectiveness is strictly aggregative across students within a classroom. Operationally, regardless of how student performance is distributed within the classroom, the class average is chosen to represent class performance (Shavelson et al., 1986:52).

One of the reasons that the measurement of time-on-task became a favorite topic of research in evaluation studies was that it emphasized curriculum content and coverage, giving teachers another motive to neglect reflective communication in the classroom. It does not seem to matter whether students gain a deeper understanding or integrate the subject matter; what matters is that they give the "right" answer. Indeed, what test results demonstrate is a superficial but overall coverage of the curriculum. Critical thinking about subjects by either teachers or students is discouraged by our very measurement of teacher effectiveness through standardized testing.

If the essence of teaching is cognitive content and cognitive structure of knowledge, it has no support in the actual practice of evaluating teacher effectiveness and student achievement through standardized testing. We must be more aware of both the limitations of testing and the alternatives proposed by evaluation researchers. One such alternative is the students' response patterns (Shavelson et al., 1986) analyzed in the school setting (Burstein, 1980). Another alternative is for teachers to affect the selection and coverage of curriculum content, the actual organization of topics viewed as more congruent with students' experience and needs, the selection of frameworks and formats for structuring knowledge, and the creation of a classroom atmosphere suitable for promoting students' self-esteem and stimulating their commitment to learn. This would allow degrees of freedom to permit teachers a gradual departure from topic coverage and increased use of personal strategies to accommodate cultural differences among students.

Abuse of standardized tests may penalize all student populations and their teachers by creating a classroom environment filled with quick, superficial, and uninteresting coverage of mandated subjects. The penalties for teachers of linguistic minority students are still more painful and discouraging. Actual abilities of linguistic minority students and their cognitive gains are least likely to be detected through standardized tests for the following reasons:

1. Tests are in English, a language many of them are unfamiliar with and cannot handle well enough to deal with the subtle semantic differences required to infer meaning.
2. The cultural values assumed in tests, and experiences required to make inferences, have not yet been acquired by these children, or those acquired are contradictory to the ones they learned at home.
3. Test-taking ability of minority students has not been developed to the level of their mainstream peers.
4. Linguistic minority students' grasp of the subject matter is often fragmentary and incomplete. Consequently, their performance in recalling is slower and less clear.
5. Most gains in cognitive structuring and integration of knowledge cannot show up in tests that allow a prescribed amount of time for completion.

## Teachers' Dilemmas and Difficulties

Teachers of linguistic minority children are well aware of the struggles through which their students must go before they can begin to show gains in test scores. The dilemmas these teachers face require further analysis because the teacher's role is, in the final analysis, internalized by decisions made in an attempt to resolve such dilemmas. Six typical problems are discussed here.

**Departure from Prescribed Curriculum**  Among teachers' dilemmas is whether to abide by curriculum requirements or simply to decide on their own what is best for students. Teachers of linguistic minorities often agonize over tests given to their students because they anticipate the resulting stereotypes and subsequent penalties with which students will be met in society. Teachers may feel they have become part of an "oppressive society" that unfairly misclassifies and mistreats such children:

> Bilingual teachers, caught between the accepted practices they are required to follow and the sound theories and research that contradict those practices, are especially vulnerable to attack. Most bilingual teachers were not educated in bilingual programs, nor have they had the experience of teaching in bilingual schools that receive full society support. In many instances they themselves have been victims of language oppression and racism; thus, in order to empower their students to overcome conditions of domination and oppression, they must first be empowered themselves (Ada, 1986:386).

**Ambivalence about the Function of Schools**    Another concern of teachers working with linguistic and other minorities is that in their own experience they have become painfully aware that schooling is not necessarily opening the door of opportunity for which minority people came to this country in the first place. Liberal teachers point at the school as the institution par excellence in charge of reproducing a social order in which minorities continue to be deprived of participation in the political, economic, and social institutions of our society (Ogbu, 1974, 1978; Giroux, 1983; Aronowitz & Giroux, 1985; Ada, 1986; Cummins, 1986).

Current social movements such as the English-Only initiative and new laws on immigration, the attacks on bilingual education, and the popular belief that mother-tongue maintenance hinders English acquisition in linguistic minority students (the so-called "subtractive bilingualism" theory) have placed teachers in a precarious position. Many of them know that research contradicts notions of subtractive bilingualism and overwhelmingly supports the idea of enrichment or "additive bilingualism." That is, bilingualism increases people's cognitive flexibility and provides them with a new instrument for communication with speakers of other languages (Peal & Lambert, 1962; Cummins, 1981b, 1986; Lambert & Tucker, 1972; Skutnabb-Kangas, 1984; Dolson, 1985; Hakuta, 1986; and many others).

A very practical consequence of continued support for use of the mother tongue is that students can maintain communication across generations with family members and continue to appreciate their cultural heritage. Encouraging children to abandon the home language may often result in serious cultural conflict between children and their parents that will, eventually, weaken family unity and increase students' isolation. This isolation will be compounded by the student's isolation in school during the early period of integration and second-language acquisition.

Based on the notion advanced by Freire (1973) and Giroux (1983), Ada has suggested that schools should not reproduce the social system as is, with its inequities, by pursuing "traditional reproductive education," but should promote "transformative education" by engaging in "critical analysis and reconstruction of the social reality through meaningful dialogue between teachers and students" (1986:387–388). This position has been advanced by proponents of bilingual education (Ada, 1986; Cummins, 1986) as well as by other scholars who are working on first- and second-language literacy projects with linguistic minority families (Delgado-Gaitan, 1987a,b).

**Bureaucratic Constraints**   The belief by teachers working with minorities that their training did not prepare them for the job is shared by other teachers and voiced in similar terms. They feel as inadequate in handling the classroom as they do in meeting the demands of the bureaucratic school organization, with chains of supervisory personnel reinforcing adherence to the curriculum and evaluating teacher effectiveness as discussed above.

The observation has been made that school organization was originally intended to replicate the chain of command in business and military organizations. Schools are uniquely unsuited for such a model because learning is best acquired in settings in which the teacher and the student take an active role in determining what is to be processed cognitively and how.

The world of business and organizational accountability has been translated into literal adherence to a certain code of behavior, viewed as a mechanism leading to predictable and automatic productivity. In military organizations, accountability ensures automatic responses and adherence to orders from superiors regardless of personal interpretive judgements of the relationship between the order and its intended purpose. We cannot order learning outcomes in school, nor can we predict ''productivity'' as a function of prescribed curricula and teacher behavior. Learning is a uniquely individual response that cannot be controlled. Teaching, in turn, is also unique if it is conceived of as assisting the learner to acquire and structure knowledge.

**Inadequacy in Language Mastery**   Formal teaching and learning settings such as schools create some necessary and many unnecessary constraints that may suppress teachers' self-initiated efforts to gain competency in the students' language and/or to interact reflectively with students. As a consequence, the quality of instruction suffers. Lack of public support for target languages, along with political pressure placed on teachers to use English, has caused a great deal of controversy and lack of morale among teachers who were making efforts to learn their students' languages. In turn, lack of mastery of target languages has become the focus of further controversy about the effectiveness of bilingual instruction (Ada, 1986).

In bilingual education, lack of mastery of the language of instruction causes serious problems for teachers; it affects their classroom management, their clarity in explaining subject matter, and the quality of relationships with native speakers of that language. If a teacher does not know the target language well, children's linguistic and cognitive development also suffers, because they are deprived of guidance and feedback in situations where correct and precise use of the language is required to understand a concept or the logical foundations of reasoning.

Language control (first in the mother tongue and later in the second language) is, for school-age children, the most crucial instrument of communication with their teacher. The teacher's lack of mastery of the student's mother tongue, particularly during the period of transition from mother tongue to second language instruction, profoundly affects teacher–student relationships, students' self-esteem, and their overall psychological well-being.

There are academic domains within certain subjects for which the student needs to clarify certain understandings, including logical relationships such as cause–effect, antecedent–consequence, part–whole, and others. The use of appropriate and precise discourse in efforts to link logic to language requires total mastery of that language in the social and cultural context, as well as an internalization of sociocultural norms as they translate into linguistic and paralinguistic forms. In other words, total mastery of a language does not take place without a good grasp of the culture that accompanies that language. Quality instruction requires mastery of both.

**Ambivalence about Role**    The teacher of linguistic minority children, for example in ESL classes, is asked to perform in the most difficult circumstances and to fulfill the most difficult of roles. He or she is the interpreter of American sociocultural norms for students who are not familiar with such norms. But he or she is also asked to serve as referee between the students' home cultural norms and those of our school system and society. The integration of values and the inculcation of "hidden curriculum" values (Warren, 1982) involve patterns of unintended miscommunication, inadequate mastery of languages other than English, and constraints placed on teachers such as the method of evaluation of teaching effectiveness and the required rigorous coverage of prescribed curricula.

A psychological factor compounds teachers' difficulties in coming to grips with their role, and their dilemma in seeing themselves as instruments of the "traditional reproductive educational system" or the "transformative educational system" discussed above. This factor results in the increasing feeling of isolation that teachers experience. Anything and everything can be misconstrued as poor compliance with curriculum requirements and with orders from superiors. If there is a clear ideological conflict between principal and teacher, the principal has the power to prove lack of teacher effectiveness on the basis of students' low test scores. The teacher may have done a fantastic job working with a group that began at a much lower skill level and, if the job were assessed in the home language with alternative methods, might indeed have facilitated significant student progress in subject matter and English acquisition. But linguistic minority students' low performance on standardized tests, designed for mainstream student populations and taken in a language unknown to minorities, hides teachers' efforts and obscures students' progress.

The teacher of minority students may feel exposed by poor test results and may search for ways of protecting his or her position and psychological well-being. The teacher may resist the pressure from peers and superiors to accept test results as a reflection of minority students' capabilities, rather than as a problem with testing methods. Treating students in accordance with traditional interpretations of standardized tests is practically impossible for such teachers, yet school administrators may insist on compliance. Therein lies the conflict.

**Teachers' Isolation**    The isolation of teachers is a most painful experience, and is probably linked very closely to the burn-out syndrome many experience. Some teachers take months to develop small support groups, but after they feel comfortable with each other and trust their peers, they begin to share stories of anxiety and deeply painful experiences in their daily practice. The pain comes from teachers' uncertainty about their self-identity, from lack of confidence, and from desperate and unsuccessful efforts to help children while at the same time attempting to comply with orders from superiors.

The most important role of linguistic minority teachers is to assist children in the acquisition of critical thinking and communicative skills in the English language required to reach a high literacy level. If teachers have internalized this role, they should be given ample freedom to organize their classrooms and structure learning activities to suit the varied needs of their students. But for teachers to use such freedom wisely, they need to be assisted by more experienced teachers and support groups. Organization of the classroom is particularly important today, since recent reports indicate the need for educational reform if this country is to maintain its fast pace of technological development. The United States appears to be losing the opportunity to maintain its pace in technological development due to low literacy levels and high rates of attrition in high school students:

> The official reform reports, ranging from a *A Nation at Risk* to the Carnegie Forum's *A Nation Prepared*, call for a restructuring of schools and of teacher education to the end of raising the levels of literacy in accord with the requirements of an economy based on high technology. The mass of students in the schools, including the one third who will be "minorities," are to be enabled to develop "higher order skills" in preparation for "the unexpected, the nonroutine world" they will face in the future. The implicit promise is that, if the quality of teachers is improved (and "excellent" teachers rewarded and recognized), the majority of young people will be equipped for meaningful participation in an advanced knowledge-based economy wholly different from the mass-production economy familiar in the past (Greene, 1986:438).

If only all reformist movements did not end by designing new testing instruments and new gates to keep minority students and their teachers more isolated from mainstream educational opportunities. Many female teachers of linguistic minority students feel silenced by the bureaucratic organization of school for two reasons: one, because the educational system is run by men, who depend on each other to maintain control of the system; and two, because teaching minority students has a low-status stigma attached to it. Lewis and Simon (1986), based on Hartmann (1984), have characterized educational organization in general as a "patriarchy" because of the systematic use of power by men to control women. Silencing female teachers increases their isolation and despair. The formerly unchallenged privileges of male superiors over female teachers must be challenged if the quality of education and classroom instruction is to improve.

The teaching process as translated by the roles teachers of linguistic minority students must play and the difficult circumstances in which they teach were presented above. The discussion now turns to the actual communication between teachers and students during the teaching/learning process.

## THE SOCIAL ORGANIZATION OF
## THE CLASSROOM

Teachers who have internalized their role as educators responsible not for reproducing the social order but for creating a new order congruent with a transformative philosophy of education (Ada, 1986), as well as teachers who have resolved self-identity problems through reflective cultural analysis or other means, still may need assistance in organizing actual learning activities in the classroom. A fundamental prerequisite for the organization of specific curriculum activities is a basic understanding of the culture of the school and that of the classroom. School organization will be discussed in the next chapter, in the context of the support teachers need from administrators in implementing programs for linguistic minorities. Classroom organization goes beyond classroom management or simple monitoring of classroom activities into a realization of the steps that permit teachers to play their role and, thus, to teach effectively. Classroom organization is discussed here.

### The Structure of the Classroom in Its Cultural Context

Discussion of the social organization of the classroom involves the fabric of communication through moment-to-moment interaction. It also involves the meaning attributed to immediate and observable actions by teachers and students (Erickson, 1977, 1986; Erickson & Mohatt, 1982). One of the main concerns in the study of classroom social organization is the structure of events, such as the sequence of interactions in the teaching of a lesson, and the nature of student participation in different parts of the event. A second concern is the meaning that various participants seem to give to a certain activity (a set of structured actions) and to any specific action (the unit of interactional analysis) within that activity. A third concern is with the contextual variables of interaction: place and time, the physical and emotional circumstances of events, and the influence of variables on the behavior of teachers and students (Erickson, 1986).

The purpose of examining the social and structural organization of classroom activities is to see how effectively the teacher plays his or her role in stimulating critical thinking skills in students and assisting them to acquire knowledge. The fundamental aspects of classroom interaction are examined to reveal participation patterns and the use of strategies to interpret meanings. Such an examination is important because the essence of teaching and learning is communicating understanding and internalizing it to communicate more effectively. In the home environment, long before children are grouped into formal school classes, they accumulate knowledge about learning and structure in ways that permit them to make inferences and internalize understandings. These processes take place during the early period of socialization and are usually reinforced in preliminary encounters with school. Cognitive development is thus linked with daily tasks that have purpose and require the organization of activities/actions to accomplish that purpose. The meaningfulness of actions and activities must first be comprehended in their social context and then internalized intrapsychologically (Vygotsky, 1962, 1978; Wertsch, 1985).

Simple questions as to whether or not a student is on task have different meanings when observed from the perspective of participation structures. Students try to make sense of text within prescribed organizational formats controlled by the teacher. The immediate social and cultural context of the classroom determines the appropriateness and legitimacy of students' attempts to understand or to generate text, as well as to make inferences that will lead to meaningful interpretation of a variety of classroom activities in the rapid flow of interactional events. In this sense, a student's "emic" (insider) view of being on task might be in conflict with that of the teacher. Another possibility is that a student's view of cooperation (as assistance given to a peer from the same culture) may be interpreted by the teacher as cheating or copying (Delgado-Gaitan & Trueba, 1985). What is more important, given the information we have about students' home environments, observation of participant structures in the classroom indicates that the teacher's concept of "relevant topics" in a writing exercise, for example, may be in clear contrast with students' concerns (Trueba, 1987b).

## A Context-Specific Approach to Teacher Effectiveness

Traditional assessment of teacher effectiveness seems to assume that there is a causal relationship between uniform, standard mainstream teacher classroom performance and interaction with students (as guided by prescriptive curricula and norms inculcated during teacher training) and student achievement. It is assumed that if the teacher does everything he or she has been taught to do, students will necessarily achieve. Of course, simple classroom observations show that different student groups have different backgrounds, interests, learning styles, and learning motivations that determine their responses to teacher performance. However, the process of classroom interaction has been reduced to a formulaic, rehearsed, predetermined "performance" by the teacher, rather than a reflective interaction with a specific audience whose input determines the selection of materials and the organization of instruction. As Erickson puts it:

> From an interpretive point of view, teacher effectiveness is a matter of the nature of the social organization of classroom life—what we have called the enacted curriculum—whose construction is largely, but not exclusively, the responsibility of the teacher as instructional leader. This is a matter of local meaning and local politics, of teaching a rhetoric (persuasion), and of student assent as

the grounds of legitimacy for such persuasion and leadership by a teacher (Erickson, 1986: 133).

The teacher has enormous importance in determining the politics of interaction, the credibility of students, and the reward system in the classroom. But the student is far from being a simple recipient of the teacher's wisdom. There is a two-way exchange in the classroom, with continuing negotiation over meaning, interpretations being made at different levels of abstraction, and knowledge being integrated (regardless of the sources of such knowledge). Local politics are viewed by Erickson as being at the heart of decisions made by teachers in judging students' ability. One needs to know how to persuade the teacher that one is a competent student.

## The Micropolitics of Classroom Structure

Many of the ideas grouped by earlier scholars into categories such as minority handicaps or deficit theories are now discussed as the "politics of sorting out students" (Erickson, 1986:134–139), more commonly known as the micropolitics of education. Many studies done by educational ethnographers have focused on specific aspects of classroom interaction and their consequences for the sorting out of students and judgement of their competencies (Erickson, 1977; Shultz et al., 1982; Mehan, 1979; Philips, 1982; Erickson & Mohatt, 1982; and others). Other more recent studies fit well into this category (Mehan et al., 1986; Goldman & McDermott, 1987; Suarez-Orozco, in press).

With regard to differential student success, some studies point to the roots of differential political skills in handling classroom norms of behavior: some students have problems adapting to the teacher's prescribed organization. The substantive contributions by researchers who studied the Kamehameha schools have considerably advanced our understanding of how local cultural congruence affects the organization of the classroom and students' acquisition of knowledge (see work by Gallimore et al., 1974, 1986; Au, 1980, 1981; Gallimore & Tharp, 1981; Au & Kawakami, 1982; Boggs, 1985). Scholars working in Alaska and Canada (Philips, 1982; Erickson & Mohatt, 1982) have also contributed a great deal to our understanding of culturally defined appropriate behavior in classroom interaction and its outcomes in terms of student achievement. These studies advocate cultural congruence as a means to make classroom organization more functional in teaching specific groups of children. Other important considerations beyond attempts at attaining cultural congruence must be discussed regarding the creation of an appropriate classroom organization to maximize student achievement. These issues, which reflect further refinement of the positions mentioned above, will be discussed in the context of the acquisition of literacy in English.

## TEACHING ENGLISH LITERACY

The acquisition of reading and writing skills in a second language is not only overloaded with political considerations (such as declaring illiteracy a "current crisis") but is also complicated by ambiguous and conflicting definitions of literacy. Teachers often do not understand literacy and their efforts to teach linguistic minorities how to read and write in English are often lacking because they are deprived of important information on home literacy environments.

### Definitions of Literacy

Literacy definitions beyond the general notion of ability to deal with text have been operationalized in various ways. During World War II, the United States Army invented the term "functional literacy," defined as the minimum level of literacy needed by military personnel to understand written instructions required to conduct basic military activities. This was considered to be a fifth-grade level of literacy at the time (Castell et al., 1986). At the other extreme of the definitions is the notion that literacy requires the ability to analyze complex written materials and generate cohesive (syntactically correct and semantically appropriate) text in a variety of domains, including cultural history and scientific fields. While literacy for our purposes may not have so many requirements, it is a great deal more than the technical skill of coding and decoding graphic symbols:

> We expect literacy to provide not just technical skills but also a set of prescripts about using knowledge. Literacy is not just the simple ability to read and write; but by possessing and performing these skills we exercise socially approved and approvable talents; in other words, literacy is a socially constructed phenomenon (Cook-Gumperz, 1986:1).

As most recent studies on literacy as applied to the educational setting suggest, functional literacy in English refers to students' ability to understand regular instruction at their age-group level, to read textbooks, and to follow directions, as well as to generate correct, meaningful, and appropriate text in the areas of instruction.

### Literacy and Social Participation

While we can accept a compromised operational definition of functional school literacy, we cannot lose sight of the fundamental fact that in a democratic, industrial, technologically developed society, reading and writing are essential for active participation. On the one hand, some measure of social integration is indispensable for the acquisition of high literacy levels in school. The isolation of linguistic minorities has been highly instrumental in retaining low levels of literacy. On the other hand, literacy itself is a vehicle for increased and active participation in the social, economic, and political institutions of a democratic society. Because the curriculum and teaching process are geared for a population that already has certain experiences and cultural values, linguistic minority students (and their families) are unable to participate fully in the instructional process. Such participation is, in turn, essential for gaining the cognitive and linguistic skills necessary to ensure their future active participation in society. The reading process, for example, has two dimensions: providing the student with particular content that builds a sequence of logical inferences and reasoning; and reading itself, which becomes an instrumental factor in the development of higher-level cognitive skills, regardless of the subject matter. The process of writing has similar attributes: it can create a higher level of conscious awareness of a subject matter, which becomes instrumental in the cognitive organization of future knowledge.

Empowering minority students so that they may participate fully in their education through the acquisition of English literacy requires metalinguistic awareness and the strategic use of calculated interventions to create a more suitable literacy environment in the home (Cummins, 1976, 1978, 1983, 1986; Rueda, 1987; Rueda & Mehan, 1986). It also requires that students acquire the political skills needed to deal effectively with the school bureaucracy and its lack of educational equity (Mehan et al., 1986; Goldman & McDermott, 1987).

## Literacy Crises and Politics

Literacy crises, announced from time to time, are more a political barometer of awareness about existing literacy deficiencies (at times by means of new instruments) than realistic judgements that people in the United States are somehow less literate now than in the past (Resnick & Resnick, 1977; Cook-Gumperz, 1986). Some scholars have begun to speak of the "literacy myth" and the misrepresentation of "literacy crises." They argue that what we actually have are discussions on literacy that are "surprisingly facile" and that "regardless of purpose or intent, flounder because they slight any effort to formulate a consistent and realistic definition of literacy" (Graff, 1986:63). Graff considers that failure to grasp the concept of literacy and its relative sociohistorical significance has resulted in literacy myths:

> The results of such failures surround us; they preclude our knowing even dimensions of qualitative changes in the people's ability to employ usefully or functionally the skills of reading and writing. Expectations and assumptions with respect to the primacy and priority of literacy as an index of the condition of civilization—all stand unsatisfactorily and inadequately as substitutes for a deeper, more grounded understanding (Graff, 1986:63).

Graff thinks that we have exaggerated the implications of literacy, and argues that we continue to hold a very narrow notion when we speak about literacy levels in the public and people's need to use text:

> Writings about the imputed "consequences," "implications," or "concomi-
> tants" of literacy have assigned to literacy's acquisition a truly daunting number
> of cognitive, affective, behavioral, and attitudinal effects, ranging from em-
> pathy, innovativeness, achievement orientation, "cosmopolitanism," infor-
> mation acquisition and media awareness, national identification, technological
> acceptance, rationality, commitment to democracy or to opportunism, linearity
> of thought and behavior, or urban residence! Literacy is sometimes conceived
> as a skill, but more often as symbolic or representative of attitudes and men-
> talities (Graff, 1986:65).

Graff makes points that are important particularly in the face of alarmists' denouncing of "uncontainable" waves of immigrants who speak other languages and are not literate in English. Many of these immigrants are literate in their own languages and are rapidly acquiring English literacy, but because of the increasing numbers of newcomers there is a certain sociological permanency to the idea that speakers of other languages are illiterate in English.

Granting to Graff that we have exaggerated the virtues of English literacy without fully understanding the broader notion of literacy, if we focus on the schools and operationalize literacy very pragmatically as the control of text required for academic work, the reality today is indeed discouraging. Illiteracy among minorities is very high. The obvious consequences of academic illiteracy are political and real, taking form in denial of certificates, meaning employment legitimacy is with-held. Other consequences, particularly painful for minorities, are loss of self-esteem and feelings of marginality.

Because English literacy has always been rooted in the social and cultural acceptance by immigrants of mainstream values, which encourages their incorpo-ration into the new society, literacy in minorities can be viewed by mainstream people as either an asset or a threat. Literacy was historically, and still is, viewed as the key to cultural values. In order to keep some cultural values out of reach of immigrants, social distance has been created by mainstream peoples during peak periods of immigration in order to restrict access by immigrants to employment or political positions considered the privilege of mainstream Americans. Sharing main-stream cultural heritage with low-status immigrants has been viewed as a threat to cultural integrity. Excluding immigrants from public educational institutions has also been viewed as a threat to American democracy (Castell & Luke, 1986). Immigrants themselves have historically considered their private schools as means of inculcating their own cultural and religious values in children, not only as a means of integration into the new society's employment force. Indeed, most mid-nineteenth century occupations required reading and writing skills (Graff, 1979; Castell & Luke, 1986).

Could it be true that a literacy crisis is a social crisis, which, by creating or permitting social isolation and differential participation in economic and political institutions among members of society, allows for a concentration of power in the hands of schooled people, thus perpetuating social hierarchies and qualitative differences in educational services? The fact that schools reproduce the social order and maintain the social and political power hierarchy explains the creation of curricula that primarily serve those who share certain cultural values, to the exclusion of others who do not.

The very nature of cultural differences is such that those who share less of the mainstream value orientation are penalized (Ogbu, 1974, 1978, 1981, 1987a,b; G. Spindler, 1955, 1959, 1963, 1977, 1982; Spindler & Spindler, 1983, 1987a,b,c). Penalities may come in the form of nonstimulating or irrelevant literacy materials; but such penalties are not intended. On the contrary, there is an overall policy of avoiding conspicuous advocacy of specific cultural values:

> Every attempt is made within technocratic literacy instruction to specify its "behavioral objectives" in value-neutral terminology. Consequently, explicit ideological content is absent, overridden by the instructional format and skills orientation of the literacy text. The "skills" to be taught are thus ideologically neutralized; lessons aim to improve students' ability to grasp "word meaning," "context clues," and "decoding skills" (Castell & Luke, 1986:103).

But, as could be expected and as Castell and Luke indicate, such goals and practices are far from being value neutral: "We must ask how a student can determine structure of cause and effect in a textual narrative without invoking normative rules of social context and action?" (Castell & Luke, 1986:103).

Teachers of linguistic minorities are often blamed for the high illiteracy and dropout rates among minority people. Yet if we accept the sociohistorical context of literacy and its link with cultural values, it would seem that blaming teachers for a social and cultural problem does not do much to resolve it. With reference to making sense of text beyond basic levels of integrating written/oral symbols into larger linguistic structures, that is, to comprehend text as a means for communicating specific messages effectively and clearly, our schools in general have not been very successful with minority children who speak other languages and whose access to mainstream culture is limited by isolation and poverty.

One continuing problem is the cultural value Americans attach to the use of English for literacy activities. If we postulate that reading skills transfer from one language to another, does it not make sense to teach a non-English speaking child to read in the home language? Certainly. But it also makes sense to teach this child how to read in English, along with offering other skills. The search for meaning and the interpretive process should not be linked to formal use of any language, oral or written. At the basis of literacy is this process, involving the ability to select the most likely interpretation of potential lexical items in a linguistic structure. Should we first teach reading or writing? Should we proceed in the home language or in the second language? Students should not be required to use either language, nor either format, but should be encouraged to use the language in which they can be helped best, provided that they continue to develop their inferencing abilities, and in the form they are most inclined to use without neglecting either writing or reading.

What matters is students' orientation to literacy and their becoming engaged in interpretive processes as they deal with text, either generating their own writing or reading that generated by others. Furthermore, what matters is how children cognitively process the information acquired through text, and how they integrate it into their experiential and structured (taxonomic) knowledge. Clearly, the cultural congruence of the content as a point of contact with students' cultural and experiential background is essential at the beginning of the literacy acquisition process.

## Home Literacy Background

The family background is extremely important for the development of preliteracy skills, although many families do not deal directly with the manipulation or processing of text (Delgado-Gaitan, 1987a,b). The family environment, in important and sometimes intangible ways, seems to provide the motivation behind behavioral patterns that result in higher literacy levels. For example, observing parents write notes, read newspapers or books, compose letters, engage in self-editing, help each other interpret text, and generate technical text all help the child develop an appreciation for the value of literacy. Furthermore, if a child sees siblings or parents receive rewards or status for accomplishments that presuppose control of the written language, the child is more willing to engage in writing and reading.

When literacy values do not exist in the home, and school literacy activities for minority students become incomprehensible, unrewarding, or otherwise uninteresting, students have many problems to contend with. These problems often strike teachers as unusual and difficult to understand:

1. Lack of background information regarding the content of the text, especially if previous text is required to understand specific terminology and contextual differences in its usage.
2. Lack of coding/decoding skills at the lowest inferential level, to differentiate functions of words and therefore their potential meanings.
3. Lack of motivation to engage in literacy activities, probably as a result of failure in the past.
4. Additional embarrassment resulting from an inability to identify words due to orthographic confusion, punctuation symbols, format, and other mechanics of text organization.

To compound the problem, there are serious difficulties in improving home literacy skills. Several recent ethnographic studies of literacy environments in linguistic minority students' homes demonstrate some of these difficulties (Trueba,

1984, 1987b; Trueba et al., 1984; Delgado-Gaitan, 1987a, b). These families typically have low incomes and live in crowded quarters. The rhetoric of commitment to literacy stated in personal interviews seems to contradict observations of relatively little use of text in the home, except for children's homework. The obvious difficulties students have in dealing with text, regardless of whether the home language or English is used, indicates that many of these families have been socially isolated prior to their arrival in the United States (Trueba 1984, 1987b). The following case studies can provide a better understanding of the home literacy environment of linguistic minority students and the nature of difficulties faced by their parents in attempting to support their children's academic achievement.

## THE FAMILIES OF RITA AND OFELIA, JUANA, AND PABLO: STRUGGLING WITH TEXT

To understand the problems linguistic minority students have in acquiring and using literacy in the home, one needs to see real-life situations in which economic constraints, social isolation, and survival concerns relegate literacy and academic activities to a low priority. The following case studies illustrate this point.

### Rita and Ofelia

The daughters of a single mother, Rita (14 years old) and Ofelia (12 years), have an older sister who is 19 and stays home to care for their younger sister, who has Down's syndrome. Their mother was once an elementary school teacher in Tijuana, but now they live in southern California. Three years after their arrival, all remain Spanish dominant, and the mother does not know English but is trying to learn. Rita is less fluent than Ofelia and Ofelia is the best student. In the following situation, their mother has just come home from work (at 4:30 pm). She is a teacher's aide working with Spanish-speaking first-grade children. The mother is carrying the mail in her hand, and before she says hello to her daughters, she hands the mail over to Ofelia and makes a gesture of disgust at the dirty dishes in the kitchen sink. Talking to Rita, she says:

> ¡Mira nomás! Estos platos y todo esto. Rita, tu no estas cumpliendo con tus obligaciones. Ya te he dicho que quiero que laves los trastes antes de que yo regrese del trabajo. Vete a la cocina inmediatamente.

> Look at this! These dishes and all this mess. Rita, you are not doing your chores. I have told you that I want you to wash the dishes before I come home from work. Go to the kitchen right now (translated from field notes; Trueba, 1984)

Ofelia takes the mail and sorts it out, translating for her mother and explaining the content of a bill, a sale offer, and other unimportant mail. There are some forms that have come from the school and must be filled out. Ofelia is given that task and the mother signs them. Ofelia and Rita get into a fight. Rita says to her: "It's unfair, you should help me with all these dishes." The researcher invites comments about school, but Rita does not want to talk about it. She hates school. Actually, the only thing she likes about junior high are the boys. Finally she opens up and comments:

> En sexto de primaria yo sacaba puras As. Me gustaba mucho la escuela. Pero acá, no. Aquí los Gringos lo reprueban a uno nomás así, porque que quieren. Hablan demasiado en inglés, y si te agarran hablando español, creen que estás hablando de ellos. Hay un maestro que si te ve hablando en español se enoja tanto que se pone rojo en la cara y te manda al director.

> When I was in 6th grade I got straight As. I really liked school then. But here [in junior high], no. Here these Gringo teachers flunk you just for kicks, because they want to. They speak too much in English, and if they catch you speaking Spanish, they think you are talking about them. There is a teacher that if he sees you talking in Spanish gets so mad, red in the face, and sends you to the principal (translated from field notes; Trueba, 1984).

Rita is an intelligent girl who is very articulate in Spanish. She refuses to use English even though she understands it perfectly well and speaks it fluently. Because of her resistance to cooperation with school personnel and repeated complaints from teachers and the principal, her mother has now designated Ofelia as the daughter officially in charge of all interaction with English text and English-speaking people. In this distribution of labor, Rita has become responsible for cleaning the house and doing other domestic chores. Actually, Ofelia's schoolwork shows that she struggles with English text, and at times is not very good, but she is docile and her behavior does not challenge school norms. Thus, her mother sees her as a good student. Serious errors she makes in reading contracts for the purchase of furniture on installments, labels in medications, or school notices regarding upcoming festivities show a disappointing level of literacy in the home, with no help at hand.

## Juana

Juana is a 15-year-old, living with a father who is monolingual in Spanish and a recent convert to Protestantism. Her 16-year-old sister, the single mother of a small boy, has persuaded Juana to learn to read and write in English in order to understand and disseminate evangelicalism. Juana keeps a Bible in English with her at all times, even at the kitchen table where she does her homework. As soon as she finishes her homework, she starts reading the Bible. She says she likes to write about Mexican Americans, but she needs to work on her math now. She has written a poem entitled "Cholo Life," in which she describes gang fights. Writing does not come easily to her. Here is an excerpt from one of her compositions describing a Cholo as one who:

> . . . walks slowly through the halls and spends his time with his friends. His life is never right when he drinks and smokes all night, talking back to his hifitas or hifitos [parents]. Cholos don't care. Pero Save que [But, you know what]; it don't get you nowhere, nowhere but to the pit (adapted from field notes; Trueba, 1984:34).

Juana is highly motivated to acquire English literacy, but she has no effective help in the home. In fact, she finds sentences in the English Bible to memorize in an attempt to acquire the syntax to master the language. Her written structures are still disjointed and fragmentary, but her thoughts are as powerful as her will to learn English.

## Pablo

Pablo, one of eight siblings, ages 7-16, is a 13-year-old seventh-grader. His father, monolingual in Spanish and an undocumented worker, is illiterate. He is 60 years old, and works part-time at odd jobs. His family came from Tijuana 3 years ago, and now they live in a trailer, literally on top of each other. The mother, 50 years old, can barely read in Spanish. Culturally, they have remained a traditional Mexican family in which the father has most of the authority. Both parents are extremely proud of their children and are absolutely sure that they will achieve well in school. Pablo manages to secure a corner of the small table and reads the "spelling list" aloud asking for help. There are no dictionaries, nor are there any books except for a few *novelas* (brief romance stories in the form of booklets). In spite of their poverty, both parents are involved in the school as members of the parents' advisory committee, and both closely monitor the progress of all their children, especially the younger ones. The parents seem to understand school politics fairly well. Indeed, the young children are doing very well in school and have acquired fluency in English quite rapidly. Both parents are hopeful that they will gain legal residence status so their children can be educated in this country. The children seem to be truly inspired by the idealism of their parents. They spend a great deal of time on their homework, in a situation that would discourage many other students. Too much is happening at the same time, and there is no privacy. Yet the home environment is congenial and cooperative. Much has to do with orchestration of activities by the parents and the subtle but tough control the father has over everything.

In all three families described above, there is the conviction that English literacy is essential to succeed in this country, to find a good job, and to become integrated into society. What these families do not share is the same level of understanding of what it takes to acquire English literacy, and what specific organizational changes in their lifestyle should be made to facilitate the acquisition of English literacy. The role of parents in children's acquisition of English literacy is seriously handicapped by their lack of literacy in English, and in some cases in Spanish as well.

## SUMMARY AND FINAL THOUGHTS

For teachers to assist linguistic minority children effectively in the acquisition of critical thinking skills and high levels of English literacy, they must gain a clear understanding of their roles and responsibilities. That is, their primary obligation is not the strict observance of prescribed curricula and teaching methodologies, but the consistent search for ways to involve students actively in conscious efforts to comprehend and generate text through culturally meaningful and appropriate methods. Implied is the realization that teachers must have an increased degree of freedom in determining the structure of the curriculum to meet the specific needs of linguistic minority populations. The teaching of reading and writing must be grounded in the cultural and social context of students, their relevant cultural experiences, and their stage of social integration and acculturation, rather than by assuming a universal effectiveness of either the instructional content or method.

Teachers need to search their minds and examine the social organization of their own classrooms to detect possible cultural insensitivity and to eliminate it. Teachers must see the reading and writing processes not only as necessary for obtaining needed subject-matter knowledge but as important instruments for developing cognitive skills to interpret meaning and organize knowledge. It is essential that teachers stop viewing reading practice as a routine exercise in which minority children can participate differentially in accordance with their abilities. They must begin instead to see reading as an essential process in which minority children must be able to participate actively and meaningfully.

The role of the teacher is not merely to perform in front of minority children, with the assumption that they will eventually catch up and understand. It is to ensure that children process information. If we accept the notion that literacy is a socially constructed phenomenon (Cook-Gumperz, 1986), the content of reading and writing lessons, and the active involvement of linguistic minority students in the search for meaning, are extremely important. Because active and meaningful participation in reading and writing activities is conditioned by experiences and skills usually obtained in the home, teachers' knowledge of students' home learning environment is very important.

The case studies of Rita and Ofelia, Juana, and Pablo illustrate home environments with different problems and long-term consequences. In the case of Pablo, regardless of his present performance and limited literacy in English, the trend of achievement and commitment to advancement regardless of difficulties offers the promise of academic success. The family unit is strong and functions cohesively in providing support and motivation for high academic achievement. This is true for Pablo and his siblings. On the other hand, the home of Rita and Ofelia shows signs of stress (single mother and differential role assignments given to daughters), and does not provide effective emotional rewards for the sisters, even though the family is better off financially than Pablo's.

The case of Juana is unique. While there is some general support for literacy associated with the Bible, there is no effective assistance in her academic background that may prepare her for the higher-order cognitive abilities or mastery of the English language that she and her family seem to value. Her time invested in Bible activities supersedes other school activities that may affect her legitimacy as an achiever in school. Indeed, she has only a vague notion of the social and political organization of the school. In contrast, Pablo's parents have a keen sense of politics and appropriate social and political behavior. Both parents are deeply involved in school activities.

The degree of acculturation of linguistic minority students and their families, as manifested in their understanding and acceptance of cultural values associated with academic work, determines the extent to which students share meaning structures and reach accurate text interpretation (Spindler & Spindler, 1987b,c; Trueba, 1987b). Cultural integration—the capability of students selectively to accept new cultural values and incorporate them into the cultural values of their home—increases to the extent that the teacher's role as cultural broker is internalized.

The interpretation of text, as facilitated by the teacher in programs for linguistic minorities, consists of identifying cultural and social equivalents and bringing students from their previous understandings and experiences to new understandings. This role, which is part of their main responsibility in helping students develop English literacy, requires very personal communication. Indeed, it requires the development of a one-to-one relationship between the student and the teacher (often called a dyadic relationship) that permits the student to engage in difficult academic tasks under the close supervision of the teacher. This relationship is most rewarding for children, and it facilitates the development of linguistic and cognitive skills related to the interpretation and generation of text.

## RECOMMENDED EXERCISES

1. Attend a parent-teacher conference. Describe the communication process and the outcomes of the conference. What was the parent's understanding of the exchange, and what were the teacher's assumptions about parental response? Can you make any assumptions about the parent's attitude toward the teacher, the school, and the child?
2. Attend a teachers' group meeting in which they discuss minority students' performance or classroom problems. Describe teachers' views of their problems as well as their assessment of student performance. What are the teachers' concerns? What do they consider the most difficult aspect of teaching minorities?

3. Make arrangements to visit the family of a linguistic minority child you have observed in the classroom. Through an interpreter (if necessary), inquire about family attitudes toward school, their expectations, and their understanding of school and classroom social organization. Examine the general literacy environment and the relative use of text to communicate with each other and with nonfamily members.
4. First interview individual teachers, and later groups of teachers, regarding their view of the teaching profession, their role as teachers, their problems, and their efforts to assist minority students in the acquisition of English literacy. Inquire about the degree of support and/or status (stigma) attached to teachers working with minorities.
5. Identify a support group of teachers working with minorities and meet with them. Inquire how the group functions and determine its relative success in assisting individual teachers who have problems in school. Inquire about teachers' individual job satisfaction before and after the support group was available to them.

## RECOMMENDED READINGS

Ada, 1986
Au, 1980
Britzman, 1986
Castell and Luke, 1986
Cummins, 1978, 1986
Delgado-Gaitan 1987a,b
Delgado-Gaitan and Trueba, 1985
Diaz et al., 1986
Erickson, 1986
Goelman et al., 1984
Goldman and Trueba, 1987
Graff, 1986
Ogbu, 1987a,b
Ogbu and Matute-Bianchi, 1986
Rueda, 1987
G. Spindler, 1982
Spindler and Spindler, 1987c
Trueba, 1987b
Wertsch, 1985

# 6

# Empowering Teachers to Become Effective: Teachers' Struggles and Concerns

Educators and public officials, along with government representatives, and their studies, reports, and educational research allude to contemporary educational crises. High dropout ratios, student isolation, low-quality instruction, low literacy levels among students, little public support for education, dwindling public and private financial assistance to schools and students, and other facts seem to persuade historical analysts that we are going through a crisis equal to or worse than that of the schools during the Great Depression of the 1930s (Tyack & Hansot, 1984).

## CONTEMPORARY EDUCATIONAL CRISIS

Recently, a number of national reports have pointed toward educational crises. In 1983, *A Nation at Risk* was presented by the National Commission on Excellence in Education that Secretary T.H. Bell had appointed. Soon after, there was another report called *Action for Excellence*, which was the result of a study by the Education Commission of the States' Task Force for Economic Growth. The National Science Board issued a report on the condition of mathematics and science in education, and Ernest Boyer, former Secretary of Education wrote, under the auspices of the Carnegie Foundation, *A Report on Secondary Education in America* (1983). Since then a number of state studies and local commissions have studied school unrest and lack of discipline. The public is extremely concerned about school "problems":

> Recent U.S. polls show that the public continues to rank "lack of discipline" as the most critical problem in public schools. Media exposure of such issues as physical attacks on teachers and the use of drugs in school might suggest that most public concern about school discipline amounts to concern about these sensationalized incidents. Generally speaking, most of the people polled equate discipline with respect for authority and the rules and regulations emanating from the sources of authority (Everhart, 1987:77).

Are public schools in crisis? If so, are teachers responsible for such crises? Is the poor quality of instruction the result of some failure on the part of students and their teachers, or of the educational system, or a combination of both the system and the individuals? What are the concerns of teachers today? Is the school learning environment controlled by teachers? Are the classrooms controlled by teachers? What can teachers do to improve the quality of teaching? This chapter examines current concerns of teachers regarding the school environment, teaching practice within the classroom, and the lack of professional training and support required to allow teachers to excel in teaching.

## Historical Perspective

Historical analysts have characterized current public education as suffering from "fiscal inflation and ideological deflation" (Tyack & Hansot, 1984:50). Three main problems being faced by public schools that have become more serious in the past decade are: lack of public confidence and support, lack of funds, and decreased enrollment (Tyack & Hansot, 1984). While lack of money and decreased enrollment were also experienced by schools during the Great Depression, lack of enrollment would not have been seen as a problem but an opportunity to work more efficiently with fewer students. However, the national economic crisis seemed to have spared most schools:

> Declining elementary enrollments, tax resistance, retrenchment, demands for greater efficiency, and public complaints about facts and frills are hardly new in educational history. The educators of the Great Depression would have found these trends entirely familiar. But they would have thought their peers in the 1980s incredibly affluent in comparison with the 1930s, and the economy of the 1980s healthy by comparison with the maelstrom that followed the crash of 1929 (Tyack & Hansot, 1984:34).

Both the status and the salary of teachers in the 1930s, however, were much higher, relatively speaking, than those of their peers in the 1980s. In comparison with the average worker, teachers received better salaries in 1933 than ever before or after, primarily because they had formed a united front and obtained public support, and with it additional monies from the state governments. Just prior to World War II, polls demonstrated the conviction that education was the best ever and that parents were satisfied with schools (Tyack & Hansot, 1984).

Indeed, during the Great Depression, people's willingness to sacrifice in order to provide schools with adequate financial support was remarkable:

> In comparison with the private economy, which experienced great upheavals, public schooling remained remarkably stable in funding and continued its long-term trend of institutional expansion. Even when school income remained stable, the dollars bought more because of dropping prices—a sharp contrast with the

inflation of the 1970s. Set against the transformation of the functions and scope of the federal government, the political economy of public education changed little. The politics of scarcity in education turned out to be more the politics of compromise and continuity than of conflict and change (Tyack & Hansot, 1984:35).

The lack of confidence in public education as a phenomenon following the Vietnam War, Watergate, and the Iran-Contra scandal is not surprising when other public institutions supported by the government have disappointed the people. The lack of trust in public authority and government has undermined strong belief in traditional cultural values. The recent increase in the numbers of homeless, un-employed, and disenfranchised individuals has created cynicism and disbelief in the worthiness of education and educational goals. It is not clear that, in fact, education will open opportunities for all minority students and other underprivileged people in this country (Ogbu, 1974, 1978).

## TEACHERS' CONCERNS ABOUT THE SCHOOL ENVIRONMENT

The first part of this chapter will examine variables of the school environment as they affect the quality of teaching. The discussion will include teachers' concerns about cultural sensitivity, racial and ethnic isolation of minority students, bureau-cratic control resulting in sexist policies, curriculum tightness and irrelevance, and other constraints. In addition, the chapter will deal with the role of teachers in socializing children, local politics, lack of adequate rewards for teachers, and overall lack of support and assistance for new teachers during the formative stages of their careers.

### Equity and Cultural Sensitivity

Increasing awareness of minority children's cultural values and learning styles has motivated recent writers to change the stereotypic view of minority children, taking a position derived from well-documented cultural history and that history's impact on child development. For example, Mitchell, commenting on Hale's book *Black Children: Their Roots, Culture, and Learning Styles* (1982), states:

> Hale is to be congratulated for her pioneering efforts to give content to new categories for understanding the cultural, linguistic, and intellectual behaviors of black children. She stresses the importance of recognizing that West African cultural practices and beliefs have been infused into black communities and influence socialization and child-rearing practices. Furthermore, these West African traditions are embedded in community cultural practices that directly affect cognitive development (Mitchell, 1985:355).

This point of stressing the cultural context of black children's early socialization has significant consequences for education, in contrast with the position advanced by other researchers who overemphasize "language socialization." The theory of language socialization refers to the need to acquire linguistic patterns and proficiency in standard English as a means to succeed in school or in the job market. Language socialization alone is not likely to change social status or structural opportunity for minorities, nor can it exist in a cultural vacuum, set apart from culturally rooted socialization patterns that are linguistically unique to the black family. Some critics of Heath's work (especially her book entitled *Ways with Words* [1983]), for example Rosen (1985), suggest that the emphasis on language socialization, at the expense of political, sociocultural, and economic factors, cannot account for the academic and financial success of community members:

> [It] has been contended that schools are class institutions which internally regulate their diet for different homogeneous things in our society, and so on. The relationship between schools and jobs is never a simple one, and the proposition that certification and high test scores will lead into the Promised Land is a plain and painful delusion. I think that Heath knows all this and is content at the outset to pretend a certain innocence (Rosen, 1985:449).

At the outset of her research in Roadville and Trackton, she stated her position:

> The ways of living, eating, sleeping, worshiping, using space, and filling time which surrounded these language learners would have to be accounted for as part of the milieu in which the process of language learning took place. Though I did not then set out to do so, my next years were to be spent recording and interpreting the language learning habits of the children of Roadville and Track-ton. With these accounts of worlds about which the townspeople actually knew very little, cross-cultural comparisons of the variations of language socialization in the predominant groups of the region would be possible. Using detailed facts on the interactions of the townspeople, and my ethnographies of communication in the communities of Roadville and Trackton, we could then move to answer the central question: For each of these groups, what were the effects of the preschool home and community environment on the learning of those language structures and uses which were needed in classrooms and job settings? (Heath, 1983:3–4).

The Trackton blacks and the Roadville whites "have different ways of using language in worship, for social control, and in asserting their sense of identity" (Heath, 1983:10), but the townspeople alone, blacks and whites of the mainstream middle class, "have the most familiarity with the communicative habits and per-ferences of these public institutions." In other words, language and culture are intimately related, and "the place of language in the cultural life of each social group is interdependent with the habits and values of behaving shared among members of that group" (Heath, 1983:11).

Heath describes in detail the cultural socialization of children, and the particular use of the language in teaching children how to behave. The inseparability of language and culture in most of the descriptions presented by the author makes a strong case for looking at language as *one* of the factors responsible for keeping some poor black and white rural families from achieving upper social and economic status and higher levels of education. The question is: Is deficient language socialization the cause or the effect of cultural and political isolation and poverty? Rosen refers to a passage in *Ways with Words* in which Heath clearly states: "It is easy to claim that a radical restructuring of society or the system of education is needed for the kind of cultural bridging reported in this book" (Heath 1983:369). Does Heath mean that perhaps we cannot change the social and economic organization, and the educational level of people, simply by emphasizing the appropriate use of the language? Do we need educational, social, and health programs that can open new opportunities for children at home and in school?

## The Teacher's Dilemma: Linguistic and/or Political Socialization?

Heath's advocacy for changing the role of teachers through ethnographic training is described in the context of a science project in which learners became ethnographers. In the project reported, students played an active role and became "the basic suppliers of information, thus placing the teacher in the position of becoming a resource in the same sense in which informants [students] and other community members were resources" (Heath, 1983:324). The teacher's goals for the project are:

> Improved scores on the standardized unit tests; an increased number and variety of written materials done by students; posters in acceptable form for use with other classes; a selection of artifacts to retain for next year's unit; enthusiasm and motivation for school work, and for science in particular; parent involvement; an improved self image for the [children]; increased awareness of the types of sources which could verify information; an increased diversity of opportunities for displaying knowledge and skills (Heath, 1983:325).

Convinced that all of the above, including changes in motives and attitudes resulting from the program, are either a direct by-product of linguistic skills or themselves the result of such skills, she states:

> If the students were to be able to convince others they had gained scientific knowledge from this experience, they had to be able to use the language of science and to produce acceptable scientific statements. In the teacher's terms, students displaying specific language skills should be able to:
>
> 1. make statements and back them up with an acceptable source or authority recognized in the science world;

2. ask and answer questions briefly and precisely; be direct;
3. know the vocabulary of science used in textbooks and by teachers of science;
4. avoid telling stories about their knowledge: be able to discuss an item or event for its own sake, not in terms of their direct experiences with it (Heath, 1983:325–326).

Critics have taken issue with Heath's position and the overemphasis placed on language, in the absence of other important cognitive skills related to the organization of knowledge and the ability to search for meaning through interactional context or experience. Rosen pointedly states:

> The science-cum-ethnography project is described with scarcely concealed delight, but it includes amongst its goals the mastery of "the language of science" and making "acceptable scientific statements." It would appear that this includes, "avoid telling stories about their knowledge: be able to discuss an item or event for its own sake, not in terms of their direct experiences with it." Do those suspect goals receive Heath's imprimatur? I give her the benefit of the doubt, for she must know the philosophical and linguistic debate on these matters. I never understand what it means to do something for "its own sake." And what has Heath been doing for the previous three hundred pages but telling stories about her knowledge, and not for their own sake but for ours? (Rosen, 1985:455).

Neither the motivation to acquire scientific knowledge nor the actual mastery of its content necessarily comes with linguistic proficiency. Linguistic knowledge of any particular scientific domain does not guarantee the intellectual commitment to engage in critical inquiry about scientific issues. Personal investment in intellectual endeavors is not identical with knowing how to talk about it. The process of knowledge acquisition demands an investment of time and effort that has to be given for very personal reasons, some of them totally extrinsic to the imputed self-worth of the scientific inquiry for its own sake, if that exists. How can teachers pretend that the personal experiences of the children do not count or are not relevant to the development of critical thinking skills? It must be recognized that intellectual activities have a political dimension, and that the organization of instruction is inherently a political and sociological phenomenon that creates power strata and legitimates the existing social order.

> In the end, teachers can defend successfully the enclaves they have constructed only if they have won the parents and community to their methods and can invoke their support in sustaining them. And those are "ways with words" which have to be learned too. They constitute the language of political participation. If all of us do not learn this way with words, we shall go on placing wreaths on the tombstones of projects all over the world, overcome with sadness and impotence (Rosen, 1985:456).

If we recognize that the linguistic socialization of minority students by teachers is not sufficient to bring about the urgently needed educational and social changes that will improve the quality of life for these students and their families, an important question remains. What should the role of the teacher be? That of a cultural broker who is realistic about the need for political power but not personally involved in creating political changes? Or someone who pretends that the teacher's role is politically neutral?

## Bureaucratic Control

The teacher's role, activities, rewards, and evaluation have been defined and supervised by a bureaucratic educational system that has silenced and isolated many teachers. McDonald explains that the "cellular" organization of schools as semi-autonomous teaching stations is particularly suitable for the supervision and control of the curriculum by administrators while isolating teachers. He states:

> Cellular design permits a school to grow or diminish by this teacher or that without much organizational consequence. But of course the design itself is of great organizational consequence, including the empowerment of those who coordinate the cells, the subordination of those who inhabit them, and . . . the discouragement of cooperation, inquiry, collegiality, and participation in the fashioning of a school-wide culture (McDonald, 1986:358).

On an organizational basis, the silence of teachers is only one of the effects of their isolation; it is also a mechanism for ensuring job security and protecting school authority. The price of teachers' personal silence is a collective hopelessness on the part of teachers before the administrative control of curriculum, imposition of evaluation criteria, and assessment of teacher effectiveness. McDonald describes a group of high school teachers who were tired of being silent and decided to organize group meetings:

> A concern for autonomy against the threat of curricular tightness and administrative supervision was one of the four most salient themes in the talk of the teachers (McDonald, 1986:358).

The group started by reading books about schooling and inviting theoreticians to discuss their readings and common concerns. The initial euphoria later changed into frustration and an urgency for action. The group increased their reading assignments and began to meet regularly in the form of a monthly dinner club to discuss readings and concerns. A central topic of discussion was the contemporary school reform effort, which was conceptualized and executed with almost no teacher input and "might diminish rather than enhance the power of teachers, and hurt children already at risk" (McDonald, 1986:356).

## Teachers' Response

Teachers are becoming increasingly aware of the fine line between attempts to survive as effective professionals and becoming involved collectively as a political force. Indeed, in some instances, teachers see a great need to participate in collective political action in order to gain fair treatment and be given a chance to teach well. To public insensitivity and lack of appreciation of their work, they respond with pride and assertiveness. To the nostalgic reconstructionists of past educational glories, they point out that:

> The Great Depression was not, then, an important watershed either in the financing and governance of education or in educational practice. . . . In the view of Tyack, Lowe, and Hansot, the traditional system was one mired in reaction, tied to class and racial barriers, and essentially inadequate to the needs of a modern, democratic society. At their worst, as even the most determined defenders of traditional education will admit, American schools in the 1930s were hardly worthy of the name: unheated shacks staffed by uneducated teachers and unequipped with even the most rudimentary books and equipment; schools for rural blacks that were open only a few weeks of the year; schools in poor urban areas that students and teachers alike described as ''like prisons,'' places actively hostile to learning. But it was not just the inner-city ghettos and the forgotten outposts of rural poverty whose schools were inadequate and unjust (Brinkley, 1984:457–458).

## A Meritocratic Conception of the Teacher's Role

Many teachers and liberals privately defend the federal record opposing local segregation and isolation of minorities, but they have felt constrained to maintain silence under pressure from administrators (Ada, 1986). The national debate has continued, and educational analysts are concerned about the increasing control by the federal government and the courts of educational policy and practice (see Chapter 3 for the dialogue between Shulman [1987a,b] and Sockett [1987]; also Ravitch, [1983]).

The Rand Corporation's annual report from its Center for the Study of the Teaching Profession (1987) indicates similar concerns to those voiced by Sockett and Ravitch:

> In the last year or two, the rationale for professionalizing teaching has become increasingly clear. The argument for it is similar to the arguments that led to the transformation of other occupations into professions. The primary rationale is the need to exercise quality control over a process in which, in a largely private transaction, important services are provided to clients who inevitably know less than the service providers. . . . Appropriate instructional decisions must be made at the point of service delivery. Therefore, the quality of services

delivered inevitably depends upon the capacity of the teacher to make the appropriate decisions. . . . Professions attempt to manage quality control by emphasizing quality control over personnel as a means of assuring high-quality service delivery (Wise, 1987:1).

National efforts to end racial discrimination are viewed by conservatives as vicious and misguided quota systems and reverse discrimination; bilingual education is seen as threatening the effectiveness and coherence of the educational system, and as part of a political movement led by dissenters, educational nihilists, and ethnic pressure groups.

The intimate relationship between schools, social structure, and social and economic mobility seems to contradict a meritocratic conception of schools, in which schools must serve primarily a politically and/or economically powerful elite to retain power. In a meritocratic conception of schools, teachers have the role of maintaining the social system's status quo. Today, however, teachers' responsibilities, including the challenge of pursuing a democratic conception of schools, are a great deal more demanding and complex: "Whatever we do or fail to do in resisting the conversion of our schools into brutally frank machines for social control, in the end thousands of teachers must encounter millions of students daily in classrooms" (Rosen, 1985:456). A critique of Ravitch's work is eloquently presented by Brinkley, who comments:

> Beneath all the equivocations, reservations, and digressions, this [Ravitch's] is a book that upholds the idea of the educational system as the defender of meritocracy. Schools are not well equipped, she suggests, to remake society along egalitarian lines. They are not appropriate vehicles for satisfying the narrow demands, however legitimate, of every interest group. Their purpose is to encourage, cultivate, and reward excellence; to provide opportunities for advancement to those able and willing to seize them; and to do so in ways that will reinforce society's common culture and values (Brinkley, 1984:456).

The above is not only a very elitist conception of the functions of educational institutions, but by implication it subverts teachers into becoming agents of the governing few on behalf of the affluent. In a democratic society, this conception betrays even traditional conceptions of the mainstreaming functions attributed to schools.

## Empowerment of Teachers and Students

Reacting to this view of schools, teachers talk about the need to become empowered. What do they mean? Yonemura (1986), a scholar with a long teaching career, confesses that her earliest notions of empowerment were generated by her educational experiences in the late 1920s and the reading of books such as Isaacs'

*Intellectual Growth in Young Children* (as cited by Yonemura, 1986). Yonemura views teacher empowerment as the freedom and ability to create curricula and to use teaching methods that teachers perceive as the most appropriate for children. Empowerment also means teachers' ability to open up choices for liberating children as persons and expanding their power for decision-making. In this sense, teachers' empowerment leads to students' empowerment. She describes her experiences as follows:

> During the ten years that I taught in and directed a school serving largely black and Puerto Rican children from New York City, I found that Isaacs' way of working transcended race and social class. The children with whom I worked enthusiastically seized opportunities to make sense of their world and to learn about their environment. They were active inquirers, and were able to join in writing the script of their own education by making as well as absorbing knowledge (Yonemura, 1986:474).

Teachers are asking for latitude to meet the needs of children as they know best, rather than maintaining a teaching and curriculum structure that in their opinion is inappropriate or destructive for minority children as well as for other children. Curriculum and teaching "tightness" (as referred to earlier by McDonald, 1986) forces teachers to reduce children to "passive memorizers of educational scripts to which they make no original contribution, and which do not expand and enrich their day-to-day experiences" (Yonemura, 1986:474). Good teachers have become persuaded that children are rich in experiences and should be permitted to write their own educational scripts, with the assistance of adults. Those who defend the sacredness of curricula and the untouchable character of certain teaching practices seem to view both children and teachers as "empty vessels" who need to be given digested pieces of knowledge that neatly fit a mold.

Another factor contributing to teachers' silence is, in the overwhelming experience of professional women working in fields controlled by men, the systematic lack of opportunities for women to play an active role in making decisions that affect the entire teaching profession:

> We realize that women constitute only one of many disadvantaged social groups that include people of color, people of racial and ethnic minorities, people in countries dominated politically and economically by imperialist powers, and people who must work in exploitative relations of wage labor or commodity exchange, all of whom suffer disempowerment and silencing (Lewis & Simon, 1986:458).

How are teachers, especially women teachers, silenced? This happens in many, if sometimes subtle, ways: ignoring them, imposing decisions on them, patronizing them, preventing them from moving up the promotional ladder, questioning their abilities, demeaning the significance of their contributions, and questioning their emotional stability and mental capacity. Lewis and Simon offer a number of eloquent examples in quasiexperimental academic settings in which male–female interactions were observed and documented. One of the strategies used by men is to deny women the floor or the opportunity to participate in the structuring of discourse, which is then collectively developed to represent an opinion shared by male members of the group. Lewis and Simon analyze this strategy, in the context of their graduate seminar, as follows:

> The feeling of being in a space not one's own is familiar to women in a society marked fundamentally by patriarchy. It is not that there were not ideological differences among the men in how they took up the agenda of the class or in how they envisioned its pedagogical implications. In many instances, there was more in common both pedagogically and ideologically between groups of men and women than between people of the same gender. But since the overriding issue in this class was not the politics of curriculum but rather the politics of gender, ideological differences among the men were obliterated by the desire to structure gender solidarity (Lewis & Simon, 1986:461–462).

The politics and economics of patriarchy, namely the abuse of power across gender lines to maintain economic gains, is one possible explanation for teachers' silence. The next question, however, is why teachers continue to accept the position of powerlessness they know they have. The profound roots of inner conflict between speaking out to organize politically and being a quiet, unselfish, dedicated teacher go beyond the personal choice each teacher makes. There are cultural values in conflict, and there are rapid changes taking place.

Teachers' silence is not the result of only structural tightness and imposition of inappropriate curricula and/or teaching methods. The maintenance of low wages and withholding of merit increases can become powerful instruments of teacher domination. Performance-based evaluations as a basis for pay have conspicuously failed over the last 75 years because we lack a clear and/or economical method of monitoring individual output. As a consequence, teachers "attempt behavior that makes them appear productive relative to other workers but in fact is contrary to the goals of the organization" (Murnane & Cohen, 1986:3).

Schools cannot function the way a business does, nor can productivity be measured according to universally valid criteria. The teaching profession must operate on trust, and consequently any outspoken behavior on the part of the teacher can be construed as contrary to the school organization and punished.

A Rand Report summarizing other studies indicates that:

> Contrary to modern-day assumptions, teacher shortages have been common throughout this century, and it has always been difficult to recruit and retain talented teachers. The surplus of the last decade was an exception. . . . Teachers' salaries have increased in purchasing power since the early twentieth century, but, at the same time, other occupations that require similar education and training have gradually increased their earnings relative to those of teaching. Moreover, male teachers have generally outearned their female colleagues,

white teachers have outearned minorities, and teachers in the privileged suburbs and larger cities have earned more than those in rural and smaller districts . . . (Center for the Study of the Teaching Profession, 1987:9).

Interest on the part of qualified candidates in entering the teaching profession is decreasing at a time when the need for more teachers is becoming urgent. The Rand Study states that the next few decades will see great turmoil in the teaching profession:

A majority of our teaching work force in 1992 will consist of people who are not presently employed in teaching; over a million new teachers will enter the classroom between now and then. . . . Teacher attrition is related to inefficiency in setting teacher salary levels (Center for the Study of Teaching Profession, 1987:9–10).

Beyond the lack of economic rewards, teachers have voiced other important concerns, such as their need for guidance, support, and time in order to explore new and what they hope will be more effective instructional approaches and curriculum materials.

## TEACHERS' CONCERNS ABOUT CLASSROOM WORK

The previous sections of this chapter have discussed the shared concerns teachers have with the increasing difficulties and constraints that prevent many of them from being effective instructors, regardless of their personal professional training and competence. This part of the chapter discusses the concerns individual teachers have about their classroom work, problems in dealing with mandated curricula, students' lack of commitment to learn, the lack of home support for students, the additional burdens placed on teachers' beyond daily instruction, their need to change instructional methods, and the cultural diversity of students, with its concomitant demands. Teachers as individuals are raising their voices to ask for help in dealing with excessive testing of children. Teachers need to have the time and freedom to listen to children. They require a safe work environment and they demand respect and appreciation for their work. Indeed, they are coming to the realization that as individuals they are often powerless to teach well.

### Conflicts between the Curriculum and Students' Needs

Mass education, with its compulsory attendance yet bureaucratically mandated curricula that neglect linguistically and culturally different needs, is both a cherished value and a thorn in the side of American society. As D.K. Cohen has stated: ''For most of the twentieth century, American education has been notable for its passionate embrace of the idea that quantity is quality'' (1984:11). He goes on to discuss the debate between quality and equality:

> Another old-but-good element in the debate is the argument about quality and equality. For as long as Americans have been trying to construct a public secondary school system we have chewed on this bone. The terms in which we argue it today are not that different from the terms in which we argued it twenty or sixty years ago, though many minorities have managed to claw their way into the system. . . . When we worry about quality we want to trade equality away (Cohen, 1984:12).

As a historian, Cohen offers some insights into compulsory attendance, pragmatism, and American cultural values. Compulsory education is mandated by law, but it has some economic advantages as well. While it is true that ''keeping kids in school protects many adult workers in a precarious economy,'' the nature of schools is drastically affected by two apparently conflicting values: mass education and quality education.

> Legal and economic compulsions, and the social pressures that they have generated, have helped to turn high schools into social centers for otherwise unoccupied adolescents. It is a great help to parents, to the police, to many adult workers, and to those who make public policy. Kids like it too. There is little encouragement for education in all this, however. Such reasons for going to school erode the commitment required for thoughtful work (Cohen, 1984:13).

Such a handicapped condition for schooling undermines the very foundations of learning as a free activity requiring profound commitment, personal interest, and systematic effort. To this problem we must add another, equally crucial and as difficult to resolve: the inadequacy of the curriculum. The traditional prescriptions for a quick fix of the serious deficiencies of curricula are alluded to in teacher conferences and national reports. They include ''back to basics, or more of the three Rs,'' additional course work, higher expectations and criteria for performance assessed by standardized tests, and school reorganization supported by the federal government but controlled locally. Those formulas have not worked. As Wyatt has noted:

> The implication is that reform of curriculum and instruction in our schools will solve problems that curriculum and instruction did not create. Curricular content and instructional methodology today are a reaction to the problems created by irrelevant curricula, unequal access, rigidity, neglect of diversity, and the impersonality of the school structure in the past. Curriculum and instruction should not retrogress to the technocratic imperative initially imposed by the reaction to Sputnik and now dusted off by these various reports and commissions (Wyatt, 1984:29).

Wyatt leads to the heart of the problem and decries the fact that national reports ''minimize the need for continued sensitivity to the multicultural population in today's urban schools," while they continue to increase bureaucratic controls in mandated curricula that "will not lead to educational excellence" (Wyatt, 1984:30). The silence imposed on teachers of linguistic minorities who would like to depart from mandated curricula often results in academic failure of students and frustration of teachers.

Teachers' early attempts to socialize linguistic minority children into the culture of the school, emphasizing the value of literacy and the love of books, found that the curriculum is not appealing to children because it escapes children's experience, and thus their interest and grasp of concepts. The importance of familiarity with the immediate context of literacy materials, to allow students to grasp their content and learn to make appropriate inferences, is stressed by scholars in linguistics, communication, psychology, and anthropology (Freebody and Baker, 1985; Diaz et al., 1986; Cheng, 1987; Rueda, 1987; Trueba, 1987a,b; and many others). The relationship between experience and oral and written communication is at the heart of the discussion. Relevancy of curriculum is determined by a delicate relationship between students' knowledge and experience and the curriculum content. This content includes not only general descriptive characteristics of events or facts well-known by most, but also the cognitive organization of discourse that logically ties together ideas, values, messages, and metamessages captured in text.

Irrelevant curricula do not affect only minority students' abilities to acquire literacy; they affect other children as well. Freebody and Baker point out that "decontextualization of language does not simply relate to the absence of nonverbal signals or vocal intonation, or to the reader's ability to query the writer about meaning," but to the way children think and reason (1985:382). In fact, if we accept the theoretical position of many sociolinguists and anthropologists (Frake, 1964; Cicourel, 1974; Trueba, 1987a,b; and others), language is essential in the construction of social and cultural reality and a part of the cultural reality being constructed. In that sense, textbook language is often the tip of a foreign culture for many children, including those who are losing their home language more rapidly than they are acquiring English as a second language. Textbooks are composed by mainstream speakers of English, by adults attempting to communicate with children, holding cultural assumptions peculiar to middle-class mainstream members of American culture and their interpretation of how children talk and think. The characters of the stories may be children themselves, but the voices and cognitive structures are those of adults. In this ethnocentric adult world of textbooks, the message (conscious and/or subconscious) is conformity and submission.

In their analysis of word frequency in children's textbooks, Freebody and Baker (1985) found a predominance of *little* and *small*, in contrast to *big* and *large*. Textbooks, story books, and other readers are designed to socialize children into the world of books. As Freebody and Baker suggest:

> First, they [the readers] are the early harbingers of the culture of literacy. This
> is not merely a culture in which people can decode written language; it is also
> like an informal club or lodge with hidden stylistic signs, well-kept intellectual
> and social secrets, and obscure objects of reverence. For many children, this

is a world in which they will always feel vaguely out of place, insecure, and perhaps inferior. They will see their more fortunate peers detect and soon actually produce the signs; learn, without ever having been explicitly taught, the ways of thinking; and display a genuine reverence for the objects with which they themselves can claim only an uncomfortable acquaintance (Freebody & Baker, 1985:396).

The sociocultural differences of children and their families, along with their differential ability and motivation in handling text (which has cumulative effects for classroom participation and disruption), place teachers in a serious predicament. For whom should they structure their teaching? How should they organize the information to reach individuals with such different skill and information levels? Is the students' lack of commitment to learn the main factor in teachers' demoralization and lack of commitment to teach? The curriculum materials and the prescribed delivery and organization of such materials only increase the teacher's difficulties. The roots of illiteracy for minorities can probably be found in their lack of cultural knowledge assumed by textbooks and teachers.

While the disruptive, unproductive behavior of some culturally isolated students can be microanalyzed as being caused by the ecology of the home, school, and classroom (specifically by blaming either teachers or students for the disruption), there is a need to look at the broader educational context and the developmental stages of disruption. Compulsory attendance becomes a problem for the student not so much because schooling is obligatory, but because it is unrewarding and meaningless. If it were viewed as a privilege and a unique opportunity (as in many other countries), students might have the commitment to learn, thus preventing any disciplinary disruptions. But one could also argue that if the compulsory character of school is the problem, it is the democratic ideal of mass education in combination with its compulsory character. If the commitment to learn is not shared by all students, the teacher's job is already in jeopardy. How can teachers develop a motivational structure without the backing of the family and society? Worse still, how can this be done by the teacher when students have plenty of examples at home that education does not necessarily open the gates of success for minorities? Is it a strategy for survival on the part of the teacher to withdraw the commitment to teach, to demand less academically, and to transfer low-achieving students (and their problems) to somebody else? Some liberal and neo-Marxist thinkers, as well as many advocates of the Freiran philosophy of education (see, for example, Giroux, 1983; Giroux & McLaren, 1986; Everhart, 1987; Ada, 1986; Ogbu, 1974, 1978, 1987a,b; McDermott, 1987a,b; Cummins, 1986; and others) see our educational system as perpetuating the social structure that fails and isolates the powerless and minorities. Does transferring a stratified culture that recreates an unfair or unjust social system deprive some individuals of the benefits that knowledge brings?

Teachers, however, are not only concerned with the success of minorities but also with their own role in transferring the cultural heritage and values they themselves have received. They are concerned with protecting institutional authority in the classroom in order to maintain their professional integrity and seek excellence. They keep searching for answers to the problem of teaching effectively and they are willing to examine this problem in earnest.

Everhart (1987) offers some important insights into the factors determining student behavior. He suggests that there are three main analytical approaches, the first being at the macrolevel, that examine the sociological factors that create and influence student behavior:

> Functional and neo-Marxist theories, for example, focus on how student behavior in school relates to the purposes that schools serve for the larger society. At this level of analysis, individual actions are important, but primarily insofar as they reflect issues at the macrolevel (Everhart, 1987:78).

A second approach examines microanalytical factors of student behavior, especially in cases where individuals are seen as departing from acceptable social manners and have not internalized cultural norms. If students do not seem to have internalized such norms, action is taken to resocialize them to adopt more acceptable behaviors:

> Finally, classroom discipline can be understood from a social–ecological perspective by focusing on the context of schooling itself. That is to say, we can understand school discipline as part of the ongoing dynamic created by organizations participants (students, teachers, and administrators) as they live their lives within the school as a complex social organization. From this perspective, the question of the social order of the classroom is paramount, as are such questions like: how is order possible; under what conditions do certain forms of order prevail; which factors affect the disequilibrium of the social order; what consequences result from various forms of order and disorder; and what understandings of classroom order are held by various participants (Everhart, 1987:78).

One of the reasons why reflective teaching, meaning the increased awareness of social and cultural contexts of instruction, is emphasized today by teachers is that they live and work under high levels of stress that prevent them from asking themselves questions about social order in the classroom. In situations where survival (psychological and physical) takes precedence, teaching poorly may be an adaptive strategy. Good teachers may fall back on poor teaching methods. Otherwise it would be too painful for them to attempt to communicate with students who have already lost any interest in learning, or for them to teach through the mandated curriculum, which they know is ineffective or irrelevant to the specific student population.

In their attempt to explain differential achievement of minorities, some scholars including Everhart (1987) share the theoretical assumptions of cultural ecologists (Ogbu, 1974, 1978, 1981, 1982, 1983, 1987a,b; Ogbu & Matute-Bianchi, 1986; Gibson, 1987a,b; Suarez-Orozco, 1987, in press).

Ogbu asks a central question:

> Why do some minorities successfully cross cultural boundaries and/or opportunity barriers and do well in school? Why do some other minorities lack success in crossing cultural boundaries and/or opportunity barriers and, therefore, perform less well in school? (Ogbu, 1987:317).

The explanation given by Ogbu for the differential academic success of minority students is "societal forces" plus "culturally-determined boundaries." Societal forces as an explanation are not new. Sociologists, particularly neo-Marxists, have articulated that position since the early 1950s and 1960s, and have alluded to the *job ceiling* created by economic and social macrostructures mentioned by Ogbu (1978, 1987a,b). See, for example, the discussion by Bowles and Gintis, who explain that their model of corporate enterprise examines the control of employment by capitalist employers "in their own interests and geared toward mediating the inherent conflict between capital and labor" (Bowles & Gintis, 1976:83).

The cultural ecologists' taxonomy, particularly as used by Ogbu, divides minority groups into autonomous, immigrant, or castelike categories, based on psychological responses of "types" of minorities to similar oppressive conditions.

Ogbu's position (1974, 1978, 1981, 1982, 1983, 1987a,b) has been criticized (Erickson, 1987) on the grounds that (1) it does not explain the success of many minority students (including "castelike" minorities), (2) it ignores language and tends to be reductionistic to a position of economic determinism, and (3) it lacks empirical evidence. Erickson's reaction is predictable in terms of his sociolinguistic theoretical perspective (see Erickson, 1984, 1986).

Some of the problems with Ogbu's overgeneralization and reasoning, however, need further discussion. For example, the role of culture in the acquisition of knowledge within context-specific settings may need some clarification. Perhaps Ogbu's peculiar use of castelike, immigrant, and autonomous minority types, which was based on the work by DeVos (1967, 1973, 1982, 1984), may not be applicable to some of the ethnic groups that Ogbu has identified as prototypes of each category. Is the justification for Ogbu's taxonomy psychological? He deals with the "involuntary" presence of some minorities in this country, or with their lack of motivation to achieve in school, or with their psychological response to oppression and their development of psychological boundaries in the context of acculturation. Or, is it primarily structural, that is, based on "societal forces"? In any event, what kind of empirical evidence does he present?

Ogbu has often clearly expressed the position that the system has oppressed minorities. Minorities develop a response towards mainstream cultures shaped by the nature of this systemic social exploitation. This makes sense in a broad sociohistorical sense, but it does not explain why individuals subjected to the same oppression, even from within the same ethnic group, respond differently. Ogbu views the differential response of ethnic groups as a culturally based boundary mechanism that mediates the impact of social and economic oppression, but he does not accept significant differential responses within a single ethnic group. Ogbu states that:

> *Castelike* or *involuntary minorities* are people who were *originally brought into United States society involuntarily* through slavery, conquest, or colonization. Thereafter, these minorities were relegated to menial positions and denied true assimilation into mainstream society. American Indians, Black Americans, Native Hawaiians are examples. In the case of Mexican Americans, those who later immigrated from Mexico were assigned the status of the original conquered group in the southwestern United States, with whom they came to share a sense of peoplehood or collective identity (Ogbu, 1987b:321).

This sociocultural ecological approach, inspired by the work of DeVos (1967, 1973, 1980, 1982, 1983, 1984), postulates a taxonomy of minority groups: "autonomous," "immigrant," or "castelike," and a clear methodological distinction between "macro" and "micro," and between "explanatory" and "applied" ethnography.

Ogbu's writings, in particular two major volumes, *The Next Generation* (1974) and *Minority Education and Caste* (1978), deserve a distinguished place in contemporary social anthropological thought. His impatience with microethnographers leads him to criticize the narrow focus of some research on specific cultural domains such as "communicative style," "cognitive style," "motivational style," or "classroom social organization and social relations, interaction style, and, nowadays, 'literacy' and 'writing' styles" (Ogbu, 1987b:313). An unbiased reading of the work by scholars from the Kamehameha Early Education Program (KEEP), or the Laboratory of Comparative Human Cognition (LCHC), and of their colleagues at Stanford (see, for example, Scribner & Cole, 1981; Au & Jordan, 1981; Boggs, 1985; Diaz et al., 1986; Moll, 1986; Moll & Diaz, 1987; Tharp & Gallimore, in press; Spindler & Spindler, 1983, 1987a,b,c; G. Spindler, 1982, 1987; Trueba 1987a,b, in press; Trueba & Delgado-Gaitan, 1988), suggests that the study of interactional structures is compatible with the concern for broader sociological structures and processes. These scholars explore intervention-oriented research and see no conflict in using a solid theoretical framework to improve educational policy and practice. Their research offers a clear example that intervention and ethnographic research can go hand in hand. Tharp and Gallimore (in press) have proposed the application of Vygotsky's notion of socially based cognitive development as interpreted by neo-Vygotskians (Cole & D'Andrade, 1982; Cole & Scribner, 1974; Wertsch, 1981, 1985) to teacher education. This approach promises to become extremely helpful in integrating culture theories and recognizing the significance of the cultural context of learning (see Diaz et al., 1986; Rueda, 1987; Wertsch, 1985; Scribner & Cole, 1981).

The typology of minority groups as autonomous, immigrant, or castelike is unfounded and highly stereotypic. It is built on imputed behavior and presumed psychological responses of certain members of ethnic groups, or on statistical macrosociological samples. In addition, this categorization is faulty because it is not supported by enough empirical evidence and is based on reasoning contaminated by neo-Marxist and psychoanalytical biases. This position assumes a culturally determined response to societal forces on the part of "castelike" groups, for example, and makes this unique response the criterion to differentiate one group from another. In other words, the presumed cultural response to societal forces becomes the basis of the taxonomic differences between groups and forms the structure for the interpretation of ethnographic data gathered.

The categories of "castelike," "immigrant," and "autonomous" minorities are not clearly defined, nor are they mutually exclusive, nor do they account for the internal stratification of ethnic groups. Cultural ecologists who use Ogbu's categories must also account for the similarities between refugee students, which exist at the same time as their differential academic success. Most of all, they must account for the documented success of "castelike" minorities in spite of the stereotypes and any imputed or presumed "castelike" behavior.

The next logical question is how we go from socioecological, cultural–ecological, or context-specific theoretical approaches to the practical solution of teachers' problems. Teachers are still seeking ways to become effective, and empowered professionally so that their efforts have the expected results and desired satisfaction.

## HOW TO BECOME EMPOWERED
## AS A TEACHER

The notion of empowerment has different meanings for different people depending on their place in the political spectrum. The intent here in using the concept is not to advocate or reject neo-Marxist concepts or theories, but to advocate for teachers' needs. The teacher needs a fairly clear understanding of what needs to be done, facilitated, supported, and/or funded by decision makers and teachers themselves in order to change the classroom and school setting at the local level. Professional empowerment is not a privilege of the collectivity of teachers, much less a privilege granted teachers by the power of central government offices. Professional empowerment is understood here to involve the individual teacher's possession of the conditions, means, knowledge, and skills required to teach, and it is understood as a right similar to the rights of other professionals. By implication, empowerment requires many conditions: training, support, advice, monitoring, opportunity to continue learning about teaching, time to reflect, authority and responsibility for the organizational structure of the activities constituting instruction, and, ultimately, the commitment of students to learn.

Teachers' willingness and ability to listen to students implies that students are willing to engage in constructive learning activities and have something to share. This may even be possible in school settings beset by racial tension, drug abuse, absenteeism, violence, and lack of discipline. There are some minimal conditions required to begin teaching, such as personal safety and respect for teachers' authority in the classroom. These conditions, created by the socially sanctioned order that is an integral part of our educational values, are necessary but not sufficient. Beyond that, students' commitment to learn (also part of our value system), or at least willingness to be persuaded of the need to learn, and to be motivated to invest personal time and energy in education, is part of the (implicit) reciprocal contract between students and teachers. When the nature of this contract is transformed into one in which the teacher promises to perform in front of students, to lower academic standards, or to leave students alone in exchange for physical safety, teaching is no longer teaching because there is no learning.

Because empowerment includes many conditions that can be attained only with the strong support of educational administrators, the discussion of possible empowerment projects will speak not only to teachers but also to decision-makers from time to time. Even after all the necessary conditions for good teaching are in place, actual learning may still not occur in some students. Politzer (1971) points out that individual differences are of such magnitude that learning becomes highly personal and unpredictable. Martin (1985) knows that there are moments of critical learning, such as one case during which she felt she was intruding, when a child was busy internalizing concepts, playing roles, or absorbed in other learning activities. Meier (1986), an elementary education teacher like Martin, feels that actual learning takes place in the least expected "small moments" of teacher–student interaction:

> My lesson plans, whether they are on paper or in my head, all have a beginning, a middle, and an end. They can also include preambles, introductions, asterisks, chapter headings, conclusions, footnotes, and references. Thus, although I teach seven-year-olds, my lessons often read like a graduate school lecture or a college textbook. But when I look back on a lesson and try to find out what has happened to the big things I have tried to teach, the evidence is limited. . . . The lesson plan that goes in well organized often comes back out fifteen minutes or an hour later disjointed and beaten out of shape (Meier, 1986:298–299).

There is a serious danger in intellectualizing the serious predicaments in which teachers find themselves, or the potential assistance they need to become professionally empowered. Postulating, for example, a neo-Marxist approach (radical pedagogy or others) may result in a terse discussion of the social evils of an establishment presumed inadequate to reform education, while neglecting real opportunities to assist teachers in the context of their immediate social and cultural interactions. Inquiry or intellectual discussion that has no potential solution, at least not one within reach of individual teachers or small groups of teachers, can only demoralize them and make them feel less and less empowered to act competently.

Indeed, one needs to give serious consideration to the broad sociological, economic, and cultural context of education, as a means to understand better the educational problems faced by teachers, though not created by them. It may also be desirable, according to liberal politicians, to embrace all-encompassing goals for ambitious political and educational reforms that are viewed as a fundamental solution to the problems of minority education. These broad, long-term sociopolitical concerns should not prevent teachers and administrators from engaging in serious educational changes at the local level to facilitate teachers' work. What is proposed in the following pages is a local plan, concrete even if it is tentative, to inspire teachers in their own professional development, short-term reforms, and resolution of their individual problems of internalizing and integrating their personal and professional obligations.

## The Concept of Teacher Support Groups

Teachers talking to teachers have often found the clarity and encouragement needed to face their daily instructional duties. They have also found wisdom, a sense of justice, and a deep understanding of children, particularly of those who are neglected by prejudicial educational policies and practices. Giroux and McLaren (1986) defend the position that teachers are inevitably involved in the political struggle over power by virtue of their instructional role as "transformative intellectuals":

> By the term "transformative intellectual," we refer to one who exercises forms of intellectual and pedagogical practice which attempt to insert teaching and learning directly into the political sphere by arguing that schooling represents both a struggle for meaning and a struggle over power relations. We are also referring to one whose intellectual practices are necessarily grounded in forms of moral and ethical discourse exhibiting a preferential concern for the suffering and struggles of the disadvantaged and oppressed (Giroux & McLaren, 1986:215).

There is no doubt that consciously or subconsciously teachers, as representatives of social institutions perpetuating the social order, play a role that has significant political consequences for the distribution and use of power. Related questions arise: Can teachers profitably engage in political action through their teaching? Is teaching intrinsically political? Are teachers not only justified but also obligated in certain circumstances to engage in some specific type of teaching that has consequences for change in the social order? It is not clear what Giroux and McLaren postulate. It would seem that becoming critically conscious of sociohistorical trends in educational equity, and of the needs of minority communities, could lead to logical consequences for the practice of teaching in the form of a serious commitment to educational equity. In this sense, a "transformative intellectual" holds a philosophical position that requires greater cultural congruence in curriculum and instructional methods, and greater appreciation of students' cultural, linguistic, and ethnic values.

The organization of support groups is predicated on a strong common philosophy that serves as a foundation for teachers' views of their role. This philosophical base should be flexible enough to permit individual teachers from different political creeds to associate and work together toward a common goal. The common goal must be pragmatic, such as the improvement of instructional skills or the acquisition of knowledge to resolve instructional problems, or even to gain a better understanding of the teacher's role. Perhaps a support group should be created with the clear understanding that its main purpose is to provide reciprocal assistance between members as needed for professional empowerment. The primary advocacy of political (collective) goals, over goals related to support of activities intended to improve instructional practice, may easily persuade administrators that the group is dangerous and not worthy of support. The following practical suggestions are intended to encourage teachers to explore the possibility of developing local support groups:

1. Identify a small group (four or five) of teachers interested in monthly meetings to share ideas about teaching.
2. Convoke the first meeting to explore the chemistry of the group, along with a discussion of common concerns and interests.
3. Propose the creation of a brief statement describing the purpose of meeting, any educational philosophies shared by the group, types of activities contemplated, frequency and organizational format for meetings, and expected outcomes.
4. Early on, identify a practical, small, and well-focused task to be accomplished by the group, and get to work.
5. Explore creative approaches for engaging the group in discussion of ideas, new readings, classroom experiences, views about school and children, and general job satisfaction.
6. From time to time, reflect on the group's accomplishments and share your views with other members.

Groups of teachers, often assisted by researchers and other consultants, get together periodically to offer each other unique opportunities for professional growth and for the acquisition of important new knowledge. Participation in these groups is not easy. Paley (1986) describes the instructions she received and her experiences as follows:

> There are no right or wrong answers. Get everyone talking and then find connections—person-to-person, person-to-book. The advice was sound: do the required reading, ask most of the questions, and manage to connect a number of the ideas that arise at each meeting. Unfortunately, I did not fare too well; something was missing from my performance—a simple ingredient called *curiosity*. I was not truly interested in the people sitting around the table or curious about what they might think or say. Mainly, I wanted to keep the discussion moving and to avoid awkward silences (Paley, 1986:18).

It is not easy for these groups to share honest information about daily events, for many reasons. Teachers may feel they are in competition with each other, and

that sharing problems is tantamount to recognizing deficiencies in one's own performance. Beyond lack of confidence in performance, teaching may become so
stressful that talking about it is painful and emotionally taxing. Consider the following situation as an example of some problems discussed in a teacher support
group. It consists of excerpts from field notes taken by this author during a research
project in a local elementary school.

## TEACHERS REFLECT TOGETHER:
## A CASE STUDY

I had been coming to Grove Elementary School for almost a year. I knew all
of the teachers in the bilingual program and had several of them as students at the
university. I felt comfortable with them and thought they liked me too. We had
been meeting once a month for 8 months, at their request, to discuss the problems
of linguistic minority students in class, especially those in the bilingual classrooms.
The meetings took place after classes in a comfortable lounge, where coffee and
cookies were served. The group started with eight teachers but gradually was reduced
to six: two Anglo women, two Mexican American women, one Mexican American
man, and a Spanish-speaking black Caribbean woman.

They acted most affectionate with each other and opened up the meeting with
casual comments about events that had taken place recently or were coming up.
The discussion of classroom problems was originally focused on children known
to several of them. They would provide rich descriptions of classroom conflicts in
which children were involved: fights, unresponsiveness, distractions, and so on.
Some anecdotes were amusing and were shared in a good spirit of affection for the
children. No teacher would talk about serious matters in front of the others. They
would rather spend the time discussing readings and general matters than sharing
personal concerns.

About 6 months after the meetings had started, in a situation where the teachers
and I would get together or see each other for reasons related to a research project
(not to offer assistance of any kind), the meetings began to change: they lasted
longer, and teachers, one by one, began to open up and share very painful experiences during the course of the year. The black Caribbean teacher, an attractive
and articulate young woman, and the first black teacher in the school, described a
personal experience as follows:

> I leave my backdoor open to my room and the fourth and fifth graders play and
> a lot of the days I'll hear, "Nigger, nigger, nigger, nigger, nigger, nigger!"
> My first year here I couldn't take it, I could not take it. I remember one day I
> had my door open and I heard this boy saying it and, he said it good and loud,
> I think he probably knew my door was open, I thought he knew my door was
> open and he was gonna get back at me. I went charging out and I was looking
> all around, I was looking for that kid—five hundred kids on the playground—

and I was looking for this kid who said that and sure enough I got him and I said, "You, right there, against the wall!" "But, but, but," he started this big thing, "Well, that's what my Mom said." I said, "I don't care how ignorant your parents are, I don't care." . . . I told him, "Well, you say whatever you want to say, this and that. You can say stupid or whatever, but you don't call people names talking about their color." I laid the kid out like he was a twenty-five year old person and understood x, y, z. He was only in fifth grade, about ten years old. . . . I still see that kid and I talk to him and I feel really bad.

Other teachers began to share their problems. They freely spoke of their home situations, and how they would have trouble sleeping at night because they were thinking about specific children who would not respond. A second-grade teacher, also in tears, pulled out of her pocket a little note which was passed around. The note was written by a Spanish-speaking girl: "Ojala y muera (I wish I was dead)." The teacher commented: "Rosa Maria just sits in a corner and does not talk to anybody in any language. I do not know what to do." Teachers began to console each other and make funny comments in an attempt to inject some humor after the depressing events described.

In the next session the teachers, with humor but also somewhat angry, discussed the recent mandate from the principal (on behalf of the Superintendent). It was: "The use of Spanish on the school premises is forbidden except for instructional purposes during bilingual classes." The purpose of the ordinance was to "prevent division and miscommunication." It really was, in the teachers' view, an attempt to control the flow of information and the political cohesiveness of the bilingual teachers (12 of 26 were bilingual teachers and fluent speakers of both Spanish and English).

Meetings began to focus on curriculum matters and joint projects, while urgent concerns would occasionally be vented. The readings and theoretical discussions decreased as curriculum projects took up the teachers' time, but they became more focused on useful purposes. The group members began to see each other socially outside of school and to offer each other personal support when they needed it.

## CONCLUDING REMARKS

This chapter has focused on the need for teachers to become professionally empowered in a time of educational crises and political upheavals. Teachers' share concerns over the school learning environment that affect the quality of instruction. Concerns such as equity and cultural sensitivity of peers, superiors, and community were presented. The chapter discussed the dilemma faced by teachers regarding linguistic and/or political socialization of students; that is, to what extent educational problems can be solved by teaching minority children to speak the language of mainstream children, in the absence of other equally necessary skills and knowledge. Extremely important to modern teachers is their concern for the bureaucratic controls of curriculum and teaching methods, and their need for additional flexibility and support. We also discussed teachers' strong feelings about becoming an active part of a constructive reform effort, rather than passively perpetuating the social order on behalf of a meritocratic elite.

A discussion of teachers' individual concerns for the quality of their classroom learning environments and academic activities was presented. Teachers' somewhat handicapped condition in a public educational system that postulates both mass and compulsory education was discussed. As a consequence of our system, many students do not have the commitment to learn; they see the curriculum and instructional methods as irrelevant or unwanted, and consequently become disruptive. Some practical suggestions were made in this chapter, including the development of local support groups whose main function is to facilitate teachers' professional empowerment in order to cope with modern educational challenges. To maintain effective and fruitful support groups it takes a great deal of trust, as well as a serious investment of time and energy in interpersonal relationships. The instrumental, and almost invisible, role of the principal is essential. The principal should provide rewards to teachers' groups and foster cooperativeness as a working model for all school personnel. While doing so, the principal must protect this group from expending their energies on matters that are less relevant to professional development and instructional improvement. However, the principal must respect the autonomy of these groups and treat them as colleagues in decision-making matters.

## RECOMMENDED EXERCISES

1. Take your notes from all previous exercises—field notes, reports on activities, classes attended, readings—and ask yourself one or two fundamental questions organized into components. These questions should reflect your present thinking about the issues you have been discussing in class. Define your terms and articulate the issue, its components, and its significance; then proceed to write about them. Your synthesis and current thoughts must reflect primarily your own views and experience rather than what you have read. These experiences should include the discussions you have had with friends, teachers, and minority students themselves.

2. After you have finished the first assignment, analyze your thoughts in contrast with some of the readings you did during the course. What are the major disagreements? Where do you feel that your insights make more sense in attempts to analyze the educational problems of minority students, the low quality of instruction by their teachers, or the inherent structural problems of the schools as social institutions? Your experience and knowledge must be brought to bear on the theoretical positions you have examined, and you must attempt to restructure, qualify, or change the reasoning you found in print.

3. Organize a small group of students, perhaps four or five, to discuss the results of the two previous assignments. Listen to what they have to say.

After giving an opportunity to each of your peers to express his or her thoughts, describe and contrast your own findings and your current theoretical direction (as distinct from any in print). Negotiate with your peers some areas of consensus and any mutually reinforcing insights into the problems discussed. Write up a cooperative joint summary and share it with other groups.

## RECOMMENDED READINGS

Ada, 1986
Cheng, 1987
Cohen, 1984
Cummins, 1983, 1984, 1986
DeVos, 1973, 1980, 1983
Erickson, 1987
Everhart, 1987
Gibson, 1987a,b
Giroux and McLaren, 1986
Gold and Tempes, 1987
Jones, 1976
Martin, 1985
McDermott, 1987a,b
Meier, 1986
Ogbu 1974, 1978, 1987a,b
Paley, 1986
Rosen, 1985
Rueda, 1987
Shulman, 1987a,b
Sockett, 1987
Tharp and Gallimore, in press
Trueba, 1987a,b
Wise, 1987

# CHAPTER 7

# Program Execution: Planning, Implementation, and Evaluation

It is certainly important to recognize, as in previous chapters, the demographic, sociolinguistic, and cultural characteristics of linguistic minority populations, along with their special needs, problems, and hopes, and the attempts by school personnel to serve them. It is also important to understand the political undercurrents and legal mandates that inspire specific instructional approaches on behalf of minorities. But all of the above would have no significance if an educational program never became a reality. Therefore, we must turn our attention to the process of program execution itself in each of its three main phases: planning, implementation, and evaluation.

## THE NATURE OF THE PROGRAM EXECUTION PROCESS

The three phases of execution are intimately related as integral components of a single, indivisible, and continuing process. Furthermore, this dynamic process consists of cycles of planning–implementation–evaluation units in which the last phase of a previous cycle determines the direction of the first phase in the next cycle. This process is so essential to a good program that if the planning–implementation–evaluation cycles were terminated due to unpredicted circumstances, the program would also be terminated or its effectiveness seriously compromised. Consequently, a deeper understanding of the linkages between phases is needed for program organizers to succeed. To discuss the nature of these phases of program execution some clarification of terms is in order.

### Basic Concepts

Planning, the first phase of the program execution process, consists of preliminary organizational efforts aimed at developing a holistic concept of the program based on a theoretical framework (pedagogical foundations), an overall curriculum design with its methodological approaches and short- and long-term goals (program's expected impact), and the particular delivery modes (terms of language use and distribution). This phase clarifies the relationship of delivery modes to the general curriculum design and its pedagogical foundations. The selection of instructional methods (including delivery modes) refers to the incremental steps required to implement the curriculum design.

Implementation, the second phase, consists of the chronological transition from plans to practice. The timely realization of plans, which is at the heart of the execution process, involves accomplishing each of the tasks planned for each step:

1. Recruitment and selection of instructional personnel on the basis of criteria developed in the previous phase.
2. Identification of the eligible pool of students and their selection in accordance with previously discussed criteria.
3. Preparation of facilities in light of student needs and the curriculum design chosen.
4. Coordination with other school programs focused on the same student population, especially with regard to instructional activities and staff responsibilities.
5. Definition of management responsibilities and their structural distribution in the school system.
6. Development of fiscal accountability and other administrative controls.
7. Development of internal monitoring systems by which peers and superiors share information and assistance.
8. Development of locally appropriate methods to assess instructional effectiveness systematically.

Additional considerations relevant to the politics of implementation and evaluation will be discussed below. The purpose of presenting these concepts now is to establish the broad parameters for the discussion of the process of execution.

Evaluation, the third and final organizational phase, consists of global assessment of the extent to which the curriculum design has been implemented, its effectiveness, teacher and student performance, and differential impact on students. Student performance is measured not only by standardized instruments but also in local and individual contexts, specifically in content areas of the curriculum, and with reference to students' intellectual and emotional growth. Evaluation aims to describe the various levels of student participation and performance, as well as significant outcomes. However, the implementation of a curriculum design must focus on the support given to teachers during the execution of instructional tasks called for in the curriculum design. Teacher-assisted performance is most important for program success. Assisted performance requires the development of mechanisms to monitor progress, to collect data on student and teacher performance, and to generate recommendations for improvement.

Evaluation methodology can include observational methods (including video-

and audiotaping techniques in the natural setting) and others that help teachers to understand the participation and performance levels of students undergoing cultural and linguistic transition. Final evaluations are generally based on the accomplishment of established goals, and systematic assessment is made of actual outcomes and performance in contrast to expected outcomes and performance. Program evaluation could answer questions regarding the role of teachers in fostering meaningful and active student participation in instructional activities where congruence between activities and students' cultural values is maximized.

The curriculum design is expected to be demonstrably functional for students' linguistic and cognitive skill levels. The intent of the evaluation is not to maintain the status quo of curriculum designs and teaching styles, but to search for new ways to maximize students' learning. Consequently, a departure from a planned curriculum created with insufficient knowledge about students' skill levels or incorrect assumptions regarding parental/community support can be viewed as a good decision. For example, if the mode of delivery chosen as appropriate for a group of students was sheltered English, but under closer scrutiny students seem to need additional development in the home language, the curriculum can be modified accordingly to extend the home language development period.

Because the discussion of program execution can be more useful to the reader if a specific example is given, the case of an elementary bilingual education program curriculum design will be described later in the chapter. This discussion will also permit the author to raise issues of linkage between the curriculum design and the need to give teachers all the support they need to implement such a design in the context of local language policies. The evaluation phase, going beyond the assessment of outcomes, will underline qualitative approaches that are more suitable for examining the process of instruction. Finally, some recommendations are offered to aid practitioners in dealing effectively with program execution tasks.

## The Micropolitics of Program Execution

From their inception, linguistic minority education programs are frequently and inherently torn between diametrically opposing political philosophies. One of the fundamental reasons for their volatility is that these programs have come into existence not as an effort to implement "an agreed upon sound educational policy," but as a political compromise, not universally accepted or based on unquestioned pedagogical assumptions. Indeed, some groups support minority programs on the basis of deficit views of minority education. From their perspective, instructional designs should be remedial and compensatory, and their funding short-term, carefully controlled by federal and state agencies, and allocated competetively with other equally deserving causes. Therefore, planning and implementing minority student programs is often done by a central district (or state) office without consulting teachers. The program plan conforms to the government's most current (and often changing) interpretation of the rules and regulations. Naturally, failure to comply with this interpretation can seriously jeopardize funding. There are also other problems with such programs: their short-term and compensatory character makes them fail and cast a stigma on students. Other groups, however, support linguistic minority programs as a long-term enriching experience not only for minorities but also for mainstream students (see Chapter 3 and the discussion of the theoretical framework, especially the discussion of "subtractive" and "additive" bilingualism originally opened by Lambert, 1975, and followed up by the work of Cummins 1981, 1983, 1986, and Gold & Tempes, 1987). Long-term enrichment programs that capitalize on students' sociocultural background and knowledge are considered the most logical solution to minority underachievement. Contrary to what happens in short-term special remedial programs for minorities, which are inherently intrusive into the regular curriculum, long-term enrichment programs are an integral part of the mainstream curriculum and do not interfere with instructional designs for mainstream children.

Differences of opinion and philosophy are not the only problems. Some schools have multiple sources of funding with a very complex set of requirements and opposing assumptions, all affecting the same children: bilingual education Title VII federal programs, migrant education, special education, compensatory programs, enrichment programs, private foundations programs, research monies for experimental interventions, and others. No wonder teachers and principals feel overwhelmed with the paperwork and tend to view some of these programs as an organizational nightmare. This problem of teacher attitude is compounded by the "cellular isolation" of teachers (alluded to by Shulman, 1987a), the lack of coordination at the school level, and the pressure on districts to pursue multiple funding from state and federal agencies.

## Coping with Political Pressure

To handle the multiple political issues associated with the process of program execution, some school districts have hired able lawyers and accountants who have then assumed responsibilities beyond their areas of expertise. They have often taken over the whole execution process, seizing central fiscal and managerial control over the programs, and have been given the responsibility for producing all documentation requested by funding agencies relevant to program implementation and evaluation. Needless to say, this strategy, originally intended to protect school personnel and free teachers from political pressure, now has the disadvantage of giving to central office (district, or state) personnel the power to make commitments, on behalf of teachers, and to establish programs seen by teachers as potentially incompatible with other programs, or with the existing curriculum design and educational philosophy. Programs are often unsuitable for the linguistic minority students in question, or lack cost-effectiveness. In some cases, to add insult to injury, the funds obtained for linguistic minorities are used for other unrelated school purposes without penalty, through a clever fiscal system of fund combination and the lack of appropriate federal and state fiscal controls.

## Assisting Teachers' and Children's Performance

Let us assume, for the time being, that the program originators are school-based and that they have enough freedom to plan and implement a program for a well-defined linguistic minority population whose needs have already been assessed and whose support has been obtained. A number of political considerations still rightfully belong in the execution process from the very planning stages to the final evaluation. These considerations affect the entire program execution and the conception of the curriculum, its short- and long-term language policy and academic goals, the specific selection of methodologies, mode of delivery (through the home language, sheltered English, or mainstream English; see Chapter 3), choice of personnel, the criteria for recruitment and admission of eligible students, the identification of curriculum materials, the organization of space for specific instructional activities, the use of time, and the sequence of expected outcomes at set intervals in the curriculum.

In fact, the attitudes of community members and school personnel toward the use of languages other than English can drastically affect the instructional options available. Community politics—for example, conflicts between members of ethnic communities and mainstream populations—have resulted in the closure of some bilingual programs in California and Texas. The chemistry of relationships between advocates of bilingual programs and representatives of mainstream communities has a great deal to do with the smooth handling of political problems in program implementation. Temporary victories in the establishment of unwanted programs (forced into use against the will of strong local community feelings) are ephemeral and can turn into destructive ventures for children in the long run if their achievement is lower than expected. Bilingual programs, if well integrated in the school curriculum and available to nonminority students, become recognized as truly enriching for all and a good long-term investment in the future of the country. At the same time they become both emotionally and intellectually rewarding for teachers and children. The future success of minority programs may well depend upon the fortitude and imagination of innovators, who quietly pursue theoretically sound instructional practices while avoiding political controversy. Some creative principals take the role of innovators and walk through the minefield of politically divisive factions with the support of their teachers and community. Their concern for children's futures and their commitment to nurture effective teachers seems to give them the strength and inspiration necessary to accomplish tough tasks. Their work is characterized by Vygotskian assisted performance.

We must remind ourselves that educational ventures on behalf of linguistic minority students are long-term investments (especially when minorities come from socially isolated groups), and generally do not demonstrate genuine success in a short period of time. Even when we have reasons to claim success after some short-term experiment, we know that the long-term effects on students' overall adjustment to society, achievement in high school years, college, and career performance, and other manifestations of success await the test of time.

# A Fictitious School and Community Setting

This fictitious school, called Santa Eulalia Elementary School, is located in a southwestern city, let us call it San Simeon, of about half a million people, in a distressed downtown area characterized by high crime and rapid sociocultural change. The total student population is around 500, with 200 (40 percent) English-speaking students and 300 (60 percent) speakers of three other languages; from the latter 300 (60 percent) approximately 275 (55 percent) speak a single language "A," 15 other children speak language "B," and 10 speak "C" (the latter two groups constituting the remaining 5 percent).

The parents of language "A" speakers are newcomers to this country, monolingual in their native language, and hold low-skill occupations, including low-status part-time jobs that last for only several weeks at a time. It is believed that about one-third of the "A" speakers are undocumented workers. At least half of the English-speaking children come from families living outside of downtown San Simeon, in various locations characterized by higher economic status, and they are bused in; the other families live in downtown San Simeon. You are the new principal and have received clear orders from the Superintendent to organize a bilingual program, within a year, in language "A" and in English. What do you do?

## THE PLANNING PHASE

We can distinguish three components in the planning phase:

1. Setting preliminary conditions for effective planning
2. Generating a sound conception of an instructional program
3. Identifying strategies for implementation within set limitations of time and space

As we discuss the preliminary conditions for planning, the fictitious school and community must be considered, so that we can deal with concrete planning issues and raise questions about the significance of this planning phase for overall program success.

## Preliminary Conditions for Planning

Preliminary planning conditions include the organization of a planning committee and a description of its responsibilities. One such responsibility is a language survey, which is part of the overall needs assessment of linguistic minority students. Next come the recruitment and selection of teachers and teachers' aides, identification of eligible students, search for appropriate facilities, and development of a management structure to run the program. These matters will be dealt with briefly so we may concentrate our discussion on the central issues of instructional program design, its goals, curriculum, and pedagogical principles. The following is an exemplary strategy.

Find out who among your colleagues has the best bilingual program in the city. Pay a visit to him or her and ask for names of expert teachers, program directors, and other consultants. Visit the program and get a clear sense of its organization and logistics. Request documents and read them carefully so that you can ask appropriate questions regarding management and instructional design. Your first job is to organize a competent, hard-working, and congenial planning committee that will be responsible for gathering all the information necessary to start the bilingual program. You will want to appoint to this committee some of your best teachers, especially those in grades K–3, two or three bilingual parents who speak "A" and English and have leadership skills, experts from other schools, and one or two community leaders.

Your goal is to create a closely knit working team that is committed to discharging its planning responsibilities with the maximum expediency and the widest possible support. This committee has the following responsibilities:

1. Conduct a language survey.
2. Develop criteria for students' entry and exit.
3. Develop criteria for recruitment of teachers and other staff.
4. Identify facilities and other resources needed.
5. Recommend a management structure for the program.
6. Conceive of the specific instructional design and the steps required to implement it.

After consultation with some experts, this committee could first conduct a language survey of all Santa Eulalia students and their families to determine self-reported language proficiency, number of children fluent in both language "A" and English, number of limited English proficient (LEP) children, residential patterns and mobility, and relative willingness of families to place their children in a bilingual program. The accuracy of this survey is essential for implementation decisions to be made. It is important to know, for example, the number of groups to be enrolled the following year, the incremental addition of new groups, the number of children per group within a given instructional design, and the expected outcomes of the program over a period of 3–5 years.

Let us further suppose that your committee successfully finds that 230 of the "A" speakers are LEP, but 200 of them attend grades K–5. The committee also finds that the 200 English-speaking children are equally distributed from kindergarten through grade 6, between 28 and 30 per grade, and that about 100 of these children, 90 of them in grades 2–4, are permitted by their parents to participate in the "A"–English bilingual program. Therefore, the comparative distribution of eligible "A" and English speakers is as shown in Table 7.1.

Furthermore, your planning committee finds that "A"-speaking parents are

**Table 7.1.   RESULTS OF SAMPLE LANGUAGE SURVEY**

| Grade | Language group | |
|---|---|---|
| | "A" | English |
| K | 50 | 10 |
| 1 | 40 | 30 |
| 2 | 35 | 30 |
| 3 | 25 | 15 |
| 4 | 20 | 10 |
| 5 | 15 | 5 |
| 6 | — | — |
| Total | 200 | 100 |

extremely enthusiastic about having their children in bilingual programs. The committee has also identified documents from surrounding schools with bilingual education programs, with a sample curriculum for grades K–4 and information related to entry and exit criteria. The committee, originally composed of 12 people, has been reduced to about 8 people after 2 months of work, but the group continues to meet periodically with you, the principal. You feel full of creative inspiration and are determined to develop the best bilingual program in San Simeon. The committee has been divided into a public relations subcommittee, a curriculum subcommittee, and an instructional design subcommittee. You have now regrouped your entire committee and are ready to move to the next stage of the planning phase.

## Conception of the Curriculum Design

You remind the committee that the selection of the curriculum design must conform to three basic criteria:

1. The design must meet the linguistic, cultural, and academic needs of the students served collectively and, to the extent possible, individually.
2. It must reflect a relative consensus among the school personnel regarding basic educational philosophy, pedagogical principles, and values.
3. It must be based on a realistic assessment of the resources available and those to be obtained.

Your committee reviews the options available and possible decisions to be made regarding local adaptation of existing program models, wrestling with a number of issues such as the mode of delivery (the percentage of time to be given to language "A" and to sheltered or mainstream English), the ratio of speakers of "A" to English-speaking students per class, the separation of languages by means of different instructors with a clearly established schedule, policies regarding admission to and exit from the program, distribution of committee tasks via subcommittees and timetables, and the strategies used to recruit additional teachers and aides as supplements or replacements for existing teachers. You ask the committee to present a statement of policy recommending the guiding principles of the program to be established. Here is a summary of their recommendations and understandings:

1. The main purpose of the program, which has a transitional component for LEP children and an enrichment component for English-speaking children, is to help linguistic minorities integrate into the social system through active participation in school and academic achievement. In order to accomplish this purpose, two main objectives of the bilingual program have been proposed: to provide LEP children with "comprehensible input" in the home language and assist them in the acquisition of communicative and literacy skills in English required for achievement in school, and to help LEP children develop the critical thinking skills required for academic achievement that can be shown by active participation in academic activities.
2. A complementary and yet integral part of the entire program is the enrichment component, whose purpose is to offer some native English-speaking children the opportunity to acquire literacy and communicative skills in language "A" as well as in English.
3. The end result for linguistic minority children and for mainstream children must be "additive" bilingualism (as discussed in Chapter 3).

It is felt that the combination of transitional and enrichment components for LEP–mainstream children in approximate ratios of 60/40 is a healthy way of preventing social and psychological isolation of minority students. Furthermore, the committee has seen the need to establish the following guiding principles and policy statements, in an effort to arrive at a specific instructional design that can obtain the best results for speakers of both "A" and English, as well as to maximize support from school administrators, teachers, community representatives, and state authorities:

1. Use of the two languages may be clearly separated by schedule and by instructors, each associated only with one language.
2. All students in grades K and 1 (speakers of language "A" as well those of English) should be given ample opportunity to develop their home language, and may receive instruction at least 80 percent of the time in that language.
3. Grades 2 and 3 may offer LEP students the opportunity for greater exposure to sheltered or mainstream English, and consequently about 40 percent of the time instruction could be conducted in sheltered English or mainstream English. English-speaking children may also be permitted to increase their exposure to language "A" at about the same percentage.
4. Grade 4 may increase the second language instruction for LEP and their

peers to about 50 percent, using sheltered English as a means to transition to mainstream English. The use of both languages could alternate within some subject matter, without overlapping content.

5. Teachers, aides, and other staff members of the bilingual program can be assisted by an advisory committee and by other means to form a cohesive working team, and periodic in-service training may be provided to the entire group.

6. The program can start in grades K–4, with 8 bilingual classes of about 30 students each. They must try to combine children from both major linguistic groups, "A" and English, in as many activities as possible.

7. Since some LEP children may be ready to engage in mainstream English in most subjects by the fourth grade, it is important that they be permitted to retain mastery of their home language, through optional class in home language arts.

The actual proposed distribution of children in the eight groups is now as shown in Table 7.2.

With this information in mind, the planning committee develops the program organization in its structural details of subject matter, time and activities, as well as in other details of the curriculum. Committee members examine curriculum samples and organize subcommittees to explore possible adaptations of the best curricula. The LEP component of the instructional design, which represents a compromise with the broadest support, is presented in Table 7.3. A full understanding of the logistics requires further explanation.

Because one of the principles stated by the committee has been that of "comprehensible input" and language separation, it is necessary to request facilities with either two rooms for each of the eight classroom bilingual groups, or at the very least for a grade 2–3 combination and for grades 4–6. It is thought that the K–1 combination could operate within the same room, with some dividers to separate each of the learning centers.

**Table 7.2.    RELATIVE DISTRIBUTION OF SPEAKERS OF LANGUAGE "A" AND ENGLISH (E) IN EIGHT CLASSROOMS K–4**

| | Classroom groups | | | | | | | |
| | a | | b | | c | | d | |
| | A | E | A | E | A | E | A | E |
|---|---|---|---|---|---|---|---|---|
| K–1 | 22 | 10 | 22 | 10 | 23 | 10 | 23 | 10 |
| 2–3 | 20 | 15 | 20 | 15 | 20 | 15 | | |
| 4 | 20 | 10 | | | | | | |

**Table 7.3. BILINGUAL EDUCATION PROGRAM AT SANTA EULALIA ELEMENTARY SCHOOL, K-6 LEP COMPONENT**

**K-1**

| Time | Activity |
|---|---|
| 9:00– 9:15 | Opening activities |
| 9:15–10:00 | Language arts in language "A" by learning centers |
| 10:00–10:15 | Physical education |
| 10:15–11:00 | Mathematics |
| 11:00–11:15 | Recess |
| 11:15–11:35 | Social studies, music, art in learning centers |
| 11:35–12:00 | English language arts / Dismissal of kindergarten |
| 12:00– 1:00 | Lunch and recreation for first grade |
| 1:00– 2:00 | Story telling, writing, reading |
| 2:00– 2:30 | Physical education |

**2-3**

| Time | Activity |
|---|---|
| 9:00– 9:15 | Opening activities |
| 9:15–10:30 | Writing and painting, language arts in language "A" / Reading and spelling |
| 10:30–11:00 | Social studies, music, art |
| 11:00–11:15 | Recess |
| 11:15–12:15 | Mathematics and science |
| 12:15– 1:00 | Lunch and recess |
| 1:00– 2:15 | English language arts |
| 2:15– 2:30 | Physical education / Dismissal of second grade |
| 2:30– 3:00 | Writing for third grade |

**4-6**

| Time | Activity |
|---|---|
| 9:00– 9:15 | Opening activities |
| 9:15–10:30 | Language arts in language "A," reading, grammar in learning centers |
| 10:30–11:00 | Social studies, science, health in learning centers |
| 11:00–11:15 | Recess |
| 11:15–12:15 | Mathematics |
| 12:15– 1:00 | Lunch |
| 1:00– 2:00 | English language arts, reading, grammar, spelling |
| 2:00– 2:30 | Music, art |
| 2:30– 3:00 | Physical education |

Legend: , English , Language "A" , Use of Language "A" and sheltered English

166

## Planning Implementation Strategies

Table 7.3 does not tell the full story. English-speaking children in the K–1 combination classrooms have an instructional design that mirrors that of LEP children. The committee, however, is ready to discuss implementation strategies and urges you to move on with the task. The completion of the instructional design has taken them several months, and it is already February. Your intent is to start hiring new teachers in April, notify parents about program admission in May, and have the student groups organized by the end of the summer. Committee members submit the following order of priorities to you for implementation:

1. Obtain Superintendent's approval for new and/or replacement bilingual teacher positions.
2. Announce positions through all possible means, including newspapers and telephone calls.
3. Send notices to parents of eligible children (speakers of both "A" and English) to obtain their signatures of approval and intention to have their children participate in the bilingual program.
4. Inspect facilities and make arrangements to house the eight bilingual education classes suitably for the proposed instructional design.
5. Order all the required materials in language "A" and in English congruent with committee recommendations.
6. Work with current teachers to determine the composition of bilingual classroom groups for the following year.
7. Schedule meetings with current teachers to maximize support for the program and resolve potential organizational conflicts, as well as to clarify distribution of responsibilities.

## IMPLEMENTATION PHASE

There is a fine line between the planning and implementation phases. In practice, one starts where the other ends; often implementation tasks must be undertaken without discontinuing planning activities. However, after the first day of school the focus switches dramatically and signals action; but even at this point, future planning should not stop. Planning should rest on the findings and recommendations of the evaluation, which will be discussed below. The first day of class for the new program can be traumatic, even after extensive planning. Much of the trauma, however, may be minimized if you as principal have developed a good working relationship with at least some of the teachers who will be involved in the new program. It is important for the principal to take time to hold discussions with the program teachers, individually and collectively, about the specific goals of the program, the details of curriculum delivery, and some means to anticipate problems and resolve them.

The phase of implementation formally starts at Santa Eulalia Elementary School with staff meetings held a week before the first day of instruction. At this time you, the principal, have already hired and organized your program staff: a program director, eight teachers who speak the ''A'' language and eight English-speaking teachers, and/or eight teachers' aides. Lack of staffing (or of qualified staffing) can be a serious problem. If you have not been able to hire sufficient staff for all eight bilingual groups planned, you must adjust plans to accommodate existing resources, reducing the scope of efforts for the first year. You must meet with the planning committee to thank them for their invaluable contribution and invite selected members to stay on as members of a bilingual education advisory committee. This committee should be consulted if resources do not seem to warrant the scope of effort previously envisioned.

It is of critical importance that the first year of the bilingual program succeed in the eyes of all school personnel, children, parents, and district administrators. The principal and program director cannot take lightly any problems associated with lack of instructors, curriculum materials, or other important resources. There are, however, some ways to resolve temporary, unexpected shortages of personnel by hiring additional aides who are competent and supportive. There is always the risk that the program must continue operating with limited resources if administrators feel no pressure to augment support.

You now convoke a meeting of your advisory committee. They have come prepared to give you the following suggestions:

1. You as principal, along with the program director and teachers, should do your best to maintain the highest standards of academic work, and should create an environment charged with high levels of enthusiasm for program activities. Be ready to dramatize children's success in front of teachers, parents, and other community members.
2. Adopt a policy of open and established lines of communication with the program director, teachers, and parents.
3. Encourage the program director and teachers to hold frequent and regular meetings to discuss program problems and accomplishments, to develop an esprit de corps that will facilitate their intragroup communication and cooperation.
4. The director, with your help in the early stages, will regularly visit program activities in order to assess teachers' instructional effectiveness and children's academic progress.
5. You and the program director should structure in-service activities for teachers, along with built in opportunities for teachers to observe their peers in the classroom, to give each other feedback and support.
6. Finally, monthly meetings are recommended for you and the advisory committee during the first year.

It would be helpful at this point for you and the program director to go back momentarily to Table 7.3 and visualize one full day, from beginning to end, from the standpoint of the teacher and to propose alternative curricular approaches to the subjects covered. Then you and the director can observe teachers' actual performance more intensively, and can discuss with them any impressions and suggestions you may have.

Equally helpful would be to examine the curriculum following a single subject and its distribution over the entire academic year. The purpose of this exercise is to gain a deeper understanding of the pace and relative difficulty of teaching that the teachers must face in real situations. Knowing the details of subject delivery can help the principal handle the logistics of regrouping two language groups from time to time to change teachers, peers, subject matter, or the linguistic and cultural context of the instruction.

Program execution is a continuing process that does not end with implementation, but occurs daily in new and different contexts from those in previous years. With new groups of students, there is always a need to keep learning how to communicate more effectively with students, and how to engage them in learning activities. At the very heart of teachers' personal and professional survival is the need to remain active learners, to continue to reflect on daily teaching practices, and to enhance their critical thinking skills. Program implementation can significantly help teachers attain their goals of becoming better learners and reflective teachers.

Reflective classroom interaction also leads to better assessment of teaching effectiveness and better planning for the future. The role of teachers in self-regulated monitoring of teaching effectiveness must begin during the implementation phase. Incremental improvements in the quality of instruction must be noticed and recorded. But the greatest opportunity to improve teaching comes not as a function of isolated personal reflection on one's own actions as a teacher, but as a result of exchanges with peers. Peer evaluation provides support and assistance for the teacher to grow in experience and effectiveness. The following section deals with these two aspects of implementation: personal self-observation and reflection on daily teaching, which constitute the basis for self-regulated monitoring of teaching effectiveness; and the support group activities that provide outside rewards and direction.

## Self-Regulated Monitoring of Quality Instruction

One of the main purposes for developing teachers' skills in observing, recording, and reflecting on their daily practices is to counteract the rapid, uncontainable flow of demands that lead to automatic teacher responses, formulaic interaction, and simplistic pedagogical explanations for children's academic success or failure. Recently, scholars have noted an increasing tendency to regiment curriculum at the earliest stages of children's academic career in an effort to maximize their cognitive development. Martin wrote recently:

> Kindergarten used to mean brightly colored paintings, music, clay, block building, bursting curiosity, and intensive exploration. Now the kindergarten's exuberance is being muted, its color drained and spirit flattened, leaving us with

stacks of paperwork and teacher manuals. . . . One rationale for this change is that because children grow up more rapidly in the age of TV and computers, they are ready for "skill work" earlier than they used to be. Consequently, much of the day is taken up by whole-class drill in numbers, letters, and phonics, mostly through coloring and filling in commercial workbook pages. . . . This trend toward a formalized kindergarten curriculum appears to me not only mistaken—a misunderstanding of the way young children learn—but actually counterproductive. Everything I observe in my own kindergarten class contradicts the notion that children need to be corralled at this age into abstract paper and pencil exercises in order to learn (Martin, 1985:318).

Martin could have sat quietly and followed the status quo, but her need to remain effective in assisting children to learn has persuaded her to oppose current trends. She argues that one pedagogical principle inculcated in teachers—namely, to facilitate language development in children by engaging them in intensive language use—does not square with the boring paperwork. She believes that children know what they want to learn and how, but that the structural organization of the classroom is a clear obstacle. Martin observes:

Here is Teresa in dress-up clothes—long skirt, flowery hat, and high heels— talking into the toy telephone. I have already given several notices of clean-up time, and she is the only child left in the house corner. I try to signal her to stop talking, but she pretends not to see, pointedly turning her back as she continues her conversation. Finally, rather irritated, I reach my arm around her and hang up the phone, telling her that it is time to end. Teresa is outraged. She flounces out of the house corner to the furthest limits of the room where she finds an empty spot. There she reaches for an imaginary wall phone, dials into the air, and speaks into her cupped hand. Then she hangs up with an expression of relief and comes back into the group (Martin, 1985:319).

The teacher will never know exactly what was happening, but recording the incident and reflecting on it, as well as on other similar incidents, has opened her eyes to a better understanding of what the learning needs of kindergarten children are and how these needs can be met. She observes cultural and individual differences in children, and how they construct various learning environments that are incompatible with formalized regimented instruction. Children's curiosity for animals, interest in art work (both collectively and individually accomplished), excitement for scientific experiments that challenge the laws of physics, and yearning for an unlimited exploration of the environment seems to die day by day under the weight of boring drills, paperwork, and schedules. Martin's final remarks must be taken as a serious warning for the entire teaching profession:

It is extremely difficult for individual teachers to maintain their confidence in themselves and in children's potential in the face of increasing pressures from within and outside the schools. Teachers tend to be isolated in their classrooms, and even the joy of the children's amazing vitality may not be enough to sustain us in the continual battle to preserve the autonomy necessary to maintain a lively, responsive classroom. I think it might not be possible for me to remain in such a stressful job if I did not have the support of a group of colleagues with whom I meet regularly to reflect on children and teaching (Martin, 1985:320).

Self-regulated monitoring of quality instruction starts with personal reflection and is followed by peer support group discussions, which in turn may feed into reflection for action. Some of the main activities that facilitate and/or constitute self-regulated monitoring are the following:

1. Systematic observation of daily teaching activities by bringing actions to the level of clear awareness
2. Recording of main events, describing the most significant events of the day, their patterns and personal feelings about them
3. Conscious thinking associated with these events, such as possible explanations, antecedents, and/or consequences
4. Dealing with accomplishments or problems that have been highlighted or originated by the events described.
5. Considering potential improvements to be made in the teaching practice
6. Reflection on the teacher's role, including reorganization of priorities and/or pedagogical principles learned
7. Determination of possible impact of the home situation on teaching, or of teaching on the home

Keeping brief accounts of daily teaching events requires a great deal of discipline, but it eventually pays off by providing teachers with a powerful therapeutic instrument that also stimulates their critical thinking skills, while giving them a sense of control over the flow of stressful teaching activities. Teachers' journal accounts form the basis for discussion in support groups with other colleagues who are equally in need of help.

## Teacher Support Groups

Tharp and Gallimore described the development of the Kamehameha Early Education Program and the struggles of teachers. One of the teachers said:

You don't give two weeks of workshop and have someone walk into a new classroom and a new situation and then expect them to teach reading. . . . You gotta' give them more than that. Plus, I had been sick that summer and . . . I was physically run down. Even then the first week was beautiful. But the beginning of the second week, the problems started. The kids started acting up. When the problems started, all I got was criticism. I didn't get much support. I'll never forget the day. I'll never forget the day. [Two consultants] took me up to the observation deck and say, "I want you to watch Mabel teach." I had never seen anybody teach the program, ever, ever. So I took down word for word everything she said, and [the consultant] turned to me and she says, "Now can you go in and do that? . . . You go in and do what Mabel just did" (Tharp & Gallimore, in press).

Teacher isolation is, according to some scholars, the reason for the failure of educational reform and creative programs. Isolated teachers can hardly receive the assistance they need through modeling, feedback and planning. As Tharp and Gallimore indicate,

Even in successful programs, innovation and change always cost time, anxiety and uncertainty. To develop competencies and programs under this stress, it is essential that teachers have supportive interaction with peers, technical advisors, and administrators (Tharp & Gallimore, in press).

Peer support groups do not have the same functions as social gatherings, counseling therapy sessions, evaluation teams, or pressure groups, although sometimes such characteristics do surface. The most essential function of these groups is to assist peers professionally and receive some assistance from them in relation to teaching efforts that require coordination, consensus in policy, and mutual support. Effective support groups are relatively small (three to five teachers), and consist of teachers who work in the same school (or at least school district) at the same or comparable grade levels. These groups meet regularly on a voluntary basis and are long lasting when close professional working relationships develop on the basis of mutual trust and respect. The discussion of problems and insights resulting from personal reflection of group members is not enough. Additional cooperative work about instructional activities, curriculum, or extracurricular activities is an essential component of regular meetings. Reciprocity and equity are the cornerstones of cooperative teacher efforts. If the self-regulated monitoring process makes individual teachers feel incompetent, and if they are getting nowhere with their instructional approaches, other more experienced teachers can restore self-confidence and coach junior members of the support group. Junior members, of course, have a great deal to contribute with their energy, enthusiasm, and new knowledge.

The purpose of attending teacher support groups is not only to boost morale and restore confidence but also to acquire new knowledge through the intellectual stimulation resulting from interaction with other teachers. Sharing readings, curriculum materials, personal summaries of subject-matter content, art work, and so on is the basis for the development of peer learning relationships, which lead to professional growth and success in teachers. A related purpose is to observe each other, whenever possible in the natural setting, and to give each other feedback, suggestions for additional exercises, solutions to problems, encouragement during difficulties, and credit for progress made.

It should be noted that the role of the principal in facilitating peer support groups is indispensable and requires trust and self-confidence on his or her part.

The principal should offer school facilities and other resources for those who want to get together in school, and should feel free to pay occasional visits to these groups, without interfering with their efforts or attempting to control them. As a gesture of support, the principal may want to invite outside consultants to provide in-service assistance to peer teacher groups, and to offer other incentives to participants. In summary, some of the functions and activities support groups can consider are the following:

1. Assistance and nurturance of junior teachers by more experienced colleagues
2. Resolution of common problems that require joint action, coordination, and policy agreement
3. Consensus of instructional practices that affect the work of all members; for example, agreement on required skill level or subject matter knowledge in students, policy criteria for grade promotion, handling of disciplinary problems, or dealings with students' families
4. Consultation on teaching methods, curriculum structure, coverage, or other pedagogical concerns
5. Discussion of conflicts and daily sources of stress
6. Discussion of the teacher's role and job satisfaction
7. Needs related to intellectual and professional growth and the enhancement of critical thinking skills.

Support groups should keep brief records of the most important agreements, decisions, suggestions, and issues discussed in order to review them periodically. While a support group meeting can be a life-saver for a teacher experiencing a critical period, it can also be a continuous source of inspiration for teachers at all times. In order to maximize the intended benefits of these meetings, each member of the group needs to invest time and do it generously, at least in the measure that he or she receives. Also important is the need to reflect on the group meetings, attempting to record and internalize the most stimulating and significant ideas contributed by the group. This effort to internalize must be directed toward specific personal priorities and translated into well-laid plans for action. Critical thinking must be brought into teaching practice in an incremental and well-organized manner. This requires a great deal of reflection, even when the world of classroom interaction may spin at high speeds.

When well-prepared, reflective teachers have identified the issues, problems, solutions, trends, and needs, the transition from the implementation to the evaluation phase is made easier and more useful.

Tharp and Gallimore (in press) suggest a number of specific training components that can be the focus of peer group support. These components may take as long as 5 working days and consequently must be planned with the support of the principal and other administrators. The following examples have been adapted from Tharp and Gallimore's work. One component focuses on principles of behavior management, in which trainees are given reading tasks from books and journals and the training consultant directs the discussion of readings and their application to classroom activities. The use of videotape is highly recommended as an aid in focusing the discussion of application of principles.

Another component focuses on modeling and role-playing. Videotapes of teachers illustrating specific behavioral management techniques are viewed and those same techniques are then practiced for a few minutes. Each trainee may also profit from obtaining specific feedback on her or his own videotaped performance. Further detailed analysis of one's own teaching behavior may become part of the training sessions.

A more intrusive and unusual component, but one that is often helpful, is "direct coaching in the classroom" via a wireless microphone. This permits the consultant to guide teacher trainees, praise them, and establish a two-way communication. One of the teachers commented about this method:

> I remember one thing that stands out. K [the consultant] put an ear-piece in our ears. He was up on the observation deck. He could talk to us and we could hear him. He would tell us what to look for and where to go in the classroom. I always thought that was really strange. It was a really unusual experience, because half the time I was tapping the ear-piece and saying, "I can't hear you." The sound quality was very bad. The kids would look at me like, "It's God talking to Mrs. A" (Tharp & Gallimore, in press).

Feedback and continuous communication in the support groups are central elements. Teacher trainees need frequent praise, concrete individual goals, awareness of their progress, and proof of it.

## EVALUATION PHASE

The evaluation phase, as distinct from informal monitoring, which is part of the implementation phase, is discussed here in three parts.

1. The concept and purpose of evaluation: This part discusses evaluation as a concept and deals with its various components in the context of linguistic minority education programs.
2. Method, content, and focus of the evaluation: Of all the areas of concern, the ones requiring more attention are delineated. Given the purpose and focus of the evaluation, the most appropriate methods are discussed.
3. Risks and limitations of evaluation: This discussion covers the constraints and political compromises inherent in state and federal evaluations.

Evaluation research is a very extensive area with applications to many fields. In education, evaluation has attracted the attention of policy makers and government officials because it has become an indispensable instrument in the business of managing educational programs. Evaluation research and its application to social and educational issues has focused on the politics of evaluation (Rossi & Wright, 1977), the procedures for conducting evaluations in specific settings (Levine et al., 1981), the biases in the process (Berk, 1983), the requirements for good evaluative designs (Cronbach, 1982; Freeman & Rossi, 1984; Rossi & Freeman, 1985), and the basic theoretical principles specific to the education of linguistic minorities (Cummins, 1981b, 1983, 1986; Gold & Tempes, 1987). Recent work by educational anthropologists using ethnographic methods for evaluation have pointed out that evaluation of state or federal programs is often contaminated by theoretical assumptions in service to political positions, resulting in the "blamed victim" syndrome of some mandated evaluations. Fetterman (1983), in describing the situation of several programs for "disadvantaged youth," feels that the federal government adopts the cultural-deprivation theory, which attributes poor academic performance of some minority groups to a "pathology of home environment," and on this assumption program activities must be organized and evaluated:

> Programs based on this assumption attempt to change children's lives, e.g., their language and even their parents' pattern of child rearing. The child is often referred to as "disadvantaged" and "socially deprived." This is usually the reason cited for failure to learn in school (Fetterman, 1983:67).

Consequently, the evaluator does not generate questions to inquire about the rat-infested school buildings, unreadable textbooks, unsafe environments, frightened teachers, lack of ventilation and light, insensitive and prejudicial behavior of administrators, meaningless and irrelevant curriculum, meager economic support, and general chaos in many schools for minority children. If children do not learn in those environments, it must be their fault, and the evaluator must find out what else is wrong with them or their families, and how to fix it. The nature of mandated evaluations and their inherent risks are many, and they should be openly discussed by the principal, school personnel, and evaluation team.

## Evaluating Linguistic Minority Education Programs

In contrast to continuing informal in-house assessments or the monitoring of effective program operation, an evaluation is a formal, rigorous, systematic, and focused assessment of a program in essential areas. Such areas include the adequacy of instructional design, the accountability of instructional staff to the director and principal, the fulfillment of goals and objectives within the established time frame, and the cooperation of children and their families with program activities.

The purpose of the program's annual or final formal evaluation, if required by the funding agency, is clearly defined in the agency's guidelines and is presumably used as an instrument for making decisions about continuation of the program, changes in funding level, or a simple stamp of approval at the termination of program activities. To raise questions about the nature of evaluation, let us assume that, regardless of prescribed guidelines and potential political uses or abuses of evaluation, school personnel and the evaluation team have come to a combined decision that the fundamental purpose of linguistic minority program evaluation is to assess its genuine effectiveness and to discern the areas requiring attention. To put the program's effectiveness into its sociopolitical context, the evaluators must understand why and how a program was created, how its organization functions, and what the goals and objectives of program activities are. In order to identify the areas requiring attention, a series of questions must be generated.

In the case of Santa Eulalia, let us further assume that the program has been well conceptualized and implemented by a competent program director and teachers, and that its daily progress has been monitored so that most of the expected results have been obtained. How is the inquiry organized, what methods are to be used, and how is the focus going to be selected?

## Ethnographic Techniques in Evaluation

Ethnographic techniques, such as participant observation, interviews, video- and audiotaping, journal writing, and others, can be extremely useful in conducting an evaluation to gain an understanding of the social, cultural, and political context of the school and the curriculum designs. In order to discuss this type of evaluation, it is important to describe ethnography and ethnographers. As Spindler and Spindler state:

> Ethnographers attempt to record, in an orderly manner, how natives behave and how they explain their behavior. And ethnography, strictly speaking, is an orderly report of this recording. Natives are people in situations anywhere— including children and youth in schools—not just people who live in remote jungles or cozy peasant villages (1987c:17).

To produce a meaningful report of observed behavior, and of people's explanations for such behavior in the school setting, is not easy. It requires the study of human behavior in social contexts, during social interaction as constrained or determined by environmental factors.

While it is important to point out, as Fetterman does (1984:13), that there are important differences between ethnography and the so-called "ethnographic evaluation," it is essential to recognize that the use of ethnographic techniques does not constitute ethnography. Some of these techniques, however, have been instrumental in efforts to make sense of the sociopolitical and cultural context of program success. If ethnographic techniques are being used, it would help to capture the most salient methodological requirements of ethnographic approaches (taken primarily from Spindler & Spindler, 1987c; Trueba, 1987b,c; Wolcott, 1988) summarized as follows:

1. Putting into context systematic observations of behavior and the "natives' " view ("emic" perspective) of their own behavior are essential conditions for understanding behavior.
2. Emerging "theories" or inferences about observed behavior must bear on the redirection of research efforts.
3. The focus is on communicative interaction and the sociocultural knowledge presupposed by effective communication of participants' interactions.
4. Data gathering methods are generated at the location, and are designed specifically for the study at hand.
5. In conducting interviews, surveys, or observations, or using other data gathering techniques, the researcher must not impose his or her perspective nor any predetermined responses.

While it is important to recognize, as Fetterman (1984) does, that there are important differences between ethnography and ethnographic evaluation, we must also realize that any ethnographic description can become an instrument of the evaluative process. It is also important to keep in mind that evaluators using ethnographic methods are not exonerated from protecting their informants' privacy. Evaluators can fruitfully use many other data gathering methods (especially quantitative), which are often necessary to assess effectiveness, performance, and comparative competence as judged from the results of standardized texts and other teacher evaluations. The ethnographic component provides a better contextual basis for understanding why differences in achievement occur and how the organizational structure of instruction leaves out some children. Fetterman reminds us that ethnography is not a panacea:

> Ethnography has been misunderstood and misused in educational research. The misuse of ethnographic techniques, however, is due as much to overzealousness and faddishness as it is to the anthropological tradition of ritualizing methodology. Ethnography is not a panacea. It is one useful methodological tool, among others, used in addressing educational problems. The exploration and development of new frontiers requires adaptations, alterations, and innovations. This does not imply that significant compromises be made in the rigor required to conduct truly ethnographic research (Fetterman, 1984:31).

Using natural observation methods, ethnographic interviews, and other qualitative and quantitative evaluation research methods, the evaluator should explore several areas of inquiry related to the assessment of program effectiveness. The following evaluative questions for each area are suggested.

**Program Management**    Have the principal and director exercised good leadership skills, provided direction, and established clear lines of accountability? Are fiscal controls and reporting well organized? Have they monitored timely implementation of the instructional design? Have they supported teachers in their efforts to deliver quality instruction?

**Classroom Learning Environment**    Have the teachers created a stimulating and supportive learning environment in the classroom? Do teachers communicate with children well and permit them to express their feelings and ask questions? Do teachers encourage participation of all children, especially those who struggle with the second language? Do teachers understand and use the cultural background of students?

**Support for Teachers**    Are teachers encouraged to create support groups to help each other in finding solutions to daily instructional tasks, to stimulate professional growth, and to assist each other in every possible way? Are teachers free to express and implement their own suggestions to improve the instructional system? Are teachers rewarded appropriately for their efforts? Are teachers assisted with in-service counseling? Do teachers receive enough latitude to handle curriculum changes associated with a better knowledge of students' needs?

**Teacher–Parents Communication**    Is there frequent and close communication between parents and teachers? Are parents perceived as supportive by teachers and teachers by parents? Are parents critical of teachers? Are parents encouraged to assist the school as aides and in other capacities? Does the school offer additional services to parents such as counseling, literacy classes, enrichment classes, English as a second language, or others?

**Children's Academic Progress**    What are the characteristics of children's academic progress? Specifically, how do children perform in the various subjects with the assigned teachers? Are those children in the bilingual program, both LEP and English-speaking, maintaining levels of achievement comparable to those in regular classrooms? What are the trends and patterns in achievement for each subject matter and language? What is the level of literacy in the home language and in English for children in each grade or grade combination?

With the data collected and some central concerns to guide the analysis, the evaluator should produce a preliminary report addressed only to a few key persons (the principal, director, and selected members of the advisory committee). The purpose of submitting the report is to elicit reactions from school personnel, request any additional information needed, and anticipate potentially explosive political situations that may be counterproductive to the main goals of the evaluation. With careful analysis of this feedback, the evaluator can then proceed with the first complete draft of the evaluation to all school personnel. Upon receiving suggestions and revisions from school personnel, the evaluator can finally send the evaluation to the funding agency, if this is required.

Chilcott (1987) has eloquently described the dilemmas and challenges of ethnographers of education. He suggests that all ethnographic research on schools "has overtones of evaluation" but that ultimately ethnographers ought to identify those we can do something about. Then he adds:

The scientists (anthropologists or scholars in education) provide an ethnography to serve as a basis for an informed decision as to what changes can be made by the professional educator. What criteria can an ethnographer use to judge cultural behavior in the school? One, and perhaps the only, criterion that the ethnographer can use is cultural survival. Does the particular cultural behavior contribute to the survival of the individual and/or the group? The ethnographer may not approve of the behavior of a teacher or an administrator, but if this behavior contributes to the survival of the individual or the institution, the question of validity rests on the specific cultural behavior rather than the opinion of the ethnographer (Chilcott, 1987:210–211).

Perhaps one interpretation of Chilcott's statement is that survival of linguistic minority children in schools is uniquely linked to their ability to participate actively and fruitfully (on the basis of "comprehensible input" and the development of literacy skills through the home language) in the instructional process. Evaluation rightfully ought to examine the roots of the emotional, cognitive, and cultural withdrawal of minority students that leads them so often to failure in the form of dropping out, suicide, delinquency, boredom, and inability to learn. In our example at Santa Eulalia Elementary School, the evaluation team should meet with the group of teachers and the advisory committee to discuss findings and recommendations and, most of all, to give teachers the opportunity to offer alternative interpretations to those of evaluators, to make other recommendations they consider more appropriate, and, most importantly, to propose specific steps to implement those recommendations.

One of the central topics of discussion in Santa Eulalia will undoubtedly be the extent to which L1 should be used in classroom instruction as children's L2 proficiency increases and as they become more comfortable using it. It will be extremely important for teachers to be given the opportunity to read about the subject (including Rueda, 1987; Rueda & Mehan, 1986; Diaz et al., 1986, and the other readings recommended for this chapter) and to discuss their experience and knowledge with the evaluators. In the end, if teachers continue to learn and use that knowledge in their daily instructional practice, an evaluation will not impose unreasonable mandates on them, but will become an opportunity to challenge unwarranted assumptions, acquire valuable information, and improve teaching.

## SUMMARY

Program execution is a dynamic, integrated, continuing process that consists of cycles of planning, implementation, and evaluation phases. The program execution process should be realistic and responsive to the concrete needs of the student population, and it should involve key school personnel who are responsible for instruction. The role of the principal in taking initiatives and supervising progress of activities should be supported by an advisory committee, whose organization and operation should include the tactful search for broad political backing for the new program, especially from local communities.

In all phases of program execution, the advisory committee and other persons involved in the process should clearly keep in mind that the top priority is developing and implementing an adequate instructional program that meets the needs of students and is congruent with their social experiences, cultural values, and learning characteristics. During the evaluation phase, teachers should be given ample opportunity to provide the evaluation team with information and assistance, and to respond to the evaluation report.

Because in the micropolitics of program planning, implementation, and evaluation there are often constraints imposed by outside agencies, especially by those providing financial support, it is the obligation of the principal to protect the advisory committee, teachers, and evaluators from excessive political pressure and extrinsic goals. Ethnographic evaluation is recommended as an invaluable aid for conducting the evaluation phase realistically, that is, with the interests of students and their sociocultural environments in mind. This method, along with others used by the evaluation team, assists investigators in obtaining insight into the behavioral patterns of students and teachers, their conflicting cultural values, the relative effectiveness of communication during instruction, and the overall impact of linguistic minority schooling as students become integrated into the new school and society. In the final analysis, evaluation should become a means of strengthening the social ties between the teachers and children who are working cooperatively through the instructional process.

## RECOMMENDED EXERCISES

These recommendations are primarily directed toward the faculty and administration of schools. Teachers and other readers, however, may make attempts on their own to assist or become members of one of the evaluation teams.

1. Inquire about incoming evaluations of programs with which you have become familiar; request permission to examine the evaluation process. You may want to request brief interviews with team members, and/or ask to see the instruments used. If you are successful in talking with members of the evaluation team, inquire about the scope, purpose, method, and expected outcomes of the evaluation.
2. Request a copy of a previous evaluation of a program in which you have participated or have observed. Analyze the work and raise questions about documentary evidence for inferences, implied assumptions, or political considerations guiding evaluation efforts, and consequences of the evaluation.
3. From previous school observations conducted in a school in the context of other assignments, construct a brief analysis of particular instructional prac-

tices that you think should be changed. Propose specific recommendations that should be offered to the teachers and principal. Briefly describe the theoretical rationale for your analysis and the events that led you to apply such a theoretical framework.

4. In the Santa Eulalia scenario, there is a great deal of information missing. What categories of information do you think the planning committee still needs? How should this information affect the decision of this committee regarding instructional design and implementation?

5. The central areas and questions for evaluations presented at the end of the chapter are general and need to be applied to specific settings. Generate areas and questions applicable to a school situation with which you are familiar, and suggest the rationale for each addition.

## RECOMMENDED READINGS

Chilcott, 1987
Cummins, 1981, 1986
Diaz et al., 1986
Fetterman, 1983, 1984
Freeman and Rossi, 1984
Gold and Tempes, 1987
Goldman and Trueba, 1987
Levine et al., 1981
Martin, 1985
Rossi and Freeman, 1985
Spindler and Spindler, 1987a,b
Trueba, 1983, 1987a,b,c

# Conclusion

This book has taken us on a journey with linguistic minority students and their teachers in search of answers to their academic problems. In Chapter 1, after these students were identified socioculturally, and demographically, we examined hypotheses that attempted to explain their differential academic achievement and overall integration into mainstream societies. As we have seen, linguistic minorities have often been uprooted, finding themselves in new environments without the skills to communicate in the new language. Academic achievement has been viewed as linked to macrosocial and cultural factors, and to the immediate sociocultural environments of school and the community in which students live. Linguistic minority students make efforts to belong and to participate in school activities, but they are besieged with problems in their communication with others, and in their acceptance of mainstream sociocultural norms and values. Thus it becomes more difficult for them to establish dyadic teacher–student and peer–peer learning relationships. Psychological adjustment, cultural integration into the school, acquisition of communicative skills, and academic achievement are critically linked to the opportunities given to students for using their previous sociocultural experiences and knowledge, as well as their own ability to apply new ideas to those experiences.

In Chapter 2, the relationship between language, culture, and effective schooling was discussed in the context of cultural transition and adjustment. Attention to both language and culture is essential in effective classroom activities. The effective use of language requires cultural knowledge, and the transmission of cultural values necessitates linguistic skills. Linguistic minority students need to be exposed to American cultural values; this exposure is better accomplished in a nonsegregated society and school, in learning environments in which the organization of instruction is flexible, and the stress associated with public performance is minimized. In this type of environment, students are able to obtain the instrumental competencies required to participate more effectively in classroom activities and to integrate the new cultural values with those of their home culture. Reflective cultural analysis was suggested as a technique to help teachers and students internalize the nature of cultural conflicts and their solutions. Through this analysis, teachers can begin to understand children's responses to instructional organization and to teachers' behaviors, as well as grasp the different cultural assumptions behind such behaviors.

Chapter 3 examined the types of instructional programs designed for linguistic minorities, including bilingual transitional, bilingual bicultural, immersion, and pull-out programs. It was concluded that if we neglect culturally different children or, worse, if we underrate their intellectual abilities, we will not only misclassify them as "learning disabled" in school but will we create mental and emotional disabilities. To understand better children's pace in adopting new cultural values, including new linguistic and behavioral codes, it is very useful to visit their homes to learn about their culture and language. Learning about the child's home language and culture will also lead us to rethink the emphasis placed on the controversial functional distribution of home and mainstream languages in classroom instruction, and to concentrate more on the best means to accomplish pedagogical goals that are acceptable to all educators. Such goals are the acquisition of critical thinking skills, communicative skills in the language of instruction, and academic values leading to higher levels of literacy.

Chapter 4 presented, in a historical context, the modern legislative landmarks affecting linguistic minority education, including the *Brown* v. *Board of Education, Hobson* v. *Hansen, Lau* v. *Nichols, Diana* v. *State Board of Education*, and *Larry P.* v. *Wilson Riles* cases. Because of the demographic and cultural importance of Hispanics in this country, their struggle for educational equity was discussed in more detail than that of other minority groups. We learned that one of the traditional values of American democracy has been the value attached to the right to disagree and debate without losing personal liberties and/or civil rights, and without putting our national unity in jeopardy. The disagreement regarding rights of minorities to their language and culture has persisted for some time and reappears cyclically with undue force. Federal courts have typically protected a more liberal position, while local political groups continue organizing to restrict the use of languages other than English and to curtail the social, economic, and political power of ethnic minorities. These at times painful democratic processes have been punctuated by racism and intolerance, as well as by gender biases, which have serious consequences for schools and teachers. The topic of bilingual education is an example of such national debate causing educational programs for minority children to suffer, through a lack of support resulting from political division and a lack of agreement on basic pedagogical principles.

In Chapter 5, the nature and effectiveness of the instructional process were examined with an emphasis on the teaching of literacy. The social organization of the classroom was viewed in order to identify the nature of the communicative interactional events through which teachers transfer knowledge, and to see teachers' roles as they internalize them. Through the use of case studies, the reader was exposed to realistic examples of the home literacy environments of linguistic minority students. The integration of cultural values required for the acquisition of high literacy levels in English was discussed in the context of students' capability to adjust to the new setting. The teacher often plays the role of cultural broker in facilitating students' cultural integration by monitoring their responses to instructional activities.

Chapter 6 discussed the concerns expressed by teachers regarding the political turmoil surrounding their profession, and the demands imposed on them by the rapidly changing student population. Teachers are confronted with the dilemma of emphasizing either linguistic and cultural socialization or the political socialization required for academic success. Teachers are also concerned about bureaucratic centralization of classroom control and the lack of flexibility in the adaptation of curriculum materials and teaching strategies. The development of teacher support groups is discussed in the context of their empowerment and survival as competent professionals.

The seventh and final chapter described program execution as a continuing, dynamic, integrated process composed of planning, implementation, and evaluation cycles, in response to the surveyed needs of a given student population. Each phase of the process and its delicate micropolitical constraints were described in some detail. Ethnographic techniques were recommended for use in the evaluation process. They are an additional tool in efforts to obtain deeper insights into the relative effectiveness of the instructional design and its self-regulated monitoring mechanisms.

The end of the twentieth century is rapidly approaching. The children who will crowd our schools are already among us. Minority children are rapidly becoming, or have already become, the majority in a number of cities and areas of this country. Some researchers and educators are alarmed. Their sense of history is distorted by the predicted failure of minorities in schools. Their frustration feeds prejudice and compulsive rejection of languages and cultures outside the mainstream. Their fear that American society is doomed to fail in the hands of minorities takes on overtones of despair. In the meantime, many minority students quietly and consistently achieve excellence. We cannot deny the sociological phenomenon of always having large groups of minority students in school. But we lose track of those who have successfully integrated into mainstream society, including those who have selectively adopted the new, American, cultural values. In fact, some groups are so successful that universities feel compelled to establish admission quotas to protect mainstream students whose academic qualifications are not, on the average, as high. This is often the case for Asian students in technological fields, the natural sciences, mathematics, business, and other areas of study.

If it is read carefully, history demonstrates that the strength of American democracy has not only been in the freedom to disagree and debate but also in the commitment to fairness and recognition of excellence wherever it may be found. The contributions of linguistic minority children will persuade many alarmed educators that history is repeating itself, if we maintain our democratic values. As the twenty-first century approaches, we must reflect on the small lessons we have learned from examining the education of linguistic minorities. We have learned that the importance of sound and universally accepted pedagogical principles should not be overwhelmed by the political controversies of our times. We have learned that teachers of linguistic minorities are committed to becoming professionally empowered, and therefore more effective in instructional practice. We have also learned that students, if they are given a fair chance, and if they are permitted to go through the process of integration of cultural values, will succeed in learning

English as a second language and achieving successfully in school. Finally, we have learned that our school system tends to corner itself into a dead end of conflicting functions and politics, ignoring, at times, the lack of even minimal requirements for teaching to begin: safety, reasonable student willingness to learn, support from administrators, and financial and moral support from the public. Moral, humanitarian, and economic arguments can be made to motivate us to support minority education in our schools. The future of this country will be in good hands if we extend our support to minority children today.

# References

Acuña, R. (1981). *Occupied America: A history of Chicanos*. 2d ed. New York: Harper & Row.

Ada, A. F. (1986). Creative education for bilingual education teachers. *Harvard Educational Review, 56*, 4:386–394.

Alvarez, R. (1988). National politics and local responses: The nation's first successful school desegregation court case. In H. Trueba & C. Delgado-Gaitan (Eds.) *School and society: Learning content through culture* (pp. 37–52). New York: Praeger Publishers.

American Institutes for Research. (1977a). *Evaluation of the Impact of ESEA Title VII Spanish/English Bilingual Education Program, Volume I: Study Design and Interim Findings*. Palo Alto, California.

American Institutes for Research. (1977b). *Evaluation of the Impact of ESEA Title VII Spanish/English Bilingual Education Program, Volume II: Project Descriptions*. Palo Alto, California.

Andersson, T., and Boyer, M. (1971). *Bilingual schooling in the United States*, 2 vols. Washington, D.C.: Government Printing Office.

Apple, M. (1982). *Cultural and economic reproduction in education*. New York: Macmillan.

Aronowitz, S., & Giroux, H. A. (1985). *Education under siege*. South Hadley, MA: Bergin and Garvey.

Assembly Office of Research. (1986). *California 2000: A people in transition. Major issues affecting human resources*. Sacramento, CA: Joint Publications Office.

Au, K. H. (1980). Participation structures in a reading lesson with Hawaiian children: Analysis of a culturally appropriate instructional event. *Anthropology and Education Quarterly, 11*, 2:91–115.

Au, K. H. (1981). The comprehension-oriented reading lesson: Relationships to proximal indices of achievement. *Educational Perspectives, 20*, 13–15.

Au, K. H., & Jordan, C. (1981). Teaching reading to Hawaiian children: Finding a culturally appropriate solution. In H. Trueba, G. Guthrie, & K. Au (Eds.) *Culture and the bilingual classroom: Studies in classroom ethnography* (pp. 139–152). Rowley, MA: Newbury House Publishers.

Au, K. H., & Kawakami, A. J. (1982). A conceptual framework for studying in the long-term effects of comprehension instruction. *The Quarterly Newsletter of the Laboratory of Comparative Human Cognition, 6*, 4:95–100.

Berk, R. A. (1983). An introduction to sample selection bias in sociological data. *American Sociological Review, 48*, 386–398.

Bidwell, C., & Friedkin, N. (in press). The sociology of education. In N. Smelser (Ed.) *The Handbook of Sociology*.

Boas, F. (1928). *Anthropology and modern life*. New York: Morton.

Boggs, S. T. (1985). *Speaking, relating, and learning: A study of Hawaiian children at home and at school*. Norwood, NJ: Ablex Publishing Corp.

Borish, S. (1988). The winter of their discontent: Cultural compression and decompression in the life cycle of the Kibbutz adolescent. In H. Trueba & C. Delgado-Gaitan (Eds.) *School and society: Teaching content through culture* (pp. 181–199). New York: Praeger Publishers.

Bowles, S., & Gintis, H. (1976). *Schooling in capitalist America: Educational reform and the contradictions of economic life*. New York: Basic Books.

Boyer, E. (1983). *High school: A report on secondary education in America*. Princeton, NJ: Carnegie Foundation for the Advancement of Teaching.

Brinkley, A. (1984). All things to all people: Fifty years of American schools. *Harvard Educational Review, 54*, 4:452–459.

Britzman, D. (1986). Cultural myths in the making of a teacher: Biography and social strcuture in teacher education. *Harvard Educational Review, 56*, 4:442–456.

*Brown v. Board of Education of Topeka* (1954). 347 U.S. 483.

Brown, A., Campione, E., Cole, M., Griffin, P., Mehan, H., & Riel, M. (1982). A model system for the study of learning difficulties. *The Quarterly Newsletter of the Laboratory of Comparative Human Cognition, 4*, 3:39–55.

Brown, G., Rosen, H., Hill, S, & Olivas, M. (1980). *The condition of education for Hispanic Americans*. Washington, DC: United States Department of Education, National Center for Educational Statistics.

Burstein, L. (1980). Analyzing multilevel educational data: The choice of an analytical model rather than a unit of analysis. In E. Baker & E. Quellmaiz (Eds.) *Design, analysis, and policy in testing and evaluation* (pp. 81–94). Beverly Hills, CA: Sage Publications.

California State Department of Education. (1981). *Schooling and language minority students: A theoretical framework*. Los Angeles, CA: California State University, Evaluation, Dissemination and Assessment Center.

California State Department of Education. (1983). *Basic principles for the education of language-minority students: An overview*. Los Angeles, CA: California State University, Evaluation, Dissemination and Assessment Center.

California State Department of Education. (1984). *Studies on immersion education*. Los Angeles, CA: California State University, Evaluation, Dissemination and Assessment Center.

California State Department of Education. (1986). *Beyond language: social and cultural factors in schooling language minority students*. Los Angeles, CA: California State University, Evaluation, Dissemination and Assessment Center.

Camilleri, C. (1985). *Anthropologie culturelle et education*. Paris: UNESCO.

Carter, T. P., & Segura, R. D. (1979). *Mexican Americans in school: A decade of change*. New York: College Entrance Examination Board.

Castell, S. Luke, A., & MacLennan, D. (1986). On defining literacy. In S. Castell, A. Luke, & K. Egan (Eds.) *Literacy, society, and schooling: A reader* (pp. 3–14). Cambridge: Cambridge University Press.

Castell, S., & Luke, A. (1986). Models of literacy in North American schools: Social and historical conditions and consequences. In S. Castell, A. Luke, & K. Egan (Eds.)

*Literacy, society, and schooling: A reader* (pp. 87–109). Cambridge: Cambridge University Press.

Cazden, C. (1985). *The ESL teacher as advocate*. Plenary presentation to the TESOL Conference. New York.

Center for the Study of the Teaching Profession. *Annual Report, October 1986 to September 1987*, AR-3792-CSTP. Santa Monica, CA: Rand.

Cervantes, R. (1974). Problems and alternatives in testing Mexican-American students. *Integrated Education, 12*, 33–37.

Chamot, A. (1983). Toward a functional ESL curriculum in the elementary school. *TESOL Quarterly, 17*, 459–472.

Cheng, L. (1987). English communicative competence of language minority children: Assessment and treatment of language "impaired" preschoolers. In H. Trueba (Ed.) *Success or failure?: Learning and the language minority student* (pp. 49–68). New York: Newbury/Harper & Row.

Chilcott, J. H. (1987). Where are you coming from and where are you going? The reporting of ethnographic research. *American Educational Research Journal, 24*, 2:199–218.

Cicourel, A. (1974). The acquisition of social structure: Toward a developmental sociology of language and meaning. In J. D. Douglas (Ed.) *Understanding everyday life* (pp. 136–168). Chicago: Aldine.

Cohen, A. D. (1975). *A sociolinguistic approach to bilingual education: Experiments in the American Southwest*. Rowley, MA.: Newbury House.

Cohen, A. D. (1984). The condition of teachers' work. *Harvard Educational Review, 54*, 1:11–15.

Cole, M., & D'Andrade, R. (1982). The influence of schooling on concept formation: Some preliminary conclusions. *The Quarterly Newsletter of the Laboratory of Comparative Human Cognition, 4*, 2:19–26.

Cole, M., & Griffin, P. (1983). A socio-historical approach to re-mediation. *The Quarterly Newsletter of the Laboratory of Comparative Human Cognition, 5*, 4:69–74.

Cole, M., & Scribner, S. (1974). *Culture and thought: A psychological introduction*. New York: Basic Books.

Cook-Gumperz, J. (Ed.) (1986). *The social construction of literacy*. Cambridge: Cambridge University Press.

Cronbach, L. J. (1982). *Designing evaluations of educational and social programs*. San Francisco: Jossey-Bass.

Cuban, L. (1979). Shrinking enrollment and consolidation: Political and organizational impacts in Arlington, Virginia, 1973–1978. *Education and Urban Society, 11*, 367–395.

Cummins, J. (1976). The influence of bilingualism on cognitive growth: A synthesis of research findings and explanatory hypotheses. *Working Papers on Bilingualism, 9*, 1–43.

Cummins, J. (1978). Bilingualism and the development of metalinguistic awareness. *Journal of Crosscultural Psychology, 9*, 2:131–149.

Cummins, J. (1979). Linguistic interdependence and the educational development of bilingual children. *Review of Educational Research, 49*, 222–251.

Cummins, J. (1980). The cross-lingual dimensions of language proficiency: Implications for bilingual education and the optimal age issue. *TESOL Quarterly, 14*, 175–187.

Cummins, J. (1981a). The entry and exit fallacy in bilingual education. *National Association for Bilingual Education Journal, 4*, 3:26–60.

Cummins, J. (1981b). The role of primary language development in promoting educational success for language minority students. In *Schooling and language minority students: A theoretical framework* (pp. 3–49). Los Angeles: California State University at Los Angeles Evaluation, Dissemination and Assessment Center.

Cummins, J. (1983). *Heritage language education: A literature review.* Toronto: Ministry of Education, Ontario.

Cummins, J. (1984). *Bilingual special education: Issues in assessment and pedagogy.* San Diego, CA: College Hill Press.

Cummins, J. (1986). Empowering minority students: A framework for intervention. *Harvard Educational Review, 56,* 1:18–35.

Davis, C., Haub, C., & Willette, J. (1983). U. S. Hispanics: Changing the face of America. *Population Bulletin, 38,* 3:1–44.

Delgado-Gaitan, C. (1987a). Traditions and transitions in the learning process of Mexican children: An ethnographic view. In G. Spindler & L. Spindler (Eds.) *Interpretive ethnography of education: At home and abroad* (pp. 333–359). Hillsdale, NJ: Lawrence Erlbaum Associates.

Delgado-Gaitan, C. (1987b). Parent perceptions of school: Supportive environments for children. In H. Trueba (Ed.) *Success or failure?: Learning and the language minority student* (pp. 131–155). New York: Newbury House.

Delgado-Gaitan, C., & Trueba, H. (1985). Socialization of Mexican children for cooperation and competition. *Journal of Educational Equity and Leadership, 5,* 3:189–204.

DeVos, G. (1967). Essential elements of caste: Psychological determinants in structural theory. In G. DeVos & H. Wagatsuma (Eds.) *Japan's invisible race: Caste in culture and personality* (pp. 332–384). Berkeley: University of California Press.

DeVos, G. (1973). Japan's outcastes: The problem of the Burakumin. In B. Whitaker (Ed.) *The fourth world: Victims of group oppression* (pp. 307–327). New York: Schocken Books.

DeVos, G. (1980). Ethnic adaptation and minority status. *Journal of Cross-Cultural Psychology, 11,* 101–124.

DeVos, G. (1982). Adaptive strategies in U.S. minorities. In E. Jones & S.J. Korchin (Eds.) *Minority Mental Health* (pp. 74–117). New York: Praeger.

DeVos, G. (1983). Ethnic identity and minority status: Some psycho-cultural considerations. In A. Jacobson-Widding (Ed.) *Identity: Personal and socio-cultural* (pp. 90–113). Upsala: Almquist & Wiksell Tryckeri AB.

DeVos, G. (1984). Ethnic persistence and role degradation: An illustration from Japan. Paper read April, 1984 at the American–Soviet Symposium on Contemporary Ethnic Processes in the U.S.A. and the U.S.S.R. New Orleans, Louisiana.

Deyhle, D. (1987). Learning failure: Tests as gatekeepers and the culturally different child. In H. Trueba (Ed.) *Success or failure?: Learning and the language minority student* (pp. 85–108). New York: Newbury House.

*Diana v. California State Board of Education* (1970). No. C-70-37, U.S. District Court of Northern California.

Diaz, S., Moll, L. C., & Mehan, H. (1986). Sociocultural resources in instruction: A context-specific approach. In *Beyond language: Social and cultural factors in schooling language minority students* (pp. 187–230). Sacramento, CA: Bilingual Education Office, California State Department of Education.

Dollard, J. (1937). *Caste and class in a Southern town.* New Haven: Yale University Press.

Dolson, D. (1985). The effects of Spanish home language use on the scholastic performance of Hispanic pupils. *Journal of Multilingual and Multicultural Development, 6*, 2:135–155.

Drake, D. (1973). Anglo American teachers, Mexican American students, and dissonance in our schools. *Elementary School Journal, 73*, 207–213.

Duran, R. (1983). *Hispanics' education and background: Predictors of college achievement.* New York: College Entrance Examination Board.

Duran, R. (1985). Influences of language skills on bilingual's problem solving. In S. Chipman, J. Sigel, & R. Glaser (Eds.) *Thinking and learning skills, Volume 2: Current research and open questions* (pp. 187–207). Hillsdale, NJ: Lawrence Erlbaum Associates.

Durkheim, E. (1961). *Moral education.* Glencoe, IL: Free Press System.

Epstein, N. (1977). *Language, ethnicity and the schools.* Washington, D.C.: The George Washington University Institute for Educational Leadership.

Erickson, F. (1977). Some approaches to inquiry in school/community ethnography. *Anthropology and Education Quarterly, 8*, 3:58–69.

Erickson, F. (1982). Classroom discourse as improvisation: Relationships between academic task structure and social participation structure in lessons. In L. C. Wilkinson (Ed.) *Communicating in the classroom* (pp. 153–181). New York: Academic Press.

Erickson, F. (1984). School literacy, reasoning, and civility: An anthropologist's perspective. *Review of Educational Research, 54*, 4:525–544.

Erickson, F. (1986). Qualitative methods in research on teaching. In M. C. Wittrock (Ed.) *Handbook of research on teaching* (pp. 119–158). New York: Macmillan Publishing Co.

Erickson, F. (1987). Transformation and school success: The politics and culture of educational achievement. *Anthropology and Education Quarterly, 18*, 4:335–356.

Erickson, F., & Mohatt, G. (1982). Cultural organization of participation structures in two classrooms of Indian students. In G. Spindler (Ed.) *Doing the ethnography of schooling: Educational anthropology in action* (pp. 132–175). New York: Holt, Rinehart and Winston.

Estrada, L. (1986). *California's non-English speakers.* Claremont, CA: The Tomás Rivera Center.

Everhart, R. (1987). Understanding student disruption and classroom control. *Harvard Educational Review, 57*, 1:77–83.

Fetterman, D. M. (1983). Guilty knowledge, dirty hands, and other ethical dilemmas: The hazards of contract research. *Human Organization, 42*, 3:214–224.

Fetterman, D. M. (1984). Doing ethnographic educational evaluation. In D. Fetterman (Ed.) *Ethnography in educational evaluation* (pp. 13–19). Beverly Hills, CA: Sage Publications, Inc.

Figueroa, R. (1983). Test bias and Hispanic children. *The Journal of Special Education, 17*, 431–440.

Figueroa, R. (1986). *Diana revisited.* Los Angeles: National Evaluation, Dissemination and Assessment Center, California State University, Los Angeles.

Figueroa, R. (1987). The assessment of Hispanic children's intelligence. Unpublished manuscript. University of California, Davis.

Figueroa, R., Sandoval, J., & Merino, B. (1984). School psychology and limited-English-proficient children: New competencies. *Journal of School Psychology, 11*, 131–144.

Fishman, J. (1956). *Language loyalty in the United States.* The Hague: Mouton.

Fishman, J. (1976). *Bilingual education: An international sociological perspective.* Rowley, MA: Newbury House.

Fishman, J. (1977). Bilingual education: The state of social science inquiry. *Papers in applied linguistics, bilingual education series.* Arlington, VA: Center for Applied Linguistics.

Fishman, J. (1978). A gathering of vultures, the "Legion of Decency" and bilingual education in the U.S.A. *Journal of the National Association for Bilingual Education, 2,* 2:13–16.

Fishman, J. (1979). Bilingual education: What and why? In H. T. Trueba & C. Barnett-Mizrahi (Eds.) *Bilingual multicultural education and the professional: From theory to practice* (pp. 11–19). Rowley, MA.: Newbury House.

Frake, C. (1964). Notes on queries in ethnography. *American Anthropologist, 66,* 3:132–145.

Freebody, P., & Baker, C. (1985). Children's first schoolbooks: Introductions to the culture of literacy. *Harvard Educational Review, 55,*4:381–398.

Freeman, H. E., & Rossi, P. H. (1984). Furthering the applied side of sociology. *American Sociological Review, 49:* 571–580.

Freire, P. (1973). *Pedagogy of the oppressed.* New York: Seabury.

Fujita, M., & Sano, T. (1988). Children in American and Japanese day-care centers: Ethnography and reflective cross-cultural interviewing. In H. Trueba & C. Delgado-Gaitan (Eds.) *School & Society: Teaching content through culture* (pp. 73–97). New York: Praeger Publishers.

Gallimore, R., Boggs, S., & Jordan, C. (1974). *Culture, behavior and education: A study of Hawaiian-Americans.* Beverly Hills, CA: Sage Publications.

Gallimore, R., Dalton, S., & Tharp, R. (1986). Self-regulation and interactive teaching: The impact of teaching conditions on teachers' cognitive activity. *Elementary School Journal, 86,* 5: 613–631.

Gallimore, R., & Tharp, R. (1981). The interpretation of elicited imitation in a standardized setting. *Language Learning, 31,* 2:369–392.

Galvan, A., Macias, R., Magallan, R., & Orum, L. (1986). *Are English language amendments in the national interest?: An analysis of proposals to establish English as the official language of the United States.* Claremont, CA: The Tomás Rivera Center.

Genesee, F. (1981). A comparison of early and late second language learning. *Canadian Journal of Behavioral Sciences, 13,* 115–127.

Genesee, F., Tucker, G., & Lambert, W. (1975). Communication skills of bilingual children. *Child Development, 46,* 1010–14.

Gibson, M. (1987a). Playing by the rules. In G. Spindler (Ed.) *Education and cultural process: Anthropological approaches* (pp. 274–283). 2nd ed. Prospect Heights, IL: Waveland Press.

Gibson, M. (1987b). The school performance of immigrant minorities: A comparative view. *Anthropology and Education Quarterly, 18,* 4:262–275.

Gillin, J. (1955). National and regional cultural values in the United States. *Social Forces, 34,* 107–113.

Gilmore, P., & Glatthorn A. A. (1982). *Children in and out of school: Ethnography and education.* Arlington, VA: Center for Applied Linguistics.

Giroux, H. (1983). Theories of reproduction and resistance in the new sociology of education: A critical analysis. *Harvard Educational Review, 53,* 3:257–293.

Giroux, H., & McLaren, P. (1986) Teacher education and the politics of engagement: The case of democratic schooling. *Harvard Educational Review, 56*, 3:213–238.

Glenn, C. (1988). *Educating linguistic minority students.* Report, Office of Educational Equity. The Commonwealth of Massachusetts.

Goelman, H., Obert, A., & Smith, F. (Eds.) (1984). *Awakening to literacy.* London: Exeter Heinemann Educational Books.

Gold, N., & Tempes, F. (1987). *A state agency partnership with schools to improve bilingual education.* A paper presented at the Annual Meeting of the American Educational Research Association. Washington, D.C.

Goldman, S., & McDermott, R. (1987). The culture of competition in American schools. In G. Spindler (Ed.) *Education and cultural process: Anthropological approaches* (pp. 282–289). 2nd ed. Prospect Heights, IL: Waveland Press.

Goldman, S. R., & Trueba, H. T. (Eds.) (1987). *Becoming literate in English as a second language.* Norwood, NJ: Ablex Publishing Corporation.

Gonzalez, J. (1979). Coming of age in bilingual/bicultural education: A historical perspective. In H. Trueba & C. Barnett-Mizrahi (Eds.), *Bilingual multicultural education and the professional: From theory to practice* (pp. 1–10). Rowley, MA: Newbury House.

Goodlad, J. (1983). *A place called school: Prospects for the future.* New York: McGraw-Hill.

Graff, H. (1979). *The literacy myth: Literacy and the social structure in the nineteenth-century city.* New York: Academic Press.

Graff, H. (1986). The legacies of literacy: Continuities and contradictions in western society and culture. In S. Castell, A. Luke, & K. Egan (Eds.) *Literacy, society, and schooling: A reader* (pp. 61–86). Cambridge, MA: Cambridge University Press.

Greene, M. (1986). In search of a critical pedagogy. *Harvard Educational Review, 56*, 4:427–441.

Griffin, P., Newman, D., & Cole, M. (1981). Activities, actions and formal operations: A Vygotskian analysis of a Piagetian task. Unpublished manuscript. Laboratory of Comparative Human Cognition, University of California, San Diego.

Gumperz, J., & Hymes, D. (Eds.) (1964). The ethnography of communication. *American Anthropologist, 66*, 6.

Gumperz, J., & Hymes, D. (1972). *Directions in sociolinguistics: The ethnography of communication.* New York: Holt, Rinehart, and Winston.

Hakuta, K. (1986). *The mirror of language.* New York: Basic Books.

Halcon, J. (1983). A structural profile of basic Title VII (Spanish–English bilingual bicultural programs). *Journal of the National Association for Bilingual Education, 7*, 55–74.

Hale, J. (1982). *Black children: Their roots, culture, and learning styles.* Provo, UT: Brigham Young University Press.

Harris, M. (1981). *America now: The anthropology of a changing culture.* New York: Simon & Schuster.

Hartmann, H. (1984). The unhappy marriage of Marxism and feminism: Towards a more progressive union. In R. Dale, G. Esland, R. Ferguson, & M. McDonald (Eds.) *Education and the state: Politics, patriarchy, and practice* (Vol. 2, pp. 191–210). Sussex: Farmer Press.

Hatch, E. (1979). *Biography of a small town.* New York: Columbia University Press.

Haugen, E. (1978). Bilingualism, language contact, and immigrant languages in the United States: A research report 1956–1970. In J. Fishman (Ed.) *Advances in the study of societal multilingualism* (pp. 1–111). The Hague: Mouton.

Heath, S. B. (1976). A national language academy? Debate in the new nation. *International Journal of the Sociology of Language, 11*: 9–43.

Heath, S. B. (1978). *Teacher talk: Language in the classroom.* Language in Education: Theory and Practice 9. Arlington, VA: Center for Applied Linguistics.

Heath, S. B. (1983). *Ways with words: Language, life, and work in communities and classrooms.* Cambridge, MA: Cambridge University Press.

Heath, S., & Mandabach, F. (1983). Language status decisions and the law in the United States. In J. Cobarrubias & J. Fishman (Eds.) *Progress in language planning: International perspectives* (pp. 87–105). New York: Mouton.

Hernandez-Chavez, E. (1984). The inadequacy of English immersion education as an educational approach for language minority students in the United States. In *Studies on immersion education* (pp. 144–183). Sacramento: California State Department of Education.

*Hobson* v. *Hansen* (1967). 269 *F. Supp.* 401 (D.D.C.).

Hornberger, N. (1988). Iman Chay?: Quechua Children in Peru's Schools. In H. Trueba & C. Delgado-Gaitan (Eds.) *School and society: Teaching content through culture* (pp. 99–117). New York: Praeger Publishers.

Hsu, F. (1953). *Americans and Chinese: Two ways of life.* New York: Schuman.

Hsu, F. (Ed.) (1972) Psychological anthropology. In T. Parsons & E. Shils (Eds.) *Toward a general theory of action* (pp. 388–433). Cambridge: Harvard University Press.

Jacobs, L. (1987). *Differential participation and skill level in four Hmong third grade students: The social and cultural context of teaching and learning.* Doctoral Dissertation. Graduate School of Education. University of California, Santa Barbara.

John, B. (1980). Deutschunterricht fur auslandische Kinder: Zur situation in der Berliner Schule. *Deutsch Lerner, 1*: 38–45.

Jones, R. L. (Ed.) (1976). *Mainstreaming and the minority child.* Reston, VA: The Council for Exceptional Children.

Jorgensen, L. (1956). *The founding of public education in Wisconsin* (cited in Leibowitz, 1971).

Kachru, B. (1978). English in South Asia. In J. Fishman (Ed.) *Advances in the study of societal multilingualism* (pp. 477–551). The Hague: Mouton.

Keller, G. (1983). What can language planners learn from the Hispanic experience with corpus planning in the United States? In J. Cobarrubias & J. Fishman (Eds.) *Progress in language planning: International perspectives* (pp. 253–265). The Hague: Mouton.

Kirton, E. S. (1985). *The locked medicine cabinet: Hmong health care in America.* Doctoral dissertation. Department of Anthropology. University of California, Santa Barbara.

Kloss, H. (1977). *The American bilingual tradition.* Rowley, MA: Newbury House.

Kluckhohn, C. (1949). *Mirror for man.* New York: McGraw-Hill.

Kluckhohn, F. (1950). Dominant and substitute profiles of cultural orientation. *Social Forces 28*, 376–393.

Krashen, S. (1980). The theoretical and practical relevance of simple codes in second language acquisition. In R. C. Scarcella & S. D. Krashen (Eds.), *Research in second language acquisition* (pp. 7–18). Rowley, MA: Newbury House.

Krashen, S. (1981a). *Second language acquisition and second language learning.* Oxford: Pergamon Press.

Krashen, S. (1981b). Bilingual education and second language acquisition theory. In *School-*

*ing and language minority students: A theoretical framework.* California State Department of Education. Los Angeles: California State University.

Lambert, W. E. (1981). Bilingualism and language acquisition. In H. Winitz (Ed.) *Native language and foreign language acquisition* (pp. 9–22). New York: The New York Academy of Sciences.

Lambert, W. E. (1984). An overview of issues in immersion education. In *Studies on immersion education* (pp. 8–30). Sacramento: California State Department of Education.

Lambert, W., & Tucker, R. (1972). *Bilingual education of children: The St. Lambert experiment.* Rowley, MA: Newbury House.

Lapkin, S., & Cummins, J. (1984). A review of immersion education in Canada: Research and evaluation studies. In *Studies on immersion education* (pp. 58–86). Sacramento: California State Department of Education.

*Larry P. v. Riles* (1979). 343 *F. Suppl.* 1306.

*Lau v. Nichols* (1974). 414 U.S. 563–572.

Leibowitz, A. (1971). *Educational policy and political acceptance: The imposition of English as the language of instruction in American schools.* Washington, D.C.: ERIC Clearinghouse for Linguistics.

Levine, R. A., Solomon, M. A., Hellstern, G., & Wohlman, H., (Eds.) (1981). *Evaluation research and practice: Comparative and international perspectives.* Beverly Hills, CA: Sage Publications.

Lewis, M., & Simon, R. (1986). A discourse not intended for her: Learning and teaching within patriarchy. *Harvard Educational Review, 56,* 4:457–472.

Macias, J. (1987). The hidden curriculum of Papago teachers: American Indian strategies for mitigating cultural discontinuity in early schooling. In G. Spindler & L. Spindler (Eds.) *Interpretive ethnography of education: At home and abroad* (pp. 363–380). Hillsdale, NJ: New Lawrence Erlbaum Associates.

Madrid, A. (1986). Testimony on Proposition 63 delivered to the Joint Legislative Committee of the California State Legislature. Claremont, CA: The Tomás Rivera Center.

Martin, A. (1985). Back to kindergarten basics. *Harvard Educational Review 55,*3:318–320.

McDermott, R. (1987a). Achieving school failure: An anthropological approach to illiteracy and social stratification. In G. Spindler (Ed.) *Education and cultural process: Anthropological approaches* (pp. 173–209). 2nd ed. Prospects Heights, IL: Waveland Press.

McDermott, R. (1987b). The explanation of minority school failure, again. *Anthropology and Education Quarterly, 18,* 4:361–364.

McDonald, J. (1986). Raising the teacher's voice and the ironic role of theory. *Harvard Educational Review, 56,* 4:355–378.

McLaughlin, B. (1982). Theory in bilingual education: On misreading Cummins. *Selected papers in TESOL, Vol. 1.* Monterey, CA: The Monterey Institute for International Studies.

McLaughlin, B. (1985). *Second-language acquisition in childhood: Volume 2. School-age children.* 2nd ed. Hillsdale, NJ: Lawrence Erlbaum Associates.

Mead, M. (1943). *And keep your powder dry.* New York: Morrow.

Mehan, H. (1979). *Learning lessons: Social organization in the classroom.* Cambridge, MA: Harvard University Press.

Mehan, H., Hertwick, A., & Meihls, J.L. (1986). *Handicapping the handicapped: Decision making in students' educational careers.* Stanford: Stanford University Press.

Meier, D. (1986). Learning in small moments. *Harvard Educational Review, 56*, 3:298–300.

Mercer, J. (1973). *Labeling the mentally retarded.* Berkeley: University of California Press.

Mitchell, J. (1985). Black children after the eighties: Surviving the new technology. *Harvard Educational Review, 55*, 3:354–362.

Mohatt, G., & Erickson, F. (1981). Cultural differences in teaching styles in an Odawa school: A sociolinguistic approach. In H. Trueba, G. Guthrie, & K. Au (Eds.) *Culture and the bilingual classroom: Studies in classroom ethnography* (pp. 105–119). Rowley, MA: Newbury House.

Moll, L. (1986). Writing as communication: Creating strategic learning environments for students. *Theory to Practice, 26*, 2:102–108.

Moll, L., & Diaz, E. (1987). Change as the goal of educational research. *Anthropology and Education Quarterly, 18*, 4:300–311.

Murnane, R., & Cohen, D. (1986). Merit pay and the evaluation problem: Why most merit pay plans fail and a few survive. *Harvard Educational Review, 56*, 1:1–17.

Namenwirth, M. (1986). Science through a feminist prism. In R. Bleir (Ed.) *Feminist approaches to science* (pp. 18–41). New York: Pergamon Books.

National Advisory Council for Bilingual Education. (1980–81). *The prospects for bilingual education in the nation: The fifth annual report.* Washington D.C.: Office of Bilingual Education and Language Minority Affairs.

Ogbu, J. (1974). *The next generation: An ethnography of education in an urban neighborhood.* New York: Academic Press.

Ogbu, J. (1978). *Minority education and caste: The American system in cross-cultural perspective.* New York: Academic Press.

Ogbu, J. (1981). Origins of human competence: A cultural–ecological perspective. *Child Development, 52*, 413–429.

Ogbu, J. (1982). Cultural discontinuities and schooling. *Anthropology and Education Quarterly, 13*, 4:290–307.

Ogbu, J. (1983). Minority status and schooling in plural societies. *Comparative Education Review, 27*, 2:168–190.

Ogbu, J. (1987a). Variability in minority responses to schooling: Nonimmigrants vs. immigrants. In G. Spindler & L. Spindler (Eds.), *Interpretive ethnography of education: At home and abroad* (pp. 255–278). Hillsdale, NJ: Lawrence Erlbaum Associates.

Ogbu, J. (1987b). Variability in minority school performance: A problem in search of an explanation. *Anthropology and Education Quarterly, 18*, 4:312–334.

Ogbu, J., & Matute-Bianchi, M. E. (1986). Understanding sociocultural factors: Knowledge, identity and school adjustment. In *Beyond language: Social and cultural factors in schooling language minority students* (pp. 73–142). Sacramento, CA: Bilingual Education Office, California State Department of Education.

O'Malley, J. (1977). Review of interim report: Evaluation of the impact of ESEA Title VII Spanish/English bilingual education program, Vols. I and II, Memorandum to John Molina, Department of Health, Education and Welfare, National Institute of Education.

O'Malley, J. (1981). *Children's English and services study: Language minority children with limited English proficiency in the United States.* Rosslyn, VA: National Clearinghouse for Bilingual Education.

O'Malley, J. (1982). Instructional services for limited English proficient children. *Journal of the National Association for Bilingual Education, 7*, 21–36.

Paley, V. (1986). On listening to what the children say. *Harvard Educational Review, 56,* 1:18–27.

Peal, E., & Lambert, W. (1962). The relation of bilingualism to intelligence. *Psychological Monographs, 65*: 1–23.

Peshkin, A. (1978). *Growing up American: Schooling and the survival of community.* Chicago: Chicago University Press.

Philips, S. (1982). *The invisible culture: Communication in classroom and community on the Warm Springs Indian reservation.* New York: Longman.

Pike, K. (1954). Emic and etic standpoints for the description of behavior. In K. Pike (Ed.) *Language in relation to a unified theory of the structure of human behavior* (pp. 8–28). Glendale, CA: Summer Institute of Linguistics.

Politzer, R. (1971). Toward individualization in foreign language teaching. *Modern Language Journal, 55,* 207–212.

Ravitch, D. (1983). *The troubled crusade: American education, 1945–1980.* New York: Basic Books.

Resnick, D., & Resnick, L., (1977). The nature of literacy: An historical explanation. *Harvard Educational Review, 47,* 370–385.

Richards, J. B. (1987). Learning Spanish and classroom dynamics: School failure in a Guatemalan Maya community. In H. T. Trueba (Ed.) *Success or failure?: Learning and the language minority student* (pp. 109–130). New York: Newbury House.

Rist, R. (1979). On the education of guest-worker children in Germany: A comparative study of policies and programs in Bavaria and Berlin. *The School Review, 84,* 242–268.

Roosens, E. (1971). *Socio-culturele verandering in Midden-Afrika.* Antwerp: Standaard Wetenschappelijk Uitgeverij.

Roosens, E. (1981). The multicultural nature of contemporary Belgian society: The immigrant community. In A. Liphart (Ed.) *Conflict and coexistence in Belgium* (pp. 61–92). Berkeley: University of California, Institute of International Studies.

Roosens, E. (1987). Integration processes—Adolescents from minorities. Unpublished manuscript. Center for Social and Cultural Anthropology. Catholic University, Leuven, Belgium.

Rosen, H. (1985). The voice of communities and language in classrooms. *Harvard Educational Review, 55,* 4:448–456.

Rossi, P. H., & Freeman, H. E. (1985). *Evaluation: A systematic approach.* 3rd ed. Beverly Hills, CA: Sage Publications.

Rossi, P. H., & Wright, S. R. (1977). Evaluation research: An assessment of theory, practice, and politics. *Evaluation Quarterly, 1,* 5–52.

Rueda, R. (1987). Social and communicative aspects of language proficiency in low-achieving language minority students. In H. Trueba (Ed.) *Success or failure?: Learning and the language minority student* (pp. 185–197). New York: Newbury House.

Rueda, R., & Mehan, H. (1986). Metacognition and passing: Strategic interaction in the lives of students with learning disabilities. *Anthropology and Education Quarterly, 17,* 3:139–165.

Rueda,, R., Rodriguez, R., & Prieto, A. (1981). Teacher's perceptions of competencies for teaching bilingual/multicultural exceptional children. *Exceptional Children, 48,* 268–270.

Salomone, R. (1986). *Equal education under law: Legal rights and federal policy in the post-Brown era.* New York: St. Martin's Press.

San Miguel, G., Jr. (1982). Mexican American organizations and the changing politics of school desegregation in Texas, 1945–1980. *Social Science Quarterly, 63*, 701–715.

San Miguel, G., Jr. (1983). The struggle against separate and unequal schools. *History of Education Quarterly, 23*, 343–359.

San Miguel, G. Jr. (1986). *One country, one language: An historical sketch of English language movements in the United States.* Paper commissioned by the Tomás Rivera Center, Claremont, CA.

San Miguel, G., Jr. (1987). *"Let all of them take heed": Mexican Americans and the campaign for educational equality in Texas, 1910–1981.* Austin: University of Texas Press.

Saville-Troike, M. (1979). Culture, language, and education. In H. Trueba & C. Barnett-Mizrahi (Eds.) *Bilingual multicultural education and the professional: From theory to practice* (pp. 139–148). Rowley, MA.: Newbury House.

Scribner, S., & Cole, M. (1981). *The psychology of literacy.* Cambridge: Harvard University Press.

Shavelson, R., Webb, N., & Burstein, L. (1986). Measurement of teaching. In M. C. Wittrock (Ed.) *Handbook of research on teaching* (pp. 50–91). New York: Macmillan Publishing Co.

Shulman, L. (1987a). Knowledge and teaching: Foundations of the new reform. *Harvard Educational Review, 57*, 1:1–22.

Shulman, L. (1987b). Sounding an alarm: A reply to Sockett. *Harvard Educational Review, 57*, 4:473–482.

Shultz, J., Florio, S., & Erickson, F. (1982). Where's the floor? Aspects of the cultural organization of social relationships in communication at home and at school. In P. Gilmore & A. Glatthorn (Eds.) *Children in and out of school* (pp. 88–123). Arlington, VA: Center for Applied Linguistics.

Skutnabb-Kangas, T. (1978). Semilingualism and the education of migrant children as a means of reproducing the caste of assembly line workers. In N. Dittmar, H. Haberland, T. Skutnabb-Kangas, & U. Teleman (Eds.), *Papers for the first Scandanavian-German symposium on the language of immigrant workers and their children.* Roskilde, Denmark: Universetscenter.

Skutnabb-Kangas, T. (1984). *Bilingualism or not: The education of minorities.* Clevendon, UK: Multilingual Matters.

Sockett, H. (1987). Has Shulman got the strategy right? *Harvard Educational Review, 57*, 2:208–219.

Spindler, G. (1955). *Anthropology and education.* Stanford, CA: Stanford University Press.

Spindler, G. (1959). *Transmission of American culture.* The Third Burton Lecture. Cambridge: Harvard University Press.

Spindler, G. (1963). *Education and culture: Anthropological approaches.* New York: Holt, Rinehart & Winston.

Spindler, G. (1974a). Schooling in Schoenhausen: A study of cultural transmission and instrumental adaptation in an urbanizing German village. In G. Spindler (Ed.) *Education and cultural process: Toward an anthropology of education* (pp. 230–271). New York: Holt, Rinehart & Winston.

Spindler, G. (1974b). The transmission of American culture. In G. Spindler (Ed.) *Education and cultural process: Toward an anthropology of education* (pp. 279–310). New York: Holt, Rinehart & Winston.

Spindler, G. (1977). Change and continuity in American core cultural values: An anthropological perspective. In G. D. DeRenzo (Ed.) *We the people: American character and social change* (pp. 20–40). Westport, CT: Greenwood.

Spindler, G. (1982). *Doing the ethnography of schooling: Educational anthropology in action.* New York: Holt, Rinehart & Winston.

Spindler, G. (1987). Why have minority groups in North America been disadvantaged by their schools? In G. Spindler (Ed.) *Education and cultural process: Anthropological approaches* (pp. 160–172). 2nd ed. Prospect Heights, IL: Waveland Press.

Spindler, G., & Spindler, L. (1965). The Instrumental Activities Inventory: A technique for the study of the psychology of acculturation. *Southwestern Journal of Anthropology, 21,* 1:1–23.

Spindler, G., & Spindler, L. (1982). Roger Harker and Schoenhausen: From the familiar to the strange and back again. In G. Spindler (Ed.) *Doing the ethnography of schooling* (pp. 20–47). New York: Holt, Rinehart & Winston.

Spindler, G., & Spindler, L. (1983). Anthropologists view American culture. *Annual Review of Anthropology, 12*: 49–78.

Spindler, G., & Spindler, L. (1987a). *Instrumental competence, self-efficacy, linguistic minorities, schooling, and cultural therapy: A preliminary attempt at integration.* Paper presented at the Conference on Educational Anthropology: Current Research and Implications for Instruction. University of California, Santa Barbara, May 16.

Spindler, G., & Spindler, L. (1987b). Cultural dialogue and schooling in Schoenhausen and Roseville: A comparative analysis. *Anthropology and Education Quarterly, 18,* 1:3–16.

Spindler, G., & Spindler, L. (1987c). Teaching and learning how to do the ethnography of education. In G. Spindler & L. Spindler (Eds.) *Interpretive ethnography of education at home and abroad* (pp. 17–33). Hillsdale, NJ: Lawrence Erlbaum Associates.

Spindler, L. (1978). Researching the psychology of culture change and urbanization. In G. Spindler (Ed.) *The making of psychological anthropology* (pp. 187–195). Berkeley: University of California Press.

Spindler, L. (1984). *Culture change and modernization: Mini-models and case studies.* Prospect Heights, IL: Waveland Press.

Spindler, L., & Spindler, G. (1979). Changing women in men's worlds. In A. McElroy and C. Mathiasson (Eds.) *Sex roles in changing cultures: Occasional papers in anthropology. Number One.* Buffalo, NY: State University of New York at Buffalo.

Suarez-Orozco, M. (1986). Hispanic Americans: Comparative considerations and the educational problems of children. Unpublished manuscript. University of California, Santa Cruz.

Suarez-Orozco, M. (1987). Towards a psychosocial understanding of Hispanic adaptation to American schooling. In H. Trueba (Ed.) *Success or failure?: Learning and the language minority student* (pp. 156–168). New York: Newbury House/Harper & Row.

Suarez-Orozco, M. (in press). *In pursuit of a dream: New Hispanic immigrants in American schools.* Stanford University Press.

Swain, M. (1978). French immersion: Early, late or partial? *Canadian Modern Language Review, 34*: 577–585.

Swain, M. (1984). A review of immersion education in Canada: Research and evaluation studies. In *Studies on immersion education* (pp. 87–112). Sacramento: California State Department of Education.

Teitelbaum, H., & Hiller, R. (1979). Bilingual education: The legal mandate. In H. Trueba

& C. Barnett-Mizrahi (Eds.) *Bilingual multicultural education and the professional: From theory to practice* (pp. 20–53). Rowley, MA: Newbury House.

Tharp, R., & Gallimore, R. (in press). *Teaching mind and society: Theory and practice of teaching, literacy and schooling.* Cambridge University Press.

Tiedt, P., & Tiedt, I. (1986). *Multicultural teaching: A handbook of activities, information, and resources.* 2nd ed. Boston: Allyn and Bacon.

Trudgill, P. (Ed.). (1984). *Applied sociolinguistics.* Orlando, FL: Academic Press.

Trueba, H. (1979). Bilingual education models: Types and designs. In H. Trueba & C. Barnett-Mizrahi (Eds.) *Bilingual multicultural education and the professional: From theory to practice* (pp. 54–73). Rowley, MA: Newbury House.

Trueba, H. (1983). Adjustment problems of Mexican American children: An anthropological study. *Learning Disabilities Quarterly, 6,* 4:395–415.

Trueba, H. (1984). The forms, functions and values of literacy: Reading for survival. *Journal of the National Association for Bilingual Education, 9,* 1:21–39.

Trueba, H. (1986). Review of *Beyond language: Social and cultural factors in schooling language minority students.* In *Anthropology and Education Quarterly, 17,* 4: 255–259.

Trueba, H. (Ed.) (1987a). *Success or failure?: Learning and the language minority student.* New York: Newbury House/Harper & Row.

Trueba, H. (1987b). Organizing classroom instruction in specific sociocultural contexts: Teaching Mexican youth to write in English. In S. Goldman & H. Trueba (Eds.) *Becoming literate in English as a second language: Advances in research and theory* (pp. 235–252). Norwood, NJ: Ablex Corporation.

Trueba, H. (1987c). Introduction: The ethnography of schooling. In H. T. Trueba (Ed.) *Success or failure?: Learning and the language minority student* (pp. 1–13). New York: Newbury House/Harper & Row.

Trueba, H. (in press). English literacy acquisition: From cultural trauma to learning disabilities in minority students. *Linguistics and Education.*

Trueba, H., & Barnett-Mizrahi, C. (1979). (Eds.) *Bilingual multicultural education and the professional: From theory to practice.* Rowley, MA: Newbury House.

Trueba, H., & Delgado-Gaitan, C. (1988). *School and society: Learning content through culture.* New York: Praeger Publishers.

Trueba, H., Jacobs, L., & Kirton, E. (1988). *Hmong children and their families in La Playa: Cultural conflict and adjustment.* Unpublished manuscript. University of California, Santa Barbara.

Trueba, H., Moll, L., Diaz, S., & Diaz, R. (1984). *Improving the functional writing of bilingual secondary school students.* (Contract No. 400–81–0023). Washington, D.C.: National Institute of Education. ERIC, Clearinghouse on Languages and Linguistics, ED 240, 862.

Tyack, D., & Hansot, E. (1982). *Managers of virtue: Public school leadership in America, 1820–1980,* Pt. III, pp. 213–262. New York: Basic Books.

Tyack, D., & Hansot, E. (1984). Hard times, then and now: Public schools in the 1930s and 1980s. *Harvard Educational Review, 54,* 1:33–66.

U.S. Bureau of the Census (1984). 1980 U.S. Census. *Current Populations Report.* Washington, D.C.: Government Printing Office.

U.S. Department of Commerce. Bureau of the Census. (1987). *The Hispanic population in the United States: March 1986 and 1987 (Advance Report).* Washington, D.C.: U.S. Government Printing Office.

Ulibarri, D. (1982). *Limited-English proficient students: A review of national estimates.* National Center for Bilingual Research. Los Alamitos, CA: November.

Van der Plank, P. (1978). The assimilation and nonassimilation of European linguistic minorities. In J. Fishman (Ed.) *Advances in the study of societal multilingualism* (pp. 423–456). The Hague: Mouton.

Varenne, H. (1977). *Americans together: Structured diversity in a midwestern town.* New York: Teachers' College Press.

Vygotsky, L.S. (1962). *Thought and language.* Cambridge, MA: MIT Press.

Vygotsky, L. S. (1978). *Mind in society: The development of higher psychological processes.* M. Cole, V. John-Teiner, S. Scribner & E. Souberman (Eds.). Cambridge: Harvard University Press.

Wagatsuma, H., & DeVos, G. (1984). *Heritage of endurance: Family patterns and delinquency formation in urban Japan.* Berkeley, CA: University of California Press.

Waggoner, D. (1984). The need for bilingual education: Estimates from the 1980 census. *Journal of the National Association for Bilingual Education, 8,* 2:1–14.

Walker, C. (1987). Hispanic achievement: Old views and new perspectives. In H. Trueba (Ed.) *Success or failure?: Learning and the language minority student* (pp. 15–32). New York: Newbury House/Harper & Row.

Warner, W. L. (1941). *The social life of a modern community.* Yankee City Series 1. New Haven: Yale University Press.

Warren, R. (1982). Schooling, biculturalism, and ethnic identity: A case study. In G. Spindler (Ed.) *Doing the ethnography of schooling: Educational anthropology for action* (pp. 382–409). New York: Holt, Rinehart & Winston.

Wertsch, J. (1981). *The concept of activity in Soviet psychology.* New York: M.E. Sharpe.

Wertsch, J. (1985). *Vygotsky and the social formation of the mind.* Cambridge, MA: Harvard University Press.

Wise, A. E. (1987). Director's Message. In *Center for the Study of the Teaching Profession. Annual Report, October 1986 to September 1987)* (pp. 1–3). Santa Monica, CA: Rand.

Wolcott, H. (1988). "Problem finding" in qualitative research. In H. Trueba & C. Delgado-Gaitan (Eds.) *School and society: Learning content through culture* (pp. 11–35). New York: Praeger Publishers.

Wong-Fillmore, L. (1976). *The second time around: Cognitive and social strategies in second language acquisition.* Unpublished doctoral dissertation, Stanford University.

Wong-Fillmore, L. (1982). Language minority students and school participation: What kind of English is needed? *Journal of Education, 164*: 143–156.

Wyatt, C. (1984). A missing and essential element. *Harvard Educational Review, 54,* 1:28–31.

Yonemura, M. (1986). Empowerment and teacher education. *Harvard Educational Review, 56,* 4:473–480.

Zehler, A. M. (1986). *Examination of a teacher rating instrument for measuring student oral language proficiency: Validity and reliability of the SOLOM.* Unpublished manuscript. Arlington, VA: Development Associates.

Zeroulou, Z. (1985). Mobilisation familiale et réussite scolaire. *Revue Européene des Migration Internationales, 1,* 2:107–117.

# Index